Taste of Home's
CONTEST WINNING
ANNUAL RECIPES 2007

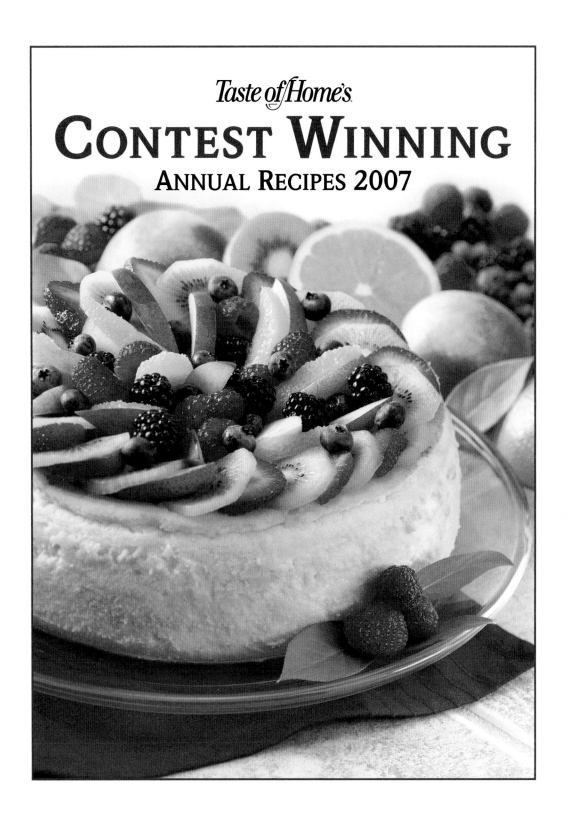

Taste of Home Books

Taste of Home's
CONTEST WINNING
ANNUAL RECIPES 2007

Editor: Michelle Bretl
Art Director: Gretchen Trautman
Vice President/Books: Heidi Reuter Lloyd
Senior Editor/Books: Mark Hagen
Layout Designers: Julie Wagner (Senior), Julie Stone
Associate Editor: Jean Steiner
Proofreader: Linne Bruskewitz
Editorial Assistant: Barb Czysz

Food Director: Diane Werner RD
Test Kitchen Manager: Karen Scales
Senior Recipe Editor: Sue A. Jurack
Recipe Editors: Mary King, Christine Rukavena
Recipe Asset System Manager: Coleen Martin
Photographers: Rob Hagen (Senior), Dan Roberts, Jim Wieland
Associate Photographer: Lori Foy
Food Stylists: Joylyn Trickel (Senior), Sarah Thompson
Set Stylist: Jennifer Bradley Vent
Photo Studio Coordinator: Suzanne Kern

Creative Director: Ardyth Cope
Senior Vice President, Editor in Chief: Catherine Cassidy
President: Barbara Newton
Founder: Roy Reiman

Taste of Home Books
© 2007 Reiman Media Group, Inc.
5400 S. 60th St., Greendale WI 53129
International Standard Book Number (10): 0-89821-522-6
International Standard Book Number (13): 978-089821-522-9
International Standard Serial Number: 1548-4157

PICTURED ON FRONT COVER:
Crustless New York Cheesecake (p. 217)

PICTURED ON BACK COVER:
Marinated Pork Chops (p. 95) and Mexican Beef and Mushrooms (p. 117).

To order additional copies of this book, write to *Taste of Home* Books, P.O. Box 908, Greendale WI 53129.
To order with a credit card, call toll-free 1-800/344-2560 or visit our Web site at **www.reimanpub.com**.

Table of Contents

Strawberry Salad Dressing, p. 45

Breakfast Upside-Down Cake, p. 80

Stuffed Baked Potatoes, p. 147

Blueberry Lattice Bars, p. 179

Cranberry Crumb Cake, p. 207

They're All Here in One Big Cookbook—359 Winners from National Recipe Contests

IT SEEMS cooks from across the country just can't get enough of prize-winning dishes. They raved about the first three editions of *Contest Winning Annual Recipes* …then clamored for more. So we knew there was just one thing to do—create this fourth edition. We think you'll agree it's the best one yet!

Contest Winning Annual Recipes 2007 is jam-packed with 359 exceptional recipes that stood out from the culinary crowd. Each dish was a prize winner in either *Taste of Home* magazine or one of its sister publications— *Quick Cooking, Light & Tasty, Country* and *Country Woman.* You get winners from five different publications in one big cookbook!

These 359 sensational dishes, all honored in national contests, include an entire year's worth of winners. It's a can't-miss collection that's truly the "cream of the crop."

Wondering how a recipe becomes a prize winner?

First, home cooks read our request for contest entries and send in their all-time best—the must-have dishes family and friends ask for again and again.

Then our expert home economists sort through the many recipes we receive and test the most promising ones. They prepare the top choices for our judging panel, which includes experienced food editors and other home economists. After much sampling (yum!), the judges pick a grand prize winner and runners-up.

Winners from Dozens of Contests

The contests spotlighted in this cookbook cover a wide range of recipes—snacks and beverages; salads and dressings; soups and stews; entrees; side dishes and condiments; breads and rolls; brownies, bars and cookies; cakes and pies; and special desserts. No matter what type of recipe you're looking for, you're sure to find it in this special collection.

For a complete list of chapters, please see the Table of Contents on page 3. Here's a quick summary of the year's worth of contests in this book and the top prize winner in each category:

- **Yeast Bread Bonanza:** Mmmmmm…who can resist the aroma of fresh-baked breads and rolls? Almond Bear Claws (p. 154) rose to the occasion in this memorable contest, capturing the grand prize.

- **Catch of the Day:** Reel in a family-size pan of cheesy Seafood Lasagna (p. 97). After one taste of this layered main dish, your gang will be hooked.

- **Gelatin Gems:** It wiggles and jiggles…and is sure to bring giggles! Make the best of ever-popular gelatin with refreshing Orange Cream Cheesecake (p. 214).

- **Garden-Fresh Beans:** Wondering what to do with your garden harvest? Snap up homey Green Bean Mushroom Pie (p. 119). Our judges agreed it was the pick of the crop.

- **Potatoes Please:** Tasty taters were at the root of this popular contest. Keep your eyes peeled for Creamy Chive Mashed Potatoes (p. 143).

- **Best Bar Cookies:** You'll have your next bake sale, church picnic or neighborhood potluck well in hand when you make scrumptious Apple Pie Bars (p. 186).

Country Potato Chowder, p. 59

Pinwheel Flank Steaks, p. 99

- **Speedy Skillet Suppers:** Broccoli Shrimp Alfredo (p. 94) looks so much like fancy restaurant fare, your family will be amazed it came together on the stove!

- **Easy Breakfasts:** How do you make morning meals fuss-free? Get started the day before by preparing an overnight recipe—Southwest Sausage Bake (p. 68).

- **Quick Microwave Dishes:** With the press of a few buttons, you can cook saucy Dressed-Up Meatballs (p. 103) and serve a satisfying, meat-and-veggies meal.

- **Tasty in 10 Minutes:** When you have a mere 10 minutes to spare, whip up decadent Chocolate Caramel Fondue (p. 213). Then pair it with your family's favorite dippers, and dessert's done!

- **Mighty Quick Muffins:** Looking for some fast favorites? When it came to golden goodies, drizzled Apple Streusel Muffins (p. 162) were tops.

- **Dessert Fixes with Mixes:** Pull from your pantry to prepare Peanut Butter Chocolate Dessert (p. 226). It uses pudding mix to give you a sweet shortcut.

- **Light Holiday Desserts:** End your Thanksgiving or Christmas dinner in a yummy but guilt-free way with a light delight—Frosty Pumpkin Pie (p. 200).

- **Berry Best Berries:** Straight from the berry patch came the juicy best for this contest. You won't want to pass up down-home Blackberry Cobbler (p. 224).

- **Creative Kabobs:** Summertime sizzles with delicious shish kabobs on the grill. Fire up and enjoy meal-in-one Oriental Steak Skewers (p. 110).

- **Apple a Day:** This versatile fruit is at the core of Bavarian Apple Tart (p. 221), an elegant and creamy dessert that'll give any meal extra appeal.

- **Terrific Turkey:** You won't have to wing it when you want to serve a tasty turkey dinner. Simply rely on comforting Turkey Biscuit Potpie (p. 90).

- **Slimmed-Down Stews:** What's better on chilly days than a piping-hot bowl of Oven Beef Stew (p. 54)? Try it, and your answer will likely be, "Nothing!"

- **Sweet Chocolate Treats:** If you're absolutely passionate about chocolate, you won't be able to resist luscious Chocolate Cake with Fudge Sauce (p. 197).

- **Rosy Rhubarb Fare:** When the time is ripe for rhubarb, turn to the top prize winner in this tongue-tingling contest—Creamy Rhubarb Crepes (p. 76).

- **Rice and Barley Banquet:** These great grains make just about any meal more flavorful and filling. Our judging panel was wild about Cranberry Rice with Caramelized Onions (p. 133).

- **Steak and Chops Are Tops:** Serve succulent Round Steak with Dumplings (p. 104), and you'll agree—this main course is a cut above the rest!

- **Blue Ribbon Winners:** Local and regional fair entries were the focus of this rewarding contest. Don't miss "the best of the best"—tasty Dill Seed Braid (p. 159).

- **Cranberry Creations:** These little gems go over big year-round. Top off your next dinner with the tangy flavor of Cran-Apple Cobbler (p. 220).

With all of these rave-review recipes, you're sure to come out a winner when you turn to *Contest Winning Annual Recipes 2007*. The only hard part? Choosing which celebrated dish to make first!

Strawberry Cream Puffs, p. 211

Cinnamon 'n' Spice Dip, p. 14

Frosty Mocha Drink, p. 25

Tomato Bread Salad, p. 19

Snacks & Beverages

Whether you need after-school munchies for the kids or elegant appetizers and drinks for guests, rely on this chapter for a wide variety of goodies and thirst-quenchers that are sure to satisfy.

Cranberry Meatballs, p. 9

Creamy Swiss Spinach Dip

Heather Millican, Fort Myers, Florida

A few ingredients and a microwave oven are all you need to throw together this warm, cheesy pleaser. It's always gone by the time the party ends. My favorite way to serve the dip is in a bread bowl with bread cubes, but it's also good with tortilla chips or French bread slices.

- 1 package (8 ounces) cream cheese, softened
- 1 teaspoon garlic powder
- 1 package (9 ounces) frozen creamed spinach, thawed
- 2 cups diced Swiss cheese
- 2 unsliced round loaves (1 pound *each*) Italian *or* French bread

1. In a small microwave-safe mixing bowl, beat cream cheese and garlic powder until smooth. Stir in spinach and Swiss cheese. Cover and microwave on high for 5-8 minutes or until cheese is melted, stirring occasionally.

2. Meanwhile, cut a 4-in. circle in the center of one loaf of bread. Remove bread, leaving 1 in. at bottom of loaf. Cut removed bread and the second loaf into 1-1/2-in. cubes. Spoon hot spinach dip into bread shell. Serve with bread cubes. **Yield:** 3-1/2 cups.

Editor's Note: This recipe was tested with an 850-watt microwave.

Berry Fruity Punch

Phyllis Shaughnessy, Livonia, New York

I created this for a summer boat trip one year, and the ruby-red punch was a big hit with everyone. Melons and pineapple are a lovely complement to the raspberries and strawberries in this refreshing thirst-quencher.

☑ Uses less fat, sugar or salt. Includes Nutrition Facts and Diabetic Exchanges.

- 2 cups unsweetened pineapple juice
- 2 cups fresh *or* frozen unsweetened raspberries
- 2 cups fresh strawberries
- 2 cups cubed honeydew
- 1 cup cubed seedless watermelon
- 3/4 cup sugar
- 1/2 teaspoon ground ginger
- 4 cups diet ginger ale, chilled
- 1 cup lime juice, chilled
- 1/2 cup lemon juice, chilled

1. In a blender or food processor, process the pineapple juice, berries and melon in batches.

2. Strain and transfer fruit mixture to a punch bowl or large pitcher. Stir in sugar and ginger. Add the ginger ale, lime and lemon juices. Serve immediately over crushed ice. **Yield:** 11 cups.

Nutrition Facts: 1 cup equals 121 calories, trace fat (trace saturated fat), 0 cholesterol, 27 mg sodium, 31 g carbohydrate, 3 g fiber, 1 g protein. **Diabetic Exchange:** 2 fruit.

🎗🎗🎗
Cranberry Meatballs
(Also pictured on page 7)

Tammy Neubauer, Ida Grove, Iowa

If my husband is able to identify cranberries in a dish, he won't eat it. So I was thrilled when he raved about these meatballs. But I knew for sure I had a winner when my grandmother asked me for the recipe!

MEATBALLS:
- 2 eggs, lightly beaten
- 1 cup cornflake crumbs
- 1/3 cup ketchup
- 2 tablespoons soy sauce
- 1 tablespoon dried parsley flakes
- 2 tablespoons dried minced onion
- 1/2 teaspoon salt
- 1/4 teaspoon pepper
- 2 pounds ground pork

SAUCE:
- 1 can (16 ounces) jellied cranberry sauce
- 1 cup ketchup
- 3 tablespoons brown sugar
- 1 tablespoon lemon juice

1. In a large mixing bowl, combine first eight meatball ingredients; crumble meat over mixture and mix well. Shape into 72 meatballs (1 in. each).

2. Place in a 15-in. x 10-in. x 1-in. baking pan. Bake at 350° for 20-25 minutes or until no longer pink. Remove from the oven; drain on paper towels.

3. In a large saucepan, combine sauce ingredients. Cook, stirring frequently, until the cranberry sauce is melted. Add the meatballs and heat through. **Yield:** 12 main-dish or 24 appetizer servings.

Aunt Frances' Lemonade

Debbie Blackburn, Camp Hill, Pennsylvania

My sister and I spent a week each summer with our Aunt Frances, who always had this thirst-quenching lemonade in a stoneware crock in the refrigerator. A cold glassful was so refreshing after a hot day.

> 5 **lemons**
> 5 **limes**
> 5 **oranges**
> 3 **quarts water**
> 1-1/2 to 2 **cups sugar**

1. Squeeze the juice from four of the lemons, limes and oranges; pour into a gallon container.

2. Thinly slice the remaining fruit and set aside for garnish. Add water and sugar; mix well. Store in the refrigerator. Serve on ice with fruit slices. **Yield:** 12-16 servings (1 gallon).

Marinated Pork Tenderloin Sandwiches

Alice Gregory, Overland Park, Kansas

These pork-filled buns score big with everyone who tries them. I like to prepare the pork ahead of time and assemble the sandwiches shortly before serving.

> 1/2 **cup soy sauce**
> 1/4 **cup packed brown sugar**
> 2 **tablespoons vegetable oil**
> 1 **teaspoon ground ginger**
> 1/2 **teaspoon ground mustard**
> 2 **garlic cloves, minced**
> 1 **pound pork tenderloin**
> 12 **dinner rolls, warmed**

1. In a large bowl, combine the soy sauce, brown sugar, oil, ginger, mustard and garlic. Pour 3/4 cup marinade into a large resealable plastic bag; add the pork. Seal bag and turn to coat; refrigerate for 12 hours or overnight, turning several times. Cover and refrigerate remaining marinade.

2. Drain and discard marinade from meat. Coat grill rack with nonstick cooking spray before starting the grill. Grill pork, uncovered, over medium heat for 7-8 minutes on each side or until a meat thermometer reads 160°. Baste with remaining marinade during the last 7 minutes of cooking.

3. Let stand for 10 minutes; carve in thin slices and serve on rolls. **Yield:** 12 servings.

Alternate cooking method: Bake tenderloin in 375° oven until meat thermometer reads 160°. Let stand for 10 minutes; carve in thin slices. Combine reserved marinade and 1 cup water. Serve with sandwiches.

🎀🎀🎀 Spicy Ribbon Potato Chips

Sue Murphy, Greenwood, Michigan

You won't settle for store-bought chips after munching these crispy, deep-fried snacks. Seasoned with chili powder and cayenne pepper, the zippy chips are surefire crowd-pleasers.

- 4 medium unpeeled baking potatoes
- 4 teaspoons salt, *divided*
- 4 cups ice water
- 1 tablespoon chili powder
- 1 teaspoon garlic salt
- 1/4 to 1/2 teaspoon cayenne pepper

Oil for deep-fat frying

1. Using a vegetable peeler or metal cheese slicer, cut potatoes into very thin lengthwise strips. Place in a large bowl; add 3 teaspoons salt and ice water. Soak for 30 minutes; drain. Place potatoes on paper towels and pat dry.

2. In a small bowl, combine the chili powder, garlic salt, cayenne and remaining salt; set aside.

3. In an electric skillet or deep-fat fryer, heat oil to 375°. Cook potatoes in oil in batches for 3-4 minutes or until deep golden brown, stirring frequently. Remove with a slotted spoon; drain on paper towels. Immediately sprinkle with seasoning mixture. Store in an airtight container. **Yield:** 6-8 servings.

🎀🎀🎀 Pineapple Pecan Cheese Ball

June Stone, Brewton, Alabama

With tangy pineapple and crunchy nuts, this cheese ball is irresistible. It also offers make-ahead convenience because it will keep for several days in the refrigerator.

- 2 packages (8 ounces *each*) cream cheese, softened
- 1 can (8 ounces) crushed pineapple, well drained
- 1/2 cup chopped green pepper
- 1/2 cup chopped green onions
- 1 teaspoon lemon-pepper seasoning
- 1 teaspoon seasoned salt
- 2 cups chopped pecans, *divided*

Assorted crackers

1. In a large mixing bowl, beat cream cheese until smooth. Stir in pineapple, green pepper, onions, seasonings and 1/2 cup nuts.

2. Turn out onto a sheet of plastic wrap and shape into a ball. Refrigerate several hours or overnight.

3. Before serving, roll cheese ball in remaining nuts. Serve with crackers. **Yield:** 12-14 servings.

🎖🎖🎖
Strawberry Salsa

Angela Packham, Oakville, Manitoba

My guests often try to guess the secret ingredient in this deliciously different salsa. No one thinks of strawberries...but many people ask for the recipe!

2-1/2 cups finely chopped fresh strawberries
1 cup chopped green pepper
2 tablespoons chopped green onions
2 tablespoons minced fresh parsley
1/3 cup prepared Catalina salad dressing
Dash hot pepper sauce
Pepper to taste
Tortilla chips

In a large bowl, combine the strawberries, green pepper, onions and parsley. Stir in the salad dressing, hot pepper sauce and pepper. Cover and refrigerate for 2 hours. Serve with tortilla chips. **Yield:** 3 cups.

Very Good Berries

When buying fresh strawberries, choose berries that are shiny, firm and very fragrant. They should be almost entirely red, although some whiteness near the cap is acceptable.

Refrigerate unwashed berries with the caps on. Wash and hull them just before using.

✿ ✿ ✿
Popcorn Nut Crunch

Midge Stolte, Blackfalds, Alberta

In my family, it just doesn't feel like Christmas until I make this yummy crunch to munch. I usually double the recipe so I can put some in tins for hostess gifts. Kept in an airtight container in a dry place, this snack will keep for up to 3 weeks.

- 2 quarts popped popcorn
- 1 cup blanched whole almonds, toasted
- 1 cup *each* pecan halves, cashews, Brazil nuts and hazelnuts, toasted
- 1-1/2 cups sugar
- 1 cup dark corn syrup
- 1/2 cup butter
- 1 teaspoon vanilla extract
- 1/2 teaspoon ground cinnamon

1. Place the popcorn and nuts in a lightly greased 5-qt. Dutch oven. Bake at 250° for 20 minutes.

2. Meanwhile, in a medium saucepan, combine sugar, corn syrup and butter; bring to a boil over medium heat, stirring constantly. Cook, without stirring, until a candy thermometer reads 290° (soft-crack stage).

3. Remove from the heat; stir in the vanilla and cinnamon. Pour a small amount at a time over the popcorn mixture, stirring constantly until the mixture is well coated.

4. Immediately spread on greased baking sheets. Cool; break into pieces. Store in airtight containers. **Yield:** about 4 quarts.

Editor's Note: We recommend that you test your candy thermometer before each use by bringing water to a boil; the thermometer should read 212°. Adjust your recipe temperature up or down based on your test.

✿ ✿ ✿
Fat Rascals

Naomi Giddis, Grawn, Michigan

This is a favorite Saturday-night treat at our house. I used to make potato patties, but when I came across this recipe for puffs, it sounded like a delicious variation. Now my family deliberately leaves some mashed potatoes in the bowl during dinner so I can make these the next day!

- 1 cup mashed potatoes
- 2 eggs, beaten
- 1/2 cup milk
- 2 cups (8 ounces) shredded American *or* cheddar cheese
- 1/2 cup flour
- 1/4 teaspoon baking powder
- Salt and pepper to taste
- Oil for deep-fat frying

In a large bowl, combine the first seven ingredients. In an electric skillet or deep-fat fryer, heat oil to 375°. Drop batter by tablespoons, 4 or 5 at a time, into the hot oil. Fry 3-4 minutes or until golden brown. Serve immediately. **Yield:** about 24 puffs.

✿ ✿ ✿
Asparagus Ham Swirls

Nancy Ingersol, Midlothian, Illinois

I came across the recipe for this hot appetizer years ago and have made it many times to share with friends and co-workers. The asparagus, ham and cheese combine to create a fun finger food.

    16 fresh asparagus spears, trimmed
     3 tablespoons Dijon mustard
    16 thin slices fully cooked ham
    16 slices process Swiss cheese
     2 eggs, beaten
     1 cup dry bread crumbs
Vegetable oil

1. In a large skillet, cook asparagus in a small amount of water until crisp-tender, about 6-8 minutes; drain well. Spread about 1 teaspoon of mustard on each ham slice. Top with one slice of cheese.

2. Place an asparagus spear at one end (trim to fit if needed). Roll up each ham slice tightly; secure with three toothpicks. Dip the ham rolls in egg, then roll in bread crumbs.

3. In an electric skillet, heat 1 in. of oil to 350°. Fry rolls, a few at a time, until golden brown, about 3-4 minutes. Drain on paper towels; keep warm. Cut each roll between the toothpicks into three pieces. **Yield:** 4 dozen.

✿ ✿ ✿
Cinnamon 'n' Spice Dip
(Also pictured on page 6)

Julie Bertha, Pittsburgh, Pennsylvania

Cinnamon, nutmeg and brown sugar dress up whipped topping in this extremely easy treat. My gang likes the dip best with apple and pear wedges, but feel free to try it with pineapple slices, strawberries or other fresh fruit.

> ✓ Uses less fat, sugar or salt. Includes Nutrition Facts and Diabetic Exchanges.

     2 cups whipped topping
    1/4 cup packed brown sugar
    1/8 to 1/4 teaspoon ground cinnamon
Dash ground nutmeg
Assorted fresh fruit

In a small bowl, combine the whipped topping, brown sugar, cinnamon and nutmeg. Serve with fruit. **Yield:** about 2 cups.

Nutrition Facts: 2 tablespoons dip (prepared with reduced-fat whipped topping; calculated without fruit) equals 66 calories, 2 g fat (2 g saturated fat), 0 cholesterol, 3 mg sodium, 11 g carbohydrate, trace fiber, 0 protein. **Diabetic Exchange:** 1/2 starch.

🎗🎗🎗
Coconut Fried Shrimp

Ann Atchison, O'Fallon, Missouri

These crisp and crunchy shrimp make a tempting appetizer or even a change-of-pace main dish. The coconut coating adds a little sweetness...and the tangy marmalade-and-honey sauce is great for dipping. It's impossible to stop munching these once you start!

1-1/4 **cups all-purpose flour**
1-1/4 **cups cornstarch**
6-1/2 **teaspoons baking powder**
   1/2 **teaspoon salt**
   1/4 **teaspoon Cajun seasoning**
1-1/2 **cups cold water**
   1/2 **teaspoon vegetable oil**
2-1/2 **cups flaked coconut**
     1 **pound uncooked large shrimp, peeled and deveined**
Additional oil for deep-fat frying
     1 **cup orange marmalade**
   1/4 **cup honey**

1. In a small bowl, combine the first five ingredients. Stir in water and oil until smooth. Place coconut in another bowl. Dip shrimp into batter, then coat with coconut.

2. In an electric skillet or deep-fat fryer, heat oil to 375°. Fry shrimp, a few at a time, for 3 minutes or until golden brown. Drain on paper towels.

3. In a saucepan, heat marmalade and honey; stir until blended. Serve as a dipping sauce for the shrimp. **Yield:** 4 servings.

🎗🎗🎗
Bacon-Cheese Appetizer Pie

Joanie Elbourn, Gardner, Massachusetts

I first made this cheesecake-like pie for an open house years ago, and everybody liked it. It's fun to have cheesecake as a savory appetizer instead of the usual sweet dessert.

Pastry for a single-crust pie
     3 **packages (8 ounces** *each***) cream cheese, softened**
     4 **eggs, lightly beaten**
   1/4 **cup milk**
     1 **cup (4 ounces) shredded Swiss cheese**
   1/2 **cup sliced green onions**
     6 **bacon strips, cooked and crumbled**
   1/2 **teaspoon salt**
   1/8 **teaspoon pepper**
   1/8 **teaspoon cayenne pepper**

1. Roll the pastry into a 13-1/2-in. circle. Fit into the bottom and up the sides of an ungreased 9-in. springform pan. Lightly prick the bottom. Bake at 450° for 8-10 minutes or until lightly browned. Cool slightly.

2. In a large mixing bowl, beat cream cheese until fluffy. Add eggs and milk; beat until smooth. Add cheese, onions, bacon, salt, pepper and cayenne; mix well. Pour into the crust.

3. Bake at 350° for 40-45 minutes or until a knife inserted near the center comes out clean. Cool 20 minutes. Remove sides of pan. Cut into thin slices; serve warm. **Yield:** 16-20 appetizer servings.

🎀🎀🎀
Cranberry Slush

Sharen Christensen, Salem, Utah

One taste of this sweet icy treat leads to another...and another! My mother-in-law makes it for family gatherings, and it never lasts long. Often, my husband and twin daughters request it as a snack or dessert.

    1 **pound fresh *or* frozen cranberries**
2-1/2 **cups cold water, *divided***
3-1/2 **cups fresh *or* frozen unsweetened raspberries**
    1 **envelope unflavored gelatin**
    2 **cups sugar**
    2 **cups ginger ale**
1-3/4 **cups raspberry ginger ale *or* additional ginger ale**

1. In a large saucepan, cook the cranberries and 1-1/2 cups water over medium heat until the berries pop, about 15 minutes. Stir in raspberries. Transfer to a blender or food processor; cover and process until smooth. Strain and discard seeds, reserving juice. Pour the juice into a 2-qt. freezer-proof container; set aside.

2. In a small saucepan, sprinkle gelatin over remaining water; let stand for 1 minute. Stir in sugar. Cook and stir over medium heat until gelatin and sugar are dissolved. Add to berry juice. Stir in 2 cups ginger ale; cover and freeze.

3. Remove from the freezer 1 hour before serving. For each serving, combine 1 cup cranberry slush with 1/4 cup raspberry ginger ale in a glass; stir well. **Yield:** 7 servings.

🎀🎀🎀
Deviled Crab Dip

Debbie Jones, California, Maryland

Blue crabs are plentiful here in Maryland, and we're always looking for new ways to enjoy them. This recipe is easy, elegant and delicious.

    1 **cup mayonnaise**
    2 **tablespoons *each* finely chopped celery, green pepper and onion**
    2 **to 3 teaspoons lemon juice**
    1 **teaspoon ground mustard**
    1 **teaspoon Worcestershire sauce**
1/4 **teaspoon salt**
1/8 **teaspoon lemon-pepper seasoning**
1/8 **to 1/4 teaspoon hot pepper sauce**
1-1/2 **cups crabmeat, drained, flaked and cartilage removed**
Assorted fresh vegetables *or* assorted crackers

In a large bowl, combine the mayonnaise, celery, green pepper, onion, lemon juice, mustard, Worcestershire sauce, salt, lemon-pepper and pepper sauce. Stir in crab. Cover and refrigerate for at least 1 hour. Serve with vegetables or crackers. **Yield:** about 2 cups.

🏅🏅🏅
Hot Cheese Dip

Ardyce Piehl, Poynette, Wisconsin

A colleague of mine brought this party-starter to a staff potluck, and everyone gave it rave reviews. It's so easy to make—you just combine the ingredients and pop it in the oven.

   2 cups (8 ounces) shredded part-skim
      mozzarella cheese
   2 cups (8 ounces) shredded cheddar cheese
   2 cups mayonnaise
   1 medium onion, minced
   1 can (4 ounces) chopped green chilies, drained
1-1/2 ounces sliced pepperoni
   1/2 cup sliced ripe olives
Rye chips, assorted crackers or assorted fresh vegetables

1. In a shallow baking dish or pie plate, combine the first five ingredients.

2. Top mixture with pepperoni and olives. Bake at 325° about 25 minutes or until bubbly. Serve with rye chips, crackers of choice or assorted fresh vegetables. **Yield:** 35 appetizer servings.

Editor's Note: Reduced-fat or fat-free mayonnaise is not recommended for this recipe.

🎀 🎀 🎀

Two-Cheese Quesadillas

Sharron Kemp, High Point, North Carolina

When we have to eat on the run, I turn to this tasty recipe because it comes together in a snap. Best of all, I can customize the ingredients to satisfy each member of my family. If someone doesn't care for onions, I simply leave them out of the quesadilla.

- 4 flour tortillas (8 inches), warmed
- 1 cup (4 ounces) shredded cheddar cheese
- 1 cup (4 ounces) shredded part-skim mozzarella cheese
- 2 small tomatoes, finely chopped
- 1/2 cup finely chopped green pepper
- 1/4 cup chopped onion

Salsa and sour cream

Place tortillas on a griddle. Sprinkle each tortilla with cheeses, tomatoes, green pepper and onion. Fold in half and press edges lightly to seal. Cook over low heat for 1-2 minutes on each side or until cheese is melted. Serve with salsa and sour cream. **Yield:** 2-4 servings.

🎀 🎀 🎀

Festive Sausage Cups

Gail Watkins, South Bend, Indiana

Using prepared pie crust speeds up preparation of these savory, filling sausage cups. They're a family favorite in our house for Thanksgiving and Christmas.

Pastry for double-crust pie (9 inches)
- 1 pound bulk spicy pork sausage
- 6 green onions, chopped
- 1 tablespoon butter
- 1/2 cup chopped canned mushrooms
- 1/4 cup thinly sliced stuffed olives
- 3/4 teaspoon salt
- 1/4 teaspoon pepper
- 1/4 cup all-purpose flour
- 2 cups heavy whipping cream
- 1 cup (4 ounces) shredded Swiss cheese

Chopped stuffed olives

1. On a lightly floured surface, roll pastry to 1/8-in. thickness. Cut with a 2-1/2-in. round cookie cutter. Press onto the bottom and up the sides of greased miniature muffin cups. Bake at 400° for 6-8 minutes or until lightly browned. Remove from pans to cool on wire racks.

2. In a large skillet, cook sausage until no longer pink; drain well and set aside. In the same skillet, saute onions in butter until tender. Add mushrooms, sliced olives, salt and pepper. Sprinkle with flour. Add cream; bring to a boil, stirring constantly. Stir in sausage. Reduce heat; simmer until thickened, about 5-10 minutes, stirring constantly.

3. Spoon into pastry cups; sprinkle with cheese. Place on ungreased baking sheets. Bake at 350° for 10 minutes or until cheese is melted. Sprinkle with chopped olives. Serve hot. **Yield:** 4 dozen.

🎗️🎗️🎗️ Tomato Bread Salad

(Also pictured on page 6)

Dodi Hardcastle, Harlingen, Texas

We look forward to tomato season each year so we can make this unique medley. It's super on warm summer days.

> 3 large tomatoes, seeded and finely chopped
> 1 medium cucumber, seeded and finely chopped
> 1/2 large sweet onion, finely chopped
> 1 cup loosely packed fresh basil, minced
> 1/4 cup olive oil
> 1 tablespoon cider vinegar
> 1 garlic clove, minced
> 1/2 teaspoon salt
> 1/4 teaspoon pepper
> 1 loaf (8 ounces) French bread

1. In a large bowl, combine tomatoes, cucumber and onion. In a small bowl, combine basil, oil, vinegar, garlic, salt and pepper. Pour over tomatoes and toss. Refrigerate for at least 1 hour.

2. Before serving, allow salad to come to room temperature. Cut bread in half lengthwise; toast under broiler until lightly browned. Top with salad. Serve immediately. **Yield:** 18 servings.

Nutrition Facts: 1 slice of bread equals 188 calories, 7 g fat (0 saturated fat), 0 cholesterol, 262 mg sodium, 28 g carbohydrate, 0 fiber, 5 g protein. **Diabetic Exchanges:** 1-1/2 starch, 1 vegetable, 1 fat.

🎗️🎗️🎗️ Crispy Chicken Wings

Nancy Lesky, La Crosse, Wisconsin

When I first prepared these irresistible baked wings, I was a beginner at cooking. And if I could make them, anybody can! They're terrific appetizers for Christmas get-togethers, picnics, softball parties...you name it.

> 2 pounds chicken wings
> 1/2 cup butter, melted
> 1/4 teaspoon garlic powder
> 2 tablespoons chopped parsley
> 1 cup dry bread crumbs
> 1/2 cup grated Parmesan cheese
> 1/2 teaspoon salt
> 1/4 teaspoon pepper

1. Cut the chicken wings in two pieces, discarding the tips of wings.

2. In a small shallow bowl, combine butter and garlic powder. In another bowl, combine remaining ingredients. Dip chicken into butter, then into crumb mixture.

3. Place on greased baking sheet; bake at 350° for 50-60 minutes or until juices run clear. **Yield:** about 20 appetizers.

Editor's Note: This recipe was prepared with the first and second sections of the chicken wings.

Rhubarb Slush Punch

Diane Haug, Neenah, Wisconsin

For years, our family has toasted special occasions with this cool thirst-quencher. It's easy to double the recipe and freeze the extra punch, so we serve it year-round.

    6 cups chopped fresh *or* frozen rhubarb, thawed
    7 cups water, *divided*
    2 cups sugar
  3/4 cup orange juice concentrate
  3/4 cup lemonade concentrate
   10 cups club soda, chilled

1. In a large saucepan, bring rhubarb and 4 cups water to a boil. Reduce heat; simmer, uncovered, for 5-8 minutes or until rhubarb is tender. Mash rhubarb; strain. Reserve juice and discard pulp. Add sugar, concentrates and remaining water to rhubarb juice. Transfer to a freezer container and freeze.

2. Remove from the freezer 30-45 minutes before serving, scraping the surface as it thaws. Place equal amounts of slush mixture and club soda in each serving glass. Serve immediately. **Yield:** 10 servings.

Editor's Note: If using frozen rhubarb, measure rhubarb while still frozen, then thaw completely. Drain in a colander, but do not press liquid out.

Apple Salsa with Cinnamon Chips

Courtney Fons, Brighton, Michigan

For a fun treat that's sure to be requested at all your parties, try this appetizer. The salsa offers good-for-you fruits, and the crunchy home-baked chips are a healthy alternative to store-bought ones.

✓ Uses less fat, sugar or salt. Includes Nutrition Facts and Diabetic Exchanges.

  6 flour tortillas (8 inches)
  3 tablespoons sugar
1-1/2 teaspoons ground cinnamon
  4 cups finely chopped Granny Smith *or* other
    tart apples (about 2 medium)
  1 cup finely chopped ripe pear
1/2 cup quartered seedless red grapes
1/2 cup chopped celery
1/4 cup chopped walnuts
  3 tablespoons orange juice
  1 tablespoon brown sugar
  2 teaspoons grated orange peel

1. Coat both sides of each tortilla with nonstick cooking spray. Combine the sugar and cinnamon; sprinkle over both sides of tortillas.

2. Cut each into eight wedges. Place on baking sheets. Bake at 400° for 4-5 minutes or until crisp.

3. Meanwhile, for salsa, in a small bowl, combine the remaining ingredients. Serve with the cinnamon chips. **Yield:** 12 servings.

Nutrition Facts: 1/2 cup salsa with 4 chips equals 141 calories, 3 g fat (trace saturated fat), 0 cholesterol, 129 mg sodium, 26 g carbohydrate, 1 g fiber, 3 g protein. **Diabetic Exchanges:** 1 starch, 1 fruit, 1/2 fat.

Grilled Pork Appetizers

Susan LeBrun, Sulphur, Louisiana

People can't seem to get enough of these tender hors d'oeuvres. Marinated in a honey-sweetened sauce, they can also make a wonderful entree when served over rice.

✓ Uses less fat, sugar or salt. Includes Nutrition Facts and Diabetic Exchanges.

  1 pound boneless whole pork loin roast
  3 tablespoons reduced-sodium soy sauce
  3 tablespoons honey
  1 tablespoon lemon juice
  1 tablespoon vegetable oil
  3 garlic cloves, minced
1/2 teaspoon ground ginger

1. Cut pork into 1/8-in. slices, then cut each slice widthwise in half. In a large resealable plastic bag, combine the remaining ingredients; add the pork. Seal bag and turn to coat; refrigerate for 2-4 hours, turning occasionally.

2. If grilling the kabobs, coat grill rack with nonstick cooking spray before starting the grill. Drain and discard marinade. Thread pork onto metal or soaked wooden skewers. Grill, uncovered, over medium heat or broil 4-6 in. from the heat for 2-3 minutes on each side or until the meat juices run clear, turning once. **Yield:** 8 servings.

Nutrition Facts: 2 ounces cooked pork equals 84 calories, 3 g fat (1 g saturated fat), 29 mg cholesterol, 80 mg sodium, 2 g carbohydrate, trace fiber, 11 g protein. **Diabetic Exchange:** 2 lean meat.

Saucy Turkey Meatballs

Janell Fugitt, Cimaron, Kansas

It's easy to turn lean ground turkey into these moist, tender meatballs. Ideal for casual get-togethers, the appetizers feature a tangy, sweet sauce that my friends find delicious.

✓ Uses less fat, sugar or salt. Includes Nutrition Facts and Diabetic Exchanges.

  1 cup old-fashioned oats
3/4 cup fat-free evaporated milk
  1 medium onion, chopped
  1 teaspoon salt
  1 teaspoon chili powder
1/4 teaspoon garlic salt
1/4 teaspoon pepper
1-1/2 pounds lean ground turkey
SAUCE:
  2 cups ketchup
1-1/2 cups packed brown sugar
1/4 cup chopped onion
  2 tablespoons Liquid Smoke, optional
1/2 teaspoon garlic salt

1. In a large bowl, combine the first seven ingredients. Crumble turkey over mixture and mix well.

2. Shape into 1-in. balls. Place in a 13-in. x 9-in. x 2-in. baking dish coated with nonstick cooking spray. Bake, uncovered, at 350° for 10-15 minutes.

3. Meanwhile, combine the sauce ingredients; pour over meatballs. Bake 30-35 minutes longer or until meat is no longer pink. **Yield:** 15 servings.

Nutrition Facts: 3 meatballs equals 217 calories, 4 g fat (1 g saturated fat), 36 mg cholesterol, 695 mg sodium, 36 g carbohydrate, 1 g fiber, 10 g protein. **Diabetic Exchanges:** 2 starch, 1 lean meat.

Crunchy Swiss and Ham Appetizers

Wendy Mitchell, Weyburn, Saskatchewan

These quick, fuss-free bites are perfect for busy cooks like me…and for hot days when you want to eat light. When I have time to entertain, I rely on these appetizers because they're always popular with guests.

  2 cups very stiff mashed potatoes
  2 cups finely chopped fully cooked ham
  1 cup (4 ounces) shredded Swiss cheese
1/2 cup mayonnaise
1/4 cup minced onion
  1 egg, well-beaten
  1 teaspoon prepared mustard
1/2 teaspoon salt
1/4 teaspoon pepper
3-1/2 cups cornflakes, crushed

1. Combine all ingredients except cornflakes; chill. Shape into 1-in. balls and roll in cornflakes.

2. Place on greased baking sheet and bake at 350° for 25-30 minutes. Serve while hot. **Yield:** about 8 dozen.

Editor's Note: Reduced-fat or fat-free mayonnaise is not recommended for this recipe.

🎀🎀🎀
Spicy Tomato Juice

Kathleen Gill, Butte, Montana

Here's a great freezer idea for fresh-picked tomatoes. Drink the flavorful juice as-is or try it in recipes that call for vegetable juice as an ingredient.

      13 pounds ripe tomatoes (about 40 medium)
       2 celery ribs, coarsely chopped
       3 medium onions, coarsely chopped
       1 medium green pepper, coarsely chopped
  1-1/2 cups chopped fresh parsley
     1/2 cup sugar
       1 tablespoon Worcestershire sauce
       4 teaspoons salt
     1/4 teaspoon hot pepper sauce
     1/4 teaspoon cayenne pepper
     1/4 teaspoon pepper

1. Quarter tomatoes; place in a 6-qt. kettle. Add the celery, onions, green pepper and parsley. Simmer, uncovered, until vegetables are tender, about 45 minutes, stirring occasionally.

2. Cool slightly; put through a sieve or food mill. Return to kettle. Add remaining ingredients; mix well. Bring to a boil. Remove from the heat; cool.

3. Pour into freezer containers, leaving 1/2-in. headspace. Freeze for up to 12 months. **Yield:** about 5 quarts.

🎀🎀🎀
Salmon Spread

Carolyn Stewart, Anchorage, Alaska

Salmon is one of our state's greatest "natural resources." This quick and creamy spread is delicious with chips, crackers or toasted French bread.

       2 cans (15 ounces *each*) salmon, drained, bones
         and skin removed
       1 tablespoon minced onion
       1 tablespoon prepared horseradish
       1 tablespoon lemon juice
       1 package (8 ounces) cream cheese, softened
       2 to 3 tablespoons mayonnaise
  1-1/2 teaspoons dried dill weed
     1/2 teaspoon salt
       1 cup (8 ounces) sour cream
Fresh dill *or* parsley, optional
Toasted bread rounds *or* crackers

In a large mixing bowl, combine first eight ingredients. Spread on a serving platter and shape into a loaf or ball. Top with sour cream. Sprinkle with dill or parsley if desired. Serve with bread rounds or crackers. **Yield:** 8-10 appetizer servings.

Picnic Beans with Dip

Martha Bergman, Cleveland Heights, Ohio

Here's a fun way to enjoy fresh-picked beans. I first sampled this creamy, well-seasoned dip at a friend's house and have made it for many years. Try it with other vegetables, too, such as broccoli, celery and carrots.

✓ Uses less fat, sugar or salt. Includes Nutrition Facts and Diabetic Exchanges.

- **1 pound fresh green *or* wax beans**
- **1/2 cup mayonnaise**
- **1/2 cup half-and-half cream**
- **6 tablespoons vegetable oil**
- **2 tablespoons white vinegar**
- **1 tablespoon Dijon mustard**
- **1 small onion, quartered**
- **1 teaspoon salt**
- **1/4 teaspoon ground coriander**
- **1/4 teaspoon dried savory**
- **1/4 teaspoon pepper**
- **1/8 teaspoon dried thyme**

1. Place beans in a saucepan and cover with water; bring to a boil. Cook, uncovered, for 8-10 minutes or until crisp-tender. Drain and rinse with cold water. Refrigerate until serving.

2. In a blender or food processor, combine the remaining ingredients. Cover and process until smooth. Refrigerate for at least 1 hour. Serve with beans for dipping. **Yield:** 1-2/3 cups dip.

Nutrition Facts: 2 tablespoons of dip (prepared with fat-free mayonnaise and fat-free half-and-half) equals 85 calories, 7 g fat (1 g saturated fat), 1 mg cholesterol, 293 mg sodium, 5 g carbohydrate, 2 g fiber, trace protein. **Diabetic Exchange:** 2 fat.

Championship Bean Dip

Wendi Wavrin Law, Omaha, Nebraska

My friends and neighbors expect me to bring this irresistible dip to every gathering. When I arrive, they ask, "You brought your bean dip, didn't you?" If there are any leftovers, we use them to make bean and cheese burritos the next day.

- **1 can (16 ounces) refried beans**
- **1 cup picante sauce**
- **1 cup (4 ounces) shredded Monterey Jack cheese**
- **1 cup (4 ounces) shredded cheddar cheese**
- **3/4 cup sour cream**
- **1 package (3 ounces) cream cheese, softened**
- **1 tablespoon chili powder**
- **1/4 teaspoon ground cumin**

Tortilla chips and salsa

In a large bowl, combine the first eight ingredients; transfer to a slow cooker. Cover and cook on high for 2 hours or until heated through, stirring once or twice. Serve with tortilla chips and salsa. **Yield:** 4-1/2 cups.

🏵 🏵 🏵
Frosty Mocha Drink
(Also pictured on page 6)

Lauren Nance, San Diego, California

I whip up this chocolate-flavored coffee drink whenever I have drop-in guests…and I automatically double the recipe because I know they'll want seconds! For a richer and creamier version, simply replace the milk with half-and-half cream.

1 cup milk
3 tablespoons instant chocolate drink mix
2 tablespoons instant coffee granules
2 tablespoons honey
1 teaspoon vanilla extract
14 to 16 ice cubes

In a blender, combine all ingredients; cover and process until smooth. Pour into chilled glasses; serve immediately. **Yield:** 4 servings.

Dilly Bean Potato Salad, p. 31

Garden Spaghetti Salad, p. 28

Cran-Raspberry Sherbet Mold, p. 35

Salads & Dressings

When it comes to sensational salads and delicious dressings, this chapter has the pick of the crop! Enjoy mouth-watering medleys of fresh veggies, pasta, rice, potatoes, seafood and much more.

Strawberry Salad Dressing, p. 45

🎗🎗🎗
Garden Spaghetti Salad

(Also pictured on page 26)

Gloria O'Bryan, Boulder, Colorado

This chock-full medley is very popular with my family, especially in summer when crisp sweet corn is fresh. I think the salad is particularly good alongside a grilled meat entree.

8 ounces spaghetti, broken into 2-inch pieces
1 tablespoon olive oil
2 cups cooked fresh *or* frozen corn
2 cups cooked fresh *or* frozen lima beans
2 medium tomatoes, peeled, seeded and chopped
3/4 cup thinly sliced green onions
1/3 cup minced fresh parsley
6 bacon strips, cooked and crumbled, *divided*
DRESSING:
1/3 cup olive oil
3 tablespoons red wine vinegar
2 tablespoons lemon juice
1 teaspoon sugar
1 teaspoon salt
1/4 teaspoon paprika
Dash pepper

1. Cook spaghetti according to package directions; rinse in cold water and drain. Place in a large bowl; toss with oil. Add the next five ingredients; stir in three-fourths of the bacon.

2. In a small bowl, whisk all dressing ingredients. Pour over spaghetti mixture; toss gently to coat. Sprinkle with remaining bacon. Serve immediately or chill. **Yield:** 10–12 servings.

🎗🎗🎗
Cajun Potato Salad

Margaret Scott, Murfreesboro, Tennessee

I have been making this mouth-watering potato salad for many years. My family prefers Cajun sausage, and thanks to a son living in New Orleans, we have a constant supply of it to use in this rave-winning recipe.

2 pounds small red potatoes
1/2 cup chopped red onions
1/2 cup sliced green onions
1/4 cup minced fresh parsley
6 tablespoons cider vinegar, *divided*
1/2 pound smoked kielbasa *or* smoked Polish sausage, sliced
6 tablespoons olive oil
1 tablespoon Dijon mustard
2 garlic cloves, minced
1/2 teaspoon pepper
1/4 to 1/2 teaspoon cayenne pepper

1. Place potatoes in a large saucepan and cover with water. Bring to a boil. Reduce heat; cover and cook for 15-20 minutes or until tender. Drain; cool completely.

2. Cut into 1/4-in. slices; transfer to a large bowl. Add onions, parsley and 3 tablespoons vinegar; toss.

3. In a medium skillet, cook sausage in oil for 5-10 minutes or until it begins to brown. Remove with slotted spoon and add to potato mixture.

4. To drippings in skillet, add mustard, garlic, pepper, cayenne pepper and remaining vinegar; bring to a boil, whisking constantly. Pour over salad; toss gently. Serve immediately. **Yield:** 6 servings.

Summer Salad with Citrus Vinaigrette

Carolyn Williams, Costa Mesa, California

We live in Orange County, and as you might guess by our county's name, there are plenty of orange trees here. This salad is one of my favorite ways to use that delightful fruit and makes a nice light supper on a hot day.

✓ Uses less fat, sugar or salt. Includes Nutrition Facts and Diabetic Exchanges.

VINAIGRETTE:
- 3 tablespoons orange juice
- 3 tablespoons red wine vinegar
- 2 teaspoons honey
- 1-1/2 teaspoons Dijon mustard
- 1 teaspoon olive oil

SALAD:
- 1 pound boneless beef sirloin steak, cut into thin strips
- 1 tablespoon vegetable oil
- 1/2 teaspoon salt, optional
- 4 cups torn romaine
- 2 large oranges, peeled and sectioned
- 1/2 cup sliced fresh strawberries
- 1/4 cup chopped walnuts, toasted, optional

1. In a small bowl, whisk the vinaigrette ingredients; set aside.

2. In a large skillet, stir-fry steak in oil for 1-2 minutes. Sprinkle with salt if desired.

3. In a large bowl, toss romaine, oranges, strawberries and steak. Add vinaigrette; toss to coat. Top with walnuts if desired. **Yield:** 4 servings.

Nutrition Facts: 1 serving (prepared without salt and walnuts) equals 291 calories, 110 mg sodium, 77 mg cholesterol, 19 g carbohydrate, 28 g protein, 12 g fat. **Diabetic Exchange:** 3 lean meat.

Curried Rice Salad

Lula Young, Newport, Arkansas

I think rice is one of the most versatile foods of all. Arkansas is the top rice-producing state in the country, so this recipe represents our region well.

- 1 can (20 ounces) pineapple tidbits
- 2 cups cooked rice, cooled
- 2 cups cubed cooked chicken
- 1/2 cup chopped celery
- 1/3 cup slivered almonds, toasted
- 1/3 cup raisins
- 1/4 cup chopped green onions
- 2/3 cup mayonnaise
- 1 tablespoon Dijon mustard
- 3/4 teaspoon curry powder
- 1/4 teaspoon salt
- Lettuce leaves, optional

1. Drain pineapple, reserving juice; set aside 1 cup pineapple and 3 tablespoons juice (refrigerate remaining pineapple and juice for another use).

2. In a large bowl, combine the rice, chicken, celery, almonds, raisins, green onions and reserved pineapple.

3. In a small bowl, combine the mayonnaise, mustard, curry powder, salt and reserved juice. Gently stir into rice mixture. Cover and refrigerate for at least 1 hour. Serve in a lettuce-lined bowl if desired. **Yield:** 8 servings.

🎀 🎀 🎀

Wild Rice Seafood Salad

Kathleen Zusan, Scandia, Minnesota

Wild rice grows naturally in the shallow lakes of our region. I'm always happy to use that ingredient in recipes like this delicious dish.

- 3 cups cooked wild rice
- 2 packages (5 ounces *each*) frozen cooked salad shrimp, thawed
- 2 cups flaked imitation crabmeat
- 1/2 cup *each* chopped sweet yellow, green and red peppers
- 1/2 cup chopped onion
- 1/2 cup red wine vinegar
- 1/4 cup olive oil
- 2 teaspoons minced fresh marjoram *or* 1/2 teaspoon dried marjoram
- 2 teaspoons minced fresh tarragon *or* 1/2 teaspoon dried tarragon
- 2 teaspoons minced fresh thyme *or* 1/2 teaspoon dried thyme
- 1 teaspoon salt
- 1/4 teaspoon pepper

1. In a large serving bowl, combine the rice, shrimp, crab, peppers and onion.

2. In a jar with a tight-fitting lid, combine the remaining ingredients; shake well. Pour over rice mixture and toss to coat. Cover and refrigerate for at least 2 hours before serving. **Yield:** 4-5 servings.

🎗🎗🎗
Speedy Southwest Salad

Kara Ann Goff, Loveland, Colorado

I used leftover corn and black beans I had in the fridge to throw together this simple layered salad. It's a big time-saver because it requires little chopping and has a quick dressing. The crunchy combination is always in demand at our house.

- 1 package (10 ounces) ready-to-serve salad greens
- 1 can (15 ounces) whole kernel corn, drained
- 1 can (15 ounces) black beans, rinsed and drained
- 1/2 cup ranch salad dressing
- 1/2 cup picante sauce
- 1 cup broken tortilla chips
- 1/2 cup shredded cheddar cheese
- 1/2 cup diced tomatoes

1. Place the greens in a large salad bowl. Top with corn and beans.

2. In a small bowl, combine the salad dressing and picante sauce; spoon over vegetables and toss to coat. Sprinkle with tortilla chips, cheese and tomatoes. Serve immediately. **Yield:** 6 servings.

🎗🎗🎗
Dilly Bean Potato Salad

(Also pictured on page 26)

Marguerite Novicke, Vineland, New Jersey

Green beans and dill pickles perk up this pretty potato salad, which gets a refreshing tang from Italian-style dressing. My grandmother made this for family gatherings, and she always comes to mind when I dish it up.

- 1 pound fresh green beans, trimmed
- 4 pounds red potatoes
- 1 medium red onion, thinly sliced and separated into rings
- 1 medium Vidalia *or* sweet onion, thinly sliced and separated into rings
- 1 cup chopped celery
- 8 dill pickles, sliced
- 2 tablespoons snipped fresh dill *or* 2 teaspoons dill weed
- 2 tablespoons minced fresh parsley
- 4 garlic cloves, minced

VINAIGRETTE:
- 3/4 cup olive oil
- 1/3 to 1/2 cup tarragon vinegar
- 1 envelope Italian salad dressing mix
- 2 tablespoons sugar
- 1 teaspoon salt
- 1 teaspoon pepper

Celery salt and seasoned salt to taste

1. Place 1 in. of water and beans in a skillet; bring to a boil. Reduce heat. Cover and simmer for 8-10 minutes or until crisp-tender; drain and set aside.

2. Meanwhile, place potatoes in a large saucepan or Dutch oven and cover with water. Bring to a boil. Reduce heat. Cover and cook for 15-20 minutes or until tender; drain and cool. Cut into 1/4-in. slices; transfer to a large bowl. Add the onions, celery, pickles, dill, parsley and garlic.

3. In a jar with a tight-fitting lid, combine the vinaigrette ingredients; shake well. Drizzle over potato mixture. Add beans; gently toss. **Yield:** 14-16 servings.

🎗🎗🎗 Cashew Snow Pea Salad

Beth Gambro, Yorkville, Illinois

I like to serve this cool and refreshing dish on hot summer days. My guests enjoy the crunchy snow peas, cauliflower and cashews tossed with a light ranch dressing.

✓ Uses less fat, sugar or salt. Includes Nutrition Facts and Diabetic Exchanges.

    3 cups fresh snow peas, halved
    2 cups chopped cauliflower
    1 cup chopped celery
 1/4 cup chopped green onions
 1/2 cup reduced-fat sour cream
 1/2 cup reduced-fat ranch salad dressing
Leaf lettuce, optional
    3 bacon strips, cooked and crumbled
 1/3 cup chopped cashews

1. In a large bowl, combine peas, cauliflower, celery and onions.

2. In a small bowl, combine the sour cream and salad dressing; pour over vegetables and toss to coat. Serve in a lettuce-lined bowl if desired. Sprinkle with bacon and cashews. **Yield:** 5 servings.

Nutrition Facts: 1 cup equals 159 calories, 10 g fat (3 g saturated fat), 12 mg cholesterol, 297 mg sodium, 12 g carbohydrate, 3 g fiber, 7 g protein. **Diabetic Exchanges:** 2 vegetable, 1-1/2 fat, 1/2 lean meat.

🎗🎗🎗 Spinach Salad with Rhubarb Dressing

Twila Mitchell, Lindsborg, Kansas

Fresh spinach is excellent with this tangy topping. A friend shared a similar salad dressing recipe with me, which I modified a bit. The rhubarb gives it rosy color and tongue-tingling flavor.

    2 cups chopped fresh or frozen rhubarb
 1/2 cup sugar
 1/4 cup white vinegar
 3/4 cup vegetable oil
    3 tablespoons grated onion
1-1/2 teaspoons Worcestershire sauce
 1/2 teaspoon salt
SALAD:
    6 cups torn fresh spinach
    6 bacon strips, cooked and crumbled
 1/2 cup fresh bean sprouts
 1/2 cup shredded cheddar cheese
    1 to 2 hard-cooked eggs, chopped

1. In a saucepan, combine rhubarb, sugar and vinegar; cook over medium heat until the rhubarb is tender, about 6 minutes. Drain, reserving about 6 tablespoons juice; discard pulp.

2. Pour juice into a jar with tight-fitting lid; add oil, onion, Worcestershire sauce and salt. Shake well. Refrigerate for at least 1 hour.

3. Just before serving, combine salad ingredients in a large bowl. Add the dressing and toss to coat. **Yield:** 6-8 servings.

Editor's Note: If using frozen rhubarb, measure rhubarb while still frozen, then thaw completely. Drain in a colander, but do not press liquid out.

Apple Cider Gelatin Salad

Cyndi Brinkhaus, South Coast Metro, California

Apple cider and crisp apples lend a hint of fall to this change-of-pace salad that's perfect for autumn and holiday gatherings. A dear neighbor lady shared the recipe with me.

  2 envelopes unflavored gelatin
1/2 cup cold water
  2 cups apple cider or juice
1/2 cup sugar
1/3 cup lemon juice
1/4 teaspoon ground cloves
Dash salt
  1 cup diced unpeeled apples
1/2 cup chopped walnuts
1/2 cup chopped celery
TOPPING:
3/4 cup sour cream
1/4 cup mayonnaise
  1 tablespoon sugar
Ground cinnamon
Cinnamon sticks, optional

1. In a small bowl, sprinkle gelatin over cold water; let stand for 1 minute.

2. In a large saucepan, bring cider to a boil; stir in the gelatin mixture and sugar until dissolved. Stir in lemon juice, cloves and salt. Pour into a large bowl. Refrigerate until slightly thickened, about 1 hour.

3. Fold in apples, walnuts and celery. Pour into a 1-qt. dish or individual dishes. Refrigerate until firm, about 2 hours.

4. For topping, in a small bowl, combine the sour cream, mayonnaise and sugar until blended. Dollop over salad; sprinkle with cinnamon. Serve with cinnamon sticks if desired. **Yield:** 6 servings.

Lentil Chicken Salad

Margaret Pache, Mesa, Arizona

This satisfying salad is a great way to use lentils. Besides the combination of textures, the tasty ingredients blend well with the creamy dressing. It merited a blue ribbon and praise from visitors at our church fair.

  2 cups shredded iceberg lettuce
  1 cup cooked lentils
  1 cup diced cooked chicken
  1 cup diced celery
1/2 cup shredded carrot
1/2 cup chopped pecans
  1 cup mayonnaise
1/4 cup chunky salsa
  4 green onions, chopped
  1 tablespoon lemon juice

In a large bowl, combine the first six ingredients. In a small bowl, combine the mayonnaise, salsa, onions and lemon juice. Pour over salad; toss gently to coat. Serve immediately. **Yield:** 4-6 servings.

🎀🎀🎀
Curried Chicken Barley Salad

Patricia Force, Winsted, Connecticut

The ingredients in this luscious summer salad sound a bit unusual, but they blend together beautifully.

5-1/3 cups water
   1 cup uncooked medium pearl barley
   2 cups frozen peas and carrots
   2 cups cubed cooked chicken
 3/4 cup salted dry roasted peanuts
   1 celery rib with leaves, finely chopped
   1 green onion, thinly sliced
DRESSING:
 1/2 cup mayonnaise
 1/2 cup plain yogurt
7-1/2 teaspoons orange marmalade
1-1/2 teaspoons spicy brown mustard
1-1/2 teaspoons curry powder

1. In a large saucepan, bring water and barley to a boil. Reduce heat; cover and simmer for 45–50 minutes or until tender.

2. Remove from the heat; let stand for 5 minutes. Drain and cool. Place 1 in. of water in another saucepan; add peas and carrots. Bring to a boil. Reduce heat; cover and simmer for 5–7 minutes or until tender. Drain and cool.

3. In a large bowl, combine the barley, peas and carrots, chicken, peanuts, celery and green onion.

4. In a small bowl, whisk together the dressing ingredients. Pour over barley mixture; toss to coat. Cover and refrigerate for 2–3 hours. **Yield:** 5–7 servings.

🎀🎀🎀
Antipasto Tossed Salad

Amy Bauman, Modesto, California

This is one of the few lettuce salads my husband will eat! Adding a little lemon juice to the bottled Italian dressing is an easy way to give it homemade flair.

✓ Uses less fat, sugar or salt. Includes Nutrition Facts and Diabetic Exchanges.

1-3/4 cups thinly sliced halved zucchini
1-1/2 cups fresh cauliflowerets
 1/4 cup thinly sliced green onions
   1 cup reduced-fat Italian salad dressing
   1 tablespoon lemon juice
 12 cups torn romaine
   2 medium tomatoes, cut into wedges
   4 large fresh mushrooms, thinly sliced
   4 ounces sliced turkey salami, julienned
   4 ounces reduced-fat provolone cheese, julienned
   1 can (2-1/4 ounces) sliced ripe olives, drained
   1 cup fat-free Italian croutons
 1/4 cup shredded Parmesan cheese

1. In a bowl, combine the zucchini, cauliflower and onions. Combine the salad dressing and lemon juice; pour over vegetables and toss to coat. Cover and refrigerate for at least 4 hours.

2. Just before serving, combine the romaine, tomatoes, mushrooms, salami, provolone and olives in a serving bowl. Add marinated vegetables; toss to coat. Top with the croutons and Parmesan cheese. **Yield:** 16 servings.

Nutrition Facts: 1 cup equals 86 calories, 5 g fat (2 g saturated fat), 12 mg cholesterol, 329 mg sodium, 7 g carbohydrate, 1 g fiber, 6 g protein. **Diabetic Exchanges:** 1/2 starch, 1/2 lean meat, 1/2 fat.

🎖 🎖 🎖
Cran-Raspberry Sherbet Mold

(Also pictured on page 26)

Judith Outlaw, Washougal, Washington

Folks who love the flavor of raspberries and cranberries rave about this tart, molded gelatin salad. It's easy to make and pretty enough for special occasions. I like to garnish it with whole cranberries and raspberries.

> **2 packages (3 ounces *each*) raspberry gelatin**
> **1-1/2 cups boiling water**
> **1 can (16 ounces) jellied cranberry sauce**
> **2 cups raspberry sherbet, softened**
> **1 tablespoon lemon juice**
> **Cranberries, raspberries, orange segments and fresh mint, optional**

1. In a large bowl, dissolve gelatin in boiling water. Stir in cranberry sauce until smooth; refrigerate for 30 minutes or until slightly thickened.

2. Fold in sherbet and lemon juice. Transfer to a 6-cup ring mold coated with nonstick cooking spray. Refrigerate until firm.

3. Unmold onto a serving platter. Fill center with cranberries and raspberries, and serve with oranges and mint if desired. **Yield:** 10-12 servings.

Unmolding Gelatin Salads

For easy removal of a gelatin salad from the mold, coat the interior of the mold with nonstick cooking spray before filling it. When ready to unmold the salad, place the serving plate or platter over the mold and invert. Then carefully lift the mold from the salad.

When unmolding a large gelatin salad, rinse the serving platter with cold water before turning the gelatin out. The moisture will allow the salad to be easily centered on the platter.

Cranberry-Chutney Turkey Salad

Andrea Yacyk, Brigantine, New Jersey

Dried cranberries give this refreshing salad sweetness while chopped pecans lend a pleasant crunch. Whether served on a lettuce leaf or stuffed inside a pita, it makes a perfect lunch or midday snack.

✓ Uses less fat, sugar or salt. Includes Nutrition Facts and Diabetic Exchanges.

- 3 cups diced cooked turkey breast
- 1/2 cup dried cranberries
- 1/3 cup chopped pecans
- 1/3 cup diced onion
- 1/3 cup diced green pepper
- 1/2 cup fat-free mayonnaise
- 1/2 cup reduced-fat sour cream
- 1 tablespoon lemon juice
- 1/2 teaspoon ground ginger
- 1/8 teaspoon cayenne pepper

Leaf lettuce

1. In a large bowl, combine the turkey, cranberries, pecans, onion and green pepper.

2. In a small bowl, combine the mayonnaise, sour cream, lemon juice, ginger and cayenne.

3. Pour over turkey mixture; stir gently to coat. Cover and refrigerate until serving. Serve in a lettuce-lined bowl. **Yield:** 6 servings.

Nutrition Facts: 2/3 cup equals 226 calories, 8 g fat (2 g saturated fat), 69 mg cholesterol, 214 mg sodium, 15 g carbohydrate, 2 g fiber, 23 g protein. **Diabetic Exchanges:** 3 very lean meat, 1 fat, 1/2 starch, 1/2 fruit.

Zesty Gazpacho Salad

Teresa Fischer, Munster, Indiana

This mouth-watering salad is excellent for a summer cookout. Because you mix it in advance, the flavors have time to blend and there's no last-minute fuss. My friends ask me to bring it whenever we get together for a meal.

- 2 medium zucchini, quartered and cut into thick slices
- 2 medium tomatoes, chopped
- 1 small ripe avocado, chopped
- 1 cup fresh or frozen corn, thawed
- 1/2 cup thinly sliced green onions
- 1/2 cup picante sauce
- 2 tablespoons minced fresh parsley
- 2 tablespoons lemon juice
- 1 tablespoon vegetable oil
- 3/4 teaspoon garlic salt
- 1/4 teaspoon ground cumin

In a bowl, combine the first five ingredients. In a small bowl, combine remaining ingredients; mix well. Pour over zucchini mixture; toss to coat. Cover and refrigerate for at least 4 hours. **Yield:** 8-10 servings.

Springtime Luncheon Salad

Julie Dillion, Boise, Idaho

I discovered this recipe when I was looking for dishes to serve on warm days. The chicken salad nestled in a molded gelatin ring makes this great for a light lunch. Even my son likes it, and he's the pickiest eater on the planet!

> 2 envelopes unflavored gelatin
> 2-1/2 cups orange juice, *divided*
> 2 cups sugar
> Dash salt
> 4 egg yolks, lightly beaten
> 3 medium navel oranges, peeled and sectioned
> 3 tablespoons lemon juice
> 1 teaspoon grated orange peel
> 1 teaspoon grated lemon peel
> 2 cups heavy whipping cream, whipped
> **CHICKEN SALAD:**
> 6 cups cubed cooked chicken
> 1 cup chopped celery
> 1 cup mayonnaise
> 1/8 teaspoon white vinegar
> Salt and pepper to taste
> 1/2 cup heavy whipping cream, whipped
> 1/2 cup sliced almonds, toasted
> Orange peel strips and fresh thyme, optional

1. In a large saucepan, sprinkle gelatin over 1 cup orange juice; let stand for 1 minute. Stir in sugar and salt. Cook and stir over low heat until gelatin and sugar are completely dissolved. Remove from the heat.

2. Stir a small amount of hot mixture into egg yolks; return all to the pan, stirring constantly. Bring to a gentle boil; cook and stir for 2 minutes longer. Remove from the heat. Stir in the orange sections, lemon juice, grated peel and remaining orange juice. Cool.

3. Fold in whipped cream. Pour into a 9-cup ring mold coated with nonstick cooking spray. Chill until set.

4. In a large bowl, combine chicken and celery. In a small bowl, combine mayonnaise, vinegar, salt and pepper; fold in whipped cream. Fold into chicken mixture.

5. Unmold gelatin onto a serving platter. Fill center with chicken salad. Sprinkle with almonds. Serve with orange peel and thyme if desired. **Yield:** 8-10 servings.

Cherry Tomato Salad

Sally Sibley, St. Augustine, Florida

This recipe evolved from a need to use the bumper crops of delicious cherry tomatoes we grow. It's become a summer favorite, especially at barbecues.

> 1 quart cherry tomatoes, halved
> 1/4 cup vegetable oil
> 3 tablespoons white vinegar
> 1/4 cup minced fresh parsley
> 1 to 2 teaspoons minced fresh basil
> 1 to 2 teaspoons minced fresh oregano
> 1/2 teaspoon salt
> 1/2 teaspoon sugar
> Lettuce leaves

Place tomatoes in a shallow bowl. In a jar with a tight-fitting lid, combine the oil, vinegar, parsley, basil, oregano, salt and sugar; shake well. Pour over tomatoes. Cover and refrigerate overnight. Serve on a bed of lettuce. **Yield:** 6-8 servings.

Grapefruit Pork Salad

Sarah Hickman, Cardington, Ohio

I found the recipe for this stir-fried pork salad years ago and have modified it a bit since. My family often requests it—especially in summer.

✓ Uses less fat, sugar or salt. Includes Nutrition Facts and Diabetic Exchanges.

1/4 cup unsweetened grapefruit juice
2 tablespoons red wine vinegar
1 tablespoon canola oil
2 teaspoons honey
1 teaspoon prepared mustard
1 teaspoon poppy seeds
1/8 plus 1/4 teaspoon salt, *divided*
1 pound pork tenderloin, julienned
1 bunch leaf lettuce, torn
1 medium grapefruit, peeled and sectioned
1 medium white grapefruit, peeled and sectioned
1-1/2 cups halved green grapes
1 cup quartered fresh strawberries

1. In a jar with a tight-fitting lid, combine the grapefruit juice, vinegar, oil, honey, mustard, poppy seeds and 1/8 teaspoon salt; shake well and set aside.

2. In a large nonstick skillet coated with nonstick cooking spray, stir-fry pork with remaining salt until no longer pink.

3. Place lettuce on a platter; top with warm pork. Arrange grapefruit, grapes and strawberries around pork. Shake dressing; drizzle over salad. **Yield:** 4 servings.

Nutrition Facts: 1 serving equals 311 calories, 10 g fat (2 g saturated fat), 62 mg cholesterol, 354 mg sodium, 30 g carbohydrate, 6 g fiber, 28 g protein. **Diabetic Exchanges:** 3 lean meat, 1-1/2 fruit, 1 fat.

Cashew Chicken Toss

Pamela Martin, Huntsville, Texas

As a home economics teacher, I gave presentations on cooking with microwave ovens when they first became popular. Back then, I shared this pretty salad and warm citrus dressing with my students. It remains one of my favorites today.

2 cans (8 ounces *each*) pineapple chunks
3 tablespoons sugar
2 teaspoons cornstarch
2 teaspoons grated orange peel
1/4 to 1/2 teaspoon dried basil
Dash pepper
1 pound boneless skinless chicken breast halves (4 ounces)
4 cups ready-to-serve salad greens
1 can (11 ounces) mandarin oranges, drained
1/3 cup cashews

1. Drain pineapple, reserving juice; set pineapple aside. In a microwave-safe bowl, combine the sugar, cornstarch, orange peel, basil and pepper. Gradually whisk in pineapple juice until blended.

2. Microwave, uncovered, on high for 2 to 2-1/2 minutes or until mixture boils and is thickened, stirring every 30 seconds. Set aside; stir occasionally.

3. Place chicken in a greased 8-in. square microwave-safe dish. Cover and microwave on high for 5-7 minutes or until juices run clear, turning every 2 minutes. Let stand, covered, for 10 minutes. Cut into thin strips.

4. Arrange the salad greens, chicken, oranges and reserved pineapple on individual plates. Drizzle with warm dressing. Sprinkle with cashews. **Yield:** 4 servings.

Editor's Note: This recipe was tested with an 850-watt microwave.

Quick Vegetable Salad

Priscilla Witthar, Marshall, Missouri

This recipe was given to me by a friend, and it's one the entire family likes. Whenever we have a family get-together, I'm asked to bring this fresh-tasting salad.

✓ Uses less fat, sugar or salt. Includes Nutrition Facts and Diabetic Exchanges.

1 can (16 ounces) whole kernel corn, drained
1 large tomato, seeded and chopped
1/2 cup chopped celery
1/2 cup chopped cucumber
1/3 cup finely chopped green pepper
1/4 cup finely chopped onion
1/4 cup sour cream
2 tablespoons mayonnaise
1 tablespoon cider vinegar
1/4 teaspoon salt, optional
1/4 teaspoon celery seed
1/8 teaspoon pepper

1. In a large salad bowl, combine the corn, tomato, celery, cucumber, green pepper and onion.

2. In a small bowl, combine the remaining ingredients; gently blend into the salad. Serve immediately. **Yield:** 8 servings.

Nutrition Facts: 1/2 cup (prepared with no-salt-added corn, reduced-fat sour cream and fat-free mayonnaise and without added salt) equals 58 calories, 1 g fat (0 saturated fat), 3 mg cholesterol, 42 mg sodium, 12 g carbohydrate, 0 fiber, 2 g protein. **Diabetic Exchanges:** 1 vegetable, 1/2 starch.

🎗🎗🎗 Spectacular Overnight Slaw

Ruth Lovett, Bay City, Texas

To create this crowd-pleasing coleslaw, I combined a number of different recipes and added some ideas of my own. As it chills overnight in the refrigerator, the flavor just keeps getting better. The slaw is a nice option for busy-day events because you prepare it ahead of time.

- 1 medium head cabbage, shredded
- 1 medium red onion, thinly sliced
- 1/2 cup chopped green pepper
- 1/2 cup chopped sweet red pepper
- 1/2 cup sliced stuffed olives
- 1/2 cup white wine vinegar
- 1/2 cup vegetable oil
- 1/2 cup sugar
- 2 teaspoons Dijon mustard
- 1 teaspoon *each* salt, celery seed and mustard seed

In a 4-qt. bowl, combine the cabbage, onion, peppers and olives. In a saucepan, combine the remaining ingredients; bring to a boil. Cook and stir for 1 minute. Pour over vegetables and stir gently. Cover and refrigerate overnight. Mix well before serving. **Yield:** 12-16 servings.

🎗🎗🎗 Southwestern Rice Salad

Rita Zagrzebski, Eagle River, Wisconsin

This meatless salad makes a robust side dish, filling lunch or satisfying snack. I'll even spoon some into low-fat tortillas for a main course.

☑ Uses less fat, sugar or salt. Includes Nutrition Facts and Diabetic Exchanges.

- 2 cups cooked long grain rice, cooled
- 1 cup cooked wild rice, cooled
- 1 can (16 ounces) kidney beans, rinsed and drained
- 1-1/2 cups frozen corn, thawed
- 1/2 cup diced red onion
- 1/2 cup diced green pepper
- 1 can (2-1/4 ounces) sliced ripe olives, drained
- 1-1/2 cups chunky salsa
- 1/2 cup reduced-fat Italian salad dressing
- 1 teaspoon ground cumin
- 1/4 teaspoon salt

In a large bowl, combine the first seven ingredients. In a jar with a tight-fitting lid, combine salsa, salad dressing, cumin and salt; shake well. Pour over rice mixture and stir to coat. Cover and refrigerate for at least 2 hours. **Yield:** 7 servings.

Nutrition Facts: 1 cup equals 257 calories, 4 g fat (1 g saturated fat), 1 mg cholesterol, 537 mg sodium, 48 g carbohydrate, 12 g fiber, 12 g protein. **Diabetic Exchanges:** 2 starch, 1 lean meat, 1 fat.

🎗🎗🎗
Warm Shrimp Salad

Judith LaBrozzi, Canton, Ohio

For a delicious change of pace, try this zesty shrimp mixture served over fresh salad greens. The blend of herbs provides plenty of zippy flavor. Pair the salad with thick slices of Italian or garlic bread.

- 1/4 cup chopped onion
- 1 garlic clove, minced
- 1 tablespoon butter
- 1 pound cooked medium shrimp, peeled and deveined
- 1/2 cup chicken broth
- 1 teaspoon dried oregano
- 1 teaspoon dried basil
- 1/2 teaspoon dried thyme
- 1/8 to 1/4 teaspoon crushed red pepper flakes
- 4 cups torn mixed salad greens

1. In a large skillet, saute the onion and garlic in butter until onion is tender. Add shrimp; cook and stir for 2 minutes. Stir in the broth and seasonings. Bring to a boil. Reduce heat; simmer, uncovered, for 4 minutes or until heated through.

2. Place salad greens on four serving plates; top with shrimp mixture. **Yield:** 4 servings.

🎗🎗🎗
Peanut Chicken Salad

Della Byers, Rosamond, California

Our former neighbor, a native of Indonesia, prepared this peanut chicken salad, which she called "sate." My family liked it so much that, after she moved away, I had to learn to make it.

- 1/3 cup soy sauce
- 3 tablespoons minced garlic
- 3 tablespoons peanut butter
- 1/4 cup minced fresh cilantro
- 1/2 teaspoon hot pepper sauce
- 4 boneless skinless chicken breast halves (4 ounces *each*)
- 4 cups torn mixed salad greens
- 4 small tomatoes, seeded and chopped
- 4 green onions, chopped
- 1 cup shredded cabbage
- 1 medium cucumber, sliced
- 1 cup honey-roasted peanuts
- 1 cup ranch salad dressing
- 2 to 4 drops hot pepper sauce

1. In a large saucepan, combine the soy sauce, garlic, peanut butter, cilantro and hot pepper sauce; cook and stir until heated through and blended. Cool to room temperature.

2. Place chicken in a large resealable plastic bag; add soy sauce mixture. Seal bag and turn to coat; refrigerate for 1 hour.

3. Drain and discard marinade. Grill chicken, uncovered, over medium heat for 3 minutes on each side. Grill 6-8 minutes longer or until juices run clear.

4. Place the salad greens, tomatoes, onions, cabbage, cucumber and peanuts on a serving platter. Slice chicken; arrange over salad.

5. In a small bowl, combine the salad dressing and hot pepper sauce. Serve with salad. **Yield:** 6 servings.

1 envelope unflavored gelatin
1 cup cold water
2 packages (3 ounces *each*) lemon gelatin
2 cups boiling water
1 can (12 ounces) frozen limeade concentrate, thawed
2 cups heavy whipping cream
3 tablespoons confectioners' sugar
Fresh strawberries

1. In a small saucepan, sprinkle unflavored gelatin over cold water; let stand for 1 minute. Bring to a boil; cook and stir until gelatin is dissolved.

2. In a large mixing bowl, dissolve lemon gelatin in boiling water. Stir in unflavored gelatin mixture and limeade concentrate. Refrigerate until slightly thickened.

3. In a small mixing bowl, beat cream until soft peaks form. Add sugar, 1 tablespoon at a time, beating until stiff peaks form. Beat the gelatin until frothy. Stir in the whipped cream.

4. Pour into an 8-cup ring mold coated with nonstick cooking spray; refrigerate until set.

5. Unmold onto a serving platter. Fill the center with strawberries. **Yield:** 10-14 servings.

🎀🎀🎀
Tart Lemon Ring Mold

Patricia Ryzow, Thousand Oaks, California

This gelatin looks as good as it tastes! With its sunny lemon color, the mold brightens up any table. I usually make two because it disappears so quickly.

🎀🎀🎀
Salad with Cran-Raspberry Dressing

Tannis Williams, Gowanstown, Ontario

I was given this recipe at my bridal shower, and it's become my all-time favorite salad. The lovely, tangy berries in the mix make it perfect for just about any occasion.

1 package (10 ounces) frozen sweetened raspberries, thawed and drained
1/4 cup sugar
2 teaspoons cornstarch
1/4 teaspoon celery seed
1/4 teaspoon ground cinnamon
1/8 teaspoon ground cloves
1/2 cup cranberry juice
1/4 cup red wine vinegar
SALAD:
1 package (6 ounces) fresh baby spinach
1 can (11 ounces) mandarin oranges, drained
1/3 cup dried cranberries
3 green onions, sliced
1/4 cup sunflower kernels
1/4 cup chopped pecans
1/4 cup slivered almonds

1. Place raspberries in a blender; cover and process until pureed. Strain and discard seeds; set puree aside.

2. In a large saucepan, combine the sugar, cornstarch, celery seed, cinnamon and cloves. Stir in the cranberry juice, vinegar and reserved raspberry puree. Bring to a boil over medium heat; cook and stir for 1 minute or until thickened. Remove from the heat; cool. Cover and refrigerate.

3. In a large salad bowl, combine the spinach, oranges, cranberries, onions, sunflower kernels, pecans and almonds. Drizzle with dressing; gently toss to coat. Refrigerate any leftover dressing. **Yield:** 12 servings.

Three-Bean Tomato Cups

Audrey Green Ballon, Kentwood, Louisiana

Cilantro and cumin give this delightful salad a bit of Mexican flair. Served in hollowed-out tomatoes, the tasty bean blend is always a nice addition to a ladies' luncheon or other special meal. Garlic lovers might want to add a second clove.

3/4 **pound fresh green beans, cut into 2-inch pieces**
1/2 **pound fresh wax beans, cut into 2-inch pieces**
1 **can (15 ounces) black beans, rinsed and drained**
1 **medium sweet red pepper, cut into 1-1/2-inch strips**
3 **green onions, sliced**
1/4 **cup minced fresh cilantro**
1/4 **cup olive oil**
3 **tablespoons red wine vinegar**
1 **teaspoon ground cumin**
1 **garlic clove, minced**
1/2 **teaspoon salt**
1/4 **teaspoon pepper**
6 **large firm tomatoes**

1. Place the green and wax beans in a saucepan and cover with water; bring to a boil. Cook, uncovered, for 8-10 minutes or until crisp-tender. Drain and place in a large bowl. Add the black beans, red pepper, onions and cilantro.

2. In a jar with a tight-fitting lid, combine the oil, vinegar, cumin, garlic, salt and pepper; shake well. Pour over bean mixture and toss to coat. Cover and refrigerate for 30 minutes.

3. Cut a 1/4-in. slice off the top of each tomato; scoop out and discard pulp. Using a slotted spoon, fill tomato cups with bean mixture. **Yield:** 6 servings.

Frosted Orange Salad

Anna Jean Key, Muskogee, Oklahoma

Pineapple, bananas and marshmallows are folded into orange Jell-O for this refreshing salad. Frosted with a creamy topping, pecans and coconut, this yummy treat is a real crowd-pleaser. I've been making it for years.

- **3 packages (3 ounces *each*) orange gelatin**
- **3 cups boiling water**
- **1 can (20 ounces) crushed pineapple**
- **3 cups cold water**
- **4 medium firm bananas, sliced**
- **2-1/2 cups miniature marshmallows**
- **1/2 cup sugar**
- **1 tablespoon all-purpose flour**
- **1 egg, lightly beaten**
- **1 package (8 ounces) cream cheese, softened**
- **1 cup heavy whipping cream, whipped**
- **3/4 cup chopped pecans, toasted**
- **1/2 cup flaked coconut, toasted**

1. In a large bowl, dissolve gelatin in boiling water. Drain pineapple, reserving juice. Stir cold water, bananas, marshmallows and pineapple into gelatin. Pour into a 13-in. x 9-in. x 2-in. dish coated with nonstick cooking spray; refrigerate until firm.

2. Meanwhile, in a large saucepan, combine sugar and flour. Stir in reserved pineapple juice until smooth. Bring to a boil over medium heat; cook and stir for 2 minutes or until thickened and bubbly. Reduce heat; cook and stir 2 minutes longer.

3. Remove from the heat. Stir a small amount of hot filling into the egg; return all to the pan, stirring constantly. Bring to a gentle boil; cook and stir 2 minutes longer. Cool.

4. In a large mixing bowl, beat cream cheese until smooth. Beat in cooled filling. Fold in whipped cream. Spread over gelatin (dish will be full). Sprinkle with nuts and coconut. **Yield:** 12 servings.

Greens 'n' Fruit Salad

Jean Martin, Raleigh, North Carolina

I created this recipe in my kitchen, and I've received a lot of compliments on it. I make the salad often for my family and have also served it to guests at brunches and dinner parties.

- **6 cups torn mixed salad greens**
- **2 medium navel oranges, peeled and sectioned**
- **1 cup halved red seedless grapes**
- **1/2 cup golden raisins**
- **1/4 cup chopped red onion**
- **1/4 cup sliced almonds**
- **4 bacon strips, cooked and crumbled**

DRESSING:
- **1/2 cup mayonnaise**
- **1/2 cup honey**
- **1/4 cup orange juice**
- **2 tablespoons grated orange peel**

In a large salad bowl, combine the first seven ingredients. In a small bowl, whisk together the mayonnaise, honey, orange juice and peel. Pour over salad; toss to coat. Refrigerate leftover dressing. **Yield:** 6 servings (1 cup dressing).

🎗🎗🎗
Roasted Green Bean Salad

Kathy Shell, San Diego, California

This easy-to-fix recipe turns homegrown green beans into something special. A tangy dill-and-mustard vinaigrette nicely coats the crisp-tender beans but still lets the fresh-picked flavor come through.

  2 pounds fresh green beans, trimmed
  3 tablespoons olive oil, *divided*
3/4 teaspoon salt, *divided*
  2 tablespoons white wine vinegar
1-1/2 teaspoons Dijon mustard
  2 tablespoons snipped fresh dill *or* 2 teaspoons dill weed
1-1/2 teaspoons sugar
1/4 teaspoon pepper

1. In a bowl, toss beans with 1 tablespoon oil and 1/2 teaspoon salt. Spread in a single layer in an ungreased 15-in. x 10-in. x 1-in. baking pan. Roast, uncovered, at 400° for 30-40 minutes or until beans are tender and lightly browned, stirring twice.

2. Meanwhile, in a small bowl, whisk the vinegar, mustard, dill, sugar, pepper and remaining salt. Slowly whisk in remaining oil. Transfer beans to a large serving bowl. Add vinaigrette and toss to coat. **Yield:** 4-6 servings.

🎗🎗🎗
Strawberry Salad Dressing

(Pictured on page 27)

Rebekah Hubbard, Las Vegas, Nevada

A bit of honey perfectly balances raspberry vinegar with strawberries in this homemade dressing. Drizzle some over mixed greens of your choice and enjoy!

 Uses less fat, sugar or salt. Includes Nutrition Facts and Diabetic Exchanges.

  1 package (20 ounces) frozen unsweetened strawberries, thawed
1/2 cup water
  3 tablespoons raspberry vinegar
  2 tablespoons honey
  2 teaspoons canola oil
  1 teaspoon reduced-sodium soy sauce
1/4 teaspoon salt
1/4 teaspoon dried thyme
1/4 teaspoon pepper
Torn mixed salad greens and sliced onion

In a blender or food processor, combine the first nine ingredients. Cover and process until smooth. Serve over greens and onion. Store in the refrigerator. **Yield:** 3 cups.

Nutrition Facts: 2 tablespoons dressing equals 17 calories, trace fat (trace saturated fat), 0 cholesterol, 33 mg sodium, 4 g carbohydrate, 1 g fiber, trace protein. **Diabetic Exchange:** Free food.

Sausage Pasta Stew, p. 48

Four-Onion Soup, p. 50

Raspberry-Cranberry Soup, p. 63

Soups & Stews

Simmer up a pot of chunky gumbo, flavor-packed chili, creamy chowder or any of the other special soups and stews here. No matter which you fix, it'll warm your family heart and soul.

Tomato Zucchini Stew, p. 65

⚜ ⚜ ⚜
Monterey Jack Cheese Soup

Susan Salenski, Copemish, Michigan

I'm constantly on the lookout for soups that are satisfying enough to make a main course. This rich and cheesy variety goes well with nachos or a loaf of bread.

> 1 cup chicken broth
> 1 large tomato, peeled, seeded and diced
> 1/2 cup finely chopped onion
> 2 tablespoons chopped green chilies
> 1 garlic clove, minced
> 2 tablespoons butter
> 2 tablespoons all-purpose flour

Salt and pepper to taste

> 3 cups milk, *divided*
> 1-1/2 cups (6 ounces) shredded Monterey Jack cheese

1. In a 3-qt. saucepan, combine the broth, tomato, onion, chilies and garlic; bring to a boil. Reduce heat; cover and simmer for 10 minutes or until vegetables are tender. Remove from the heat and set aside.

2. In another saucepan, melt butter. Stir in the flour, salt and pepper until smooth; gradually stir in 1-1/2 cups milk. Bring to a boil; cook and stir for 1 minute or until thickened. Slowly stir into vegetable mixture. Reduce heat; add cheese and remaining milk. Cook and stir over low heat until cheese is melted. Serve immediately. **Yield:** 5 servings.

⚜ ⚜ ⚜
Sausage Pasta Stew

(Also pictured on page 46)

Sarah Bowen, Upland, California

I rely on my slow cooker to prepare this chili-like specialty packed with turkey sausage, pasta and vegetables. My gang gobbles it up without realizing they're eating healthy.

 Uses less fat, sugar or salt. Includes Nutrition Facts and Diabetic Exchanges.

> 1 pound turkey Italian sausage links, casings removed
> 4 cups water
> 1 jar (26 ounces) meatless spaghetti sauce
> 1 can (16 ounces) kidney beans, rinsed and drained
> 1 medium yellow summer squash, halved lengthwise and cut into 1-inch pieces
> 2 medium carrots, cut into 1/4-inch slices
> 1 medium sweet red *or* green pepper, diced
> 1/3 cup chopped onion
> 1-1/2 cups uncooked spiral pasta
> 1 cup frozen peas
> 1 teaspoon sugar
> 1/2 teaspoon salt
> 1/4 teaspoon pepper

1. In a nonstick skillet, cook sausage links over medium heat until no longer pink; drain and place in a 5-qt. slow cooker. Add water, spaghetti sauce, kidney beans, summer squash, carrots, red pepper and onion; mix well. Cover and cook on low for 7-9 hours or until vegetables are tender.

2. Stir in the pasta, peas, sugar, salt and pepper; mix well. Cover and cook on high for 15-20 minutes or until pasta is tender. **Yield:** 8 servings.

Nutrition Facts: 1-1/3 cups equals 276 calories, 6 g fat (2 g saturated fat), 30 mg cholesterol, 1,111 mg sodium, 38 g carbohydrate, 6 g fiber, 18 g protein. **Diabetic Exchanges:** 2 lean meat, 2 vegetable, 1-1/2 starch.

Texas Beef Stew

Wilma James, Ranger, Texas

This easy, tasty dish quickly became a favorite in our household. We're big fans of foods with Southwestern flavor, and this stew pleases everyone.

1-1/4 pounds beef stew meat, cut into 1-inch pieces
    1 to 2 tablespoons vegetable oil, optional
    1/4 cup chopped onion
1-1/2 teaspoons garlic powder
    1/4 teaspoon pepper
    1 cup water
    1 can (14-1/2 ounces) diced tomatoes, undrained
    1 tablespoon ground cumin
    1 teaspoon salt

1. In a Dutch oven or large saucepan, cook beef until no longer pink, adding oil if desired; drain. Add onion, garlic powder, pepper and water; bring to a boil. Reduce heat; cover and simmer for 45 minutes or until meat is almost tender.

2. Add tomatoes, cumin and salt; return to a boil. Reduce heat; cover and simmer for 15-20 minutes or until meat is tender. **Yield:** 4 servings (1 quart).

Louisiana Gumbo

Gloria Mason, Springhill, Louisiana

For a hearty and filling supper, you can't go wrong with this stew-like dish full of chicken, sausage, ham and shrimp. Serve it with hot pepper sauce on the side so guests can add their preferred amount of "heat."

    1 broiler/fryer chicken (3 to 3-1/2 pounds), cut up
    2 quarts water
3/4 cup all-purpose flour
1/2 cup vegetable oil
1/2 cup sliced green onions
1/2 cup chopped onion
1/2 cup chopped green pepper
1/2 cup chopped sweet red pepper
1/2 cup chopped celery
    2 garlic cloves, minced
1/2 pound smoked sausage, cut into 1-inch cubes
1/2 pound fully cooked ham, cut into 3/4-inch cubes
1/2 pound fresh *or* frozen uncooked shrimp, peeled and deveined
    1 cup cut fresh *or* frozen okra (3/4-inch pieces)
    1 can (16 ounces) kidney beans, rinsed and drained
1/2 teaspoon salt
1/4 teaspoon pepper
1/4 teaspoon hot pepper sauce

1. Place the chicken and water in a Dutch oven; bring to a boil. Skim fat. Reduce heat; cover and simmer 30-45 minutes or until chicken is tender.

2. Remove chicken; cool. Reserve 6 cups broth. Remove chicken from bones; cut into bite-size pieces.

3. In a Dutch oven or soup kettle, mix flour and oil until smooth; cook and stir over medium-low heat until browned, 2-3 minutes. Stir in the onions, peppers, celery and garlic; cook for 5 minutes or until vegetables are tender. Stir in the sausage, ham and reserved broth and chicken; cover and simmer for 45 minutes.

4. Add the shrimp, okra, beans, salt, pepper and hot pepper sauce; cover and simmer 10 minutes longer or until shrimp turn pink. **Yield:** 12 servings.

🎗🎗🎗
Four-Onion Soup

(Also pictured on page 46)

Margaret Adams, Pacific Grove, California

This wonderful, rich soup is such a mainstay for our family, I feel compelled to share the recipe! Topped with toasted French bread and melted cheese, it looks as great as it tastes.

- 1 medium yellow onion
- 1 medium red onion
- 1 medium leek (white portion only)
- 5 green onions with tops
- 1 garlic clove, minced
- 2 tablespoons butter
- 2 cans (14-1/2 ounces *each*) beef broth
- 1 can (10-1/2 ounces) condensed beef consomme, undiluted
- 1 teaspoon Worcestershire sauce
- 1/2 teaspoon ground nutmeg
- 1 cup (4 ounces) shredded Swiss cheese
- 6 slices French bread (3/4 inch thick), toasted
- 6 tablespoons grated Parmesan cheese, optional

1. Slice all onions 1/4 in. thick. In a large saucepan over medium-low heat, saute onions and garlic in butter for 15 minutes or until tender and golden, stirring occasionally. Add broth, consomme, Worcestershire sauce and nutmeg; bring to a boil. Reduce heat; cover and simmer for 30 minutes.

2. Sprinkle 1 tablespoon of Swiss cheese in the bottom of six oven-proof 8-oz. bowls. Ladle hot soup into bowls. Top each with a slice of bread. Sprinkle with remaining Swiss cheese and Parmesan cheese if desired. Broil 6-8 in. from the heat or until cheese melts. Serve immediately. **Yield:** 6 servings.

🎗🎗🎗
Red Potato Soup

Bev Bosveld, Waupun, Wisconsin

I love to entertain, and this is one of my favorite recipes for guests. Onion, celery and bacon season the thin but creamy broth in this chunky soup, which always wins raves.

- 2-1/2 pounds unpeeled small red potatoes, cut into 1-inch cubes
- 1 large onion, diced
- 3 celery ribs, diced
- 3 bacon strips, diced
- 8 cups milk
- 4 cups water
- 3 tablespoons chicken bouillon granules
- 1 teaspoon salt
- 1/2 teaspoon pepper
- 3/4 cup butter, cubed
- 3/4 cup all-purpose flour
- 1 cup heavy whipping cream
- 1/2 cup minced fresh parsley
- Shredded cheddar cheese and chopped green onions

1. Place potatoes in a saucepan and cover with water. Bring to a boil. Reduce heat; cover and cook for 10-12 minutes or until tender. Drain and set aside.

2. In a Dutch oven or large soup kettle, saute the onion, celery and bacon until vegetables are tender; drain well. Add the milk, water, bouillon, salt and pepper; heat through (do not boil).

3. In a large saucepan, melt butter; stir in flour until smooth. Cook and stir over medium heat for 1 minute. Gradually add cream. Bring to a boil; cook and stir for 1-2 minutes or until thickened. Stir into soup. Add parsley and potatoes; heat through. Sprinkle with cheese and green onions. **Yield:** 18 servings (4-1/2 quarts).

 Shamrock Stew

Robin Perry, Seneca, Pennsylvania

Irish or not, you and your family are sure to enjoy this savory beef stew. The homemade dumplings make it extra special.

✓ Uses less fat, sugar or salt. Includes Nutrition Facts and Diabetic Exchanges.

  1/4 **cup all-purpose flour**
  3/4 **teaspoon salt, optional**
  1/4 **teaspoon pepper**
1-1/2 **to 2 pounds boneless beef top round steak, cut into 1-inch cubes**
    1 **tablespoon vegetable oil**
    1 **can (8 ounces) tomato sauce**
    2 **cups water**
    1 **large onion, sliced**
    1 **teaspoon dried marjoram**
    1 **bay leaf**
    1 **pound carrots, cut into 1-inch pieces**
    1 **package (10 ounces) frozen peas**
DUMPLINGS:
    1 **cup all-purpose flour**
    1 **teaspoon baking powder**
  1/4 **cup milk**
    1 **egg, lightly beaten**
    1 **tablespoon vegetable oil**
    1 **tablespoon chopped fresh parsley, optional**

1. In a large bowl, combine flour, salt if desired and pepper; set aside 2 tablespoons. Add meat to bowl and toss to coat. In a Dutch oven or large soup kettle over medium heat, cook the meat in oil until no longer pink; drain. Stir in tomato sauce, water and reserved flour mixture. Add onion, marjoram and bay leaf; bring to a boil. Reduce heat; cover and simmer for 2 hours, stirring occasionally.

2. Add carrots; cover and simmer for 45 minutes. Stir in peas. Cover and simmer for 15 minutes or until the vegetables are tender. Remove bay leaf.

3. For dumplings, in a large bowl, combine flour and baking powder. Stir in milk, egg, oil and parsley if desired. Drop by tablespoonfuls onto simmering stew. Cover and cook for 12-14 minutes or until done. Do not lift the cover. Serve immediately. **Yield:** 8 servings.

Nutrition Facts: 1/8 recipe (prepared with no-salt-added tomato sauce; calculated without added salt) equals 333 calories, 9 g fat (0 saturated fat), 95 mg cholesterol, 325 mg sodium, 36 g carbohydrate, 0 fiber, 31 g protein. **Diabetic Exchanges:** 3 lean meat, 2 vegetable, 1-1/2 starch.

🎗🎗🎗
Chili with Tortilla Dumplings

Shirley Logan, Houston, Texas

Here in Texas, we've always appreciated the bold flavors of Southwestern cooking. This chili is a special favorite—I've prepared it for a crowd and even just the two of us. The simple dumplings are a fun twist.

- **2 pounds ground beef**
- **1 medium onion, chopped**
- **2 garlic cloves, minced**
- **2 cans (16 ounces *each*) kidney beans, rinsed and drained**
- **1 can (28 ounces) diced tomatoes, undrained**
- **1 can (14-1/2 ounces) chicken broth**
- **2 to 3 tablespoons chili powder**
- **1 teaspoon ground cumin**
- **1 teaspoon dried oregano**
- **1/2 teaspoon salt**
- **4 flour tortillas (7 inches)**

1. In a large saucepan, cook the beef, onion and garlic over medium heat until beef is no longer pink; drain.

Add the next seven ingredients; bring to a boil. Reduce heat; cover and simmer for 50 minutes.

2. Halve each tortilla and cut into 1/4-in. strips. Gently stir into soup; cover and simmer for 8-10 minutes or until tortillas are softened. Serve immediately. **Yield:** 6-8 servings (2-1/4 quarts).

🎗🎗🎗
Vegetable Meatball Stew

Elaine Grose, Elmira, New York

People who sample this filling stew comment on how much they like the sweet potatoes. But they never seem to guess my secret ingredient—parsnips!

- **4 cups water**
- **2 medium peeled potatoes, cut into 1-inch cubes**
- **2 medium carrots, cut into 3/4-inch chunks**
- **1 large onion, cut into eighths**
- **2 tablespoons beef bouillon granules**
- **1 bay leaf**
- **1 teaspoon dried thyme**
- **1 teaspoon dried basil**

- **1/2 teaspoon salt**
- **1/2 teaspoon pepper**
- **1/2 cup seasoned dry bread crumbs**
- **1 egg, lightly beaten**
- **1 teaspoon Worcestershire sauce**
- **1 pound ground beef**
- **2 medium sweet potatoes, peeled and cut into 1-inch cubes**
- **2 medium parsnips, peeled and cut into 3/4-inch slices**
- **1 cup frozen peas**
- **1/3 cup all-purpose flour**
- **1/2 cup cold water**
- **1/4 teaspoon browning sauce, optional**

1. In a large Dutch oven or soup kettle, bring water to boil. Add potatoes, carrots, onion and seasonings; return to a boil. Reduce heat; cover and simmer for 10 minutes.

2. Meanwhile, in a small bowl, combine the bread crumbs, egg and Worcestershire sauce. Crumble beef over mixture and mix well.

3. Shape into 1-in. balls; add to Dutch oven along with sweet potatoes and parsnips. Bring to a boil. Reduce heat; cover and simmer for 15 minutes or until vegetables are tender.

4. Discard bay leaf. Stir in peas. Combine flour and cold water and browning sauce if desired until smooth; gradually stir into stew. Bring to a boil; cook and stir for 2 minutes or until thickened. **Yield:** 6 servings.

Mexican Bean Barley Soup

Elizabeth Cole, Mauckport, Indiana

This wonderful warm-you-up soup is always on the menu for the retreats we host on our woodland farm. Everyone enjoys the tasty vegetable broth full of beans and barley. To round out the meal, I serve a basket of onion-herb bread.

- 2 medium onions, chopped
- 3 garlic cloves, minced
- 2 tablespoons vegetable oil
- 1 medium turnip, peeled and diced
- 1 medium carrot, diced
- 2 tablespoons finely chopped jalapeno pepper
- 1-1/2 teaspoons ground cumin
- 1/2 teaspoon ground coriander
- 3 cans (14-1/2 ounces *each*) vegetable broth
- 2 cups cooked barley
- 1 can (15 ounces) pinto beans, rinsed and drained
- 2 teaspoons lemon juice

1. In a large saucepan, saute onions and garlic in oil until tender. Add the turnip, carrot and jalapeno; cook and stir until tender. Add cumin and coriander; cook and stir for 2 minutes. Add broth. Bring to a boil.

2. Reduce heat; cover and simmer for 20 minutes. Add the barley, beans and lemon juice. Simmer, uncovered, 10-15 minutes longer or until soup thickens slightly. **Yield:** 7 servings.

Editor's Note: When cutting or seeding hot peppers, use rubber or plastic gloves to protect your hands. Avoid touching your face.

Black-Eyed Pea Sausage Stew

Laura Wimbrow, Bridgeville, Delaware

I've always wanted to try black-eyed peas, and I happened to have smoked sausage on hand one night, so I invented this full-flavored stew. It's the perfect way to take the chill out of a cold evening without spending a lot of time in the kitchen.

- 1 package (16 ounces) smoked sausage links, halved lengthwise and sliced
- 1 small onion, chopped
- 2 cans (15 ounces *each*) black-eyed peas, rinsed and drained
- 1 can (14-1/2 ounces) diced tomatoes, drained
- 1 can (8 ounces) tomato sauce
- 1 cup beef broth
- 1/4 teaspoon garlic powder
- 1/4 teaspoon Cajun seasoning
- 1/4 teaspoon pepper
- 1/8 teaspoon salt
- 1/8 teaspoon cayenne pepper
- 1/8 teaspoon hot pepper sauce
- 1-1/2 cups frozen corn, thawed

In a Dutch oven or soup kettle, cook sausage and onion over medium heat until meat is lightly browned; drain. Stir in the peas, tomatoes, tomato sauce, broth and seasonings. Cook and stir for 10-12 minutes or until hot and bubbly. Stir in corn; cook 5 minutes longer or until heated through. **Yield:** 6 servings.

🎀🎀🎀
Oven Beef Stew

Debbie Patton, Westchester, Illinois

My guests never guess that this home-style stew chock-full of beef is low in fat. With a thick, flavorful sauce, this hearty dish is asked for time and again.

✓ Uses less fat, sugar or salt. Includes Nutrition Facts and Diabetic Exchanges.

2 pounds boneless beef top round roast, cut into 1-1/2-inch cubes
2 medium potatoes, peeled and cut into 1/2-inch cubes
2 medium onions, cut into eighths
3 celery ribs, cut into 1-inch pieces
4 medium carrots, cut into 1-inch slices
1 can (11-1/2 ounces) tomato juice
1/3 cup dry sherry **or** water
1/3 cup quick-cooking tapioca
1 tablespoon sugar
1 teaspoon salt
1/2 teaspoon dried basil
1/4 teaspoon pepper
2 cups fresh green beans, cut into 1-inch pieces

1. In a Dutch oven or large soup kettle, combine the beef, potatoes, onions, celery and carrots; set aside.

2. In a large bowl, combine the tomato juice, sherry or water, tapioca, sugar, salt, basil and pepper. Let stand for 15 minutes. Pour over the beef mixture. Cover and bake at 325° for 2 to 2-1/2 hours or until the meat is almost tender.

3. Add the beans; cook 30 minutes longer or until beans and meat are tender. **Yield:** 8 servings.

Nutrition Facts: 1 cup equals 268 calories, 7 g fat (2 g saturated fat), 70 mg cholesterol, 519 mg sodium, 25 g carbohydrate, 4 g fiber, 25 g protein. **Diabetic Exchanges:** 3 lean meat, 2 vegetable, 1 starch.

✿✿✿
Cheeseburger Soup

Joanie Shawhan, Madison, Wisconsin

When I requested the recipe for a cheeseburger-flavored soup served at a restaurant, they wouldn't reveal it. So I developed my own by modifying a recipe for potato soup, and I was really pleased with the results.

   1/2 pound ground beef
   3/4 cup chopped onion
   3/4 cup shredded carrots
   3/4 cup diced celery
     1 teaspoon dried basil
     1 teaspoon dried parsley flakes
     4 tablespoons butter, *divided*
     3 cups chicken broth
     4 cups diced peeled potatoes (1-3/4 pounds)
   1/4 cup all-purpose flour
     2 cups (8 ounces) process cheese (Velveeta)
 1-1/2 cups milk
   3/4 teaspoon salt
   1/4 to 1/2 teaspoon pepper
   1/4 cup sour cream

1. In a 3-qt. saucepan, cook beef until no longer pink; drain and set aside. In the same saucepan, saute onion, carrots, celery, basil and parsley in 1 tablespoon butter until vegetables are tender, about 10 minutes. Add broth, potatoes and beef; bring to a boil. Reduce heat; cover and simmer for 10-12 minutes or until potatoes are tender.

2. Meanwhile, in a small skillet, melt remaining butter. Add flour; cook and stir for 3-5 minutes or until bubbly. Add to soup; bring to a boil. Cook and stir for 2 minutes. Reduce heat to low. Add cheese, milk, salt and pepper; cook and stir until cheese melts. Remove from the heat; blend in sour cream. **Yield:** 8 servings (2-1/4 quarts).

✿✿✿
Tomato Dill Soup

Patty Kile, Greentown, Pennsylvania

I like to prepare this creamy soup ahead of time and keep it in the fridge. A steaming bowlful is great with tuna or grilled cheese sandwiches, hard rolls or a salad. You could even enjoy this soup cold.

     1 medium onion, thinly sliced
     1 garlic clove, minced
     2 tablespoons vegetable oil
     1 tablespoon butter
   1/2 teaspoon salt
 Pinch pepper
     3 large tomatoes, sliced
     1 can (6 ounces) tomato paste
   1/4 cup all-purpose flour
     2 cups water, *divided*
   3/4 cup heavy whipping cream, whipped
     1 to 2 tablespoons finely minced fresh dill
       or 1 to 2 teaspoons dill weed

1. In a large saucepan over low heat, cook onion and garlic in oil and butter until tender. Add salt, pepper and tomatoes; cook over medium-high heat for 3 minutes. Remove from the heat and stir in tomato paste.

2. In a small bowl, combine flour and 1/2 cup of water; stir until smooth. Stir into saucepan. Gradually stir in remaining water until smooth; bring to a boil over medium heat. Cook and stir for 2 minutes.

3. Place mixture in a sieve over a bowl. With the back of a spoon, press vegetables through the sieve to remove seeds and skin; return puree to pan. Add cream and dill; cook over low heat just until heated through (do not boil). **Yield:** 4 servings (1 quart).

🎖🎖🎖
Cream of Asparagus Soup

Veva Hepler, Walla Walla, Washington

It's easy to fix a batch of this smooth, comforting soup full of homemade goodness. A single steaming bowl really warms me up...but I usually can't resist going back for seconds.

- 1/2 **cup chopped onion**
- 1 **tablespoon vegetable oil**
- 2 **cans (14-1/2 ounces** *each***) chicken broth**
- 2-1/2 **pounds fresh asparagus, trimmed and cut into 1-inch pieces**
- 1/4 **teaspoon dried tarragon**
- 1/4 **cup butter, cubed**
- 1/4 **cup all-purpose flour**
- 1/2 **teaspoon salt**
- 1/4 **teaspoon white pepper**
- 3 **cups half-and-half cream**
- 1-1/2 **teaspoons lemon juice**

Shredded Swiss cheese

1. In a large saucepan, saute onion in oil until tender. Add the broth, asparagus and tarragon. Bring to a boil. Reduce heat; simmer, uncovered, for 8-10 minutes or until asparagus is tender. Cool for 10 minutes.

2. In a blender or food processor, puree the asparagus mixture, a third at a time; set aside.

3. In a Dutch oven or soup kettle, melt butter; stir in flour, salt and pepper until smooth. Cook and stir for 2 minutes or until golden. Gradually add cream. Bring to a boil; cook and stir for 2 minutes or until thickened. Reduce heat; stir in the pureed asparagus and lemon juice and heat through. Sprinkle with cheese if desired. **Yield:** 8 servings (about 2 quarts).

🎖🎖🎖
Southwest Beef Stew

Janet Brannan, Sidney, Montana

Add your family's favorite picante sauce to ground beef, black beans and corn...then watch how quickly they empty their bowls! This stew freezes well, so I keep some on hand for a quick, nutritious meal whenever I need one.

☑ Uses less fat, sugar or salt. Includes Nutrition Facts and Diabetic Exchanges.

- 2 **pounds lean ground beef**
- 1-1/2 **cups chopped onions**
- 1 **can (28 ounces) diced tomatoes, undrained**
- 1 **package (16 ounces) frozen corn, thawed**
- 1 **can (15 ounces) black beans, rinsed and drained**
- 1 **cup picante sauce**
- 3/4 **cup water**
- 1 **teaspoon ground cumin**
- 3/4 **teaspoon salt**
- 1/2 **teaspoon garlic powder**
- 1/2 **teaspoon pepper**
- 1/2 **cup shredded reduced-fat cheddar cheese**

In a Dutch oven, cook beef and onions over medium heat until meat is no longer pink; drain. Stir in the tomatoes, corn, beans, picante sauce, water, cumin, salt, garlic powder and pepper. Bring to a boil. Reduce heat; cover and simmer for 15 minutes or until corn is tender. Sprinkle with cheese. **Yield:** 8 servings.

Nutrition Facts: 1-1/3 cups equals 344 calories, 12 g fat (5 g saturated fat), 45 mg cholesterol, 847 mg sodium, 28 g carbohydrate, 7 g fiber, 31 g protein. **Diabetic Exchanges:** 4 lean meat, 1-1/2 starch, 1 vegetable.

🏅🏅🏅 Skillet Chicken Stew

Valerie Jordan, Kingmont, West Virginia

I adapted this skillet supper from a beef stew recipe many years ago. We liked the chicken version so much that I have never changed any of the ingredients or amounts—unless it was to double the recipe!

> 1/3 cup all-purpose flour
> 1/2 teaspoon salt
> Dash pepper
> 1-1/2 pounds boneless skinless chicken breasts, cut into 1-inch pieces
> 3 tablespoons butter
> 1 medium onion, sliced
> 3 celery ribs, sliced
> 2 medium potatoes, peeled and cut into 3/4-inch cubes
> 3 medium carrots, cut into 1/4-inch slices
> 1 cup chicken broth
> 1/2 teaspoon dried thyme
> 1 tablespoon ketchup
> 1 tablespoon cornstarch

1. In a large resealable plastic bag, combine the flour, salt and pepper. Add chicken, a few pieces at a time, and shake to coat.

2. In a large skillet, melt butter; cook chicken until juices run clear. Add onion and celery; cook for 3 minutes. Stir in potatoes and carrots.

3. In a small bowl, combine broth, thyme, ketchup and cornstarch; stir into skillet. Bring to a boil. Reduce heat; cover and simmer for 15-20 minutes or until the vegetables are tender. **Yield:** 4-6 servings.

🏅🏅🏅 Apple Squash Soup

Crystal Ralph-Haughn, Bartlesville, Oklahoma

This is a new twist on an old favorite—pumpkin soup. I add a little ginger and sage to apples and squash for this tasty variation. My family loves it when autumn rolls around.

 Uses less fat, sugar or salt. Includes Nutrition Facts and Diabetic Exchanges.

> 1 large onion, chopped
> 1/2 teaspoon rubbed sage
> 2 tablespoons butter
> 1 can (14-1/2 ounces) chicken broth
> 3/4 cup water
> 2 medium Granny Smith *or* other tart apples, peeled and finely chopped
> 1 package (12 ounces) frozen mashed squash, thawed
> 1 teaspoon ground ginger
> 1/2 teaspoon salt
> 1/2 cup fat-free milk

1. In a saucepan, saute onion and sage in butter for 3 minutes or until tender. Add the broth, water and apples; bring to a boil. Reduce heat; cover and simmer for 12 minutes. Add the squash, ginger and salt; return to a boil. Reduce heat; simmer, uncovered, for 10 minutes. Cool until lukewarm.

2. Process in batches in a blender or food processor until smooth; return to pan. Add milk; heat through (do not boil). **Yield:** 5 servings.

Nutrition Facts: 1 cup equals 142 calories, 6 g fat (3 g saturated fat), 13 mg cholesterol, 647 mg sodium, 22 g carbohydrate, 2 g fiber, 3 g protein. **Diabetic Exchanges:** 1 fat, 1 starch, 1/2 fruit.

🎗🎗🎗
Winter Squash Soup

Angela Liette, Sidney, Ohio

I love trying new recipes and adding different seasonings to enhance flavor. This creamy soup is a tasty way to use squash.

- 2 celery ribs, chopped
- 1 medium onion, chopped
- 1 garlic clove, minced
- 3 tablespoons butter
- 3 tablespoons all-purpose flour
- 3 cups chicken broth
- 2 cups mashed cooked butternut, acorn *or* Hubbard squash
- 2 tablespoons minced fresh parsley
- 1/2 teaspoon salt
- 1/8 to 1/4 teaspoon ground nutmeg
- 1/4 teaspoon dried savory
- 1/4 teaspoon dried rosemary, crushed
- 1/8 teaspoon pepper
- 1 cup half-and-half cream

1. In a large saucepan, saute celery, onion and garlic in butter until tender; stir in flour until blended. Gradually add the broth. Bring to a boil; cook and stir for 2 minutes or until thickened. Reduce heat; stir in the squash, parsley, salt, nutmeg, savory, rosemary and pepper. Simmer, uncovered, for 10 minutes or until heated through. Cool slightly.

2. In a blender or food processor, process soup in batches until smooth. Return to the pan and heat through. Gradually stir in cream. Cook 5 minutes longer, stirring occasionally. **Yield:** 6 servings.

🎗🎗🎗
Turkey Dumpling Stew

Becky Mohr, Appleton, Wisconsin

My mom often fixed this comforting stew when I was young, and it was always a hit. Now I make it on weekends for my own children, who like the tender dumplings.

 Uses less fat, sugar or salt. Includes Nutrition Facts and Diabetic Exchanges.

- 4 bacon strips, diced
- 1-1/2 pounds turkey breast tenderloins, cut into 1-inch pieces
- 4 medium carrots, cut into 1-inch pieces
- 2 cups water, *divided*
- 1 can (14-1/2 ounces) reduced-sodium chicken broth
- 2 small onions, quartered
- 2 celery ribs, cut into 1/2-inch pieces
- 1/4 teaspoon dried rosemary, crushed
- 1 bay leaf
- 3 tablespoons all-purpose flour
- 1/2 teaspoon salt
- 1/8 to 1/4 teaspoon pepper
- 1 cup reduced-fat biscuit/baking mix
- 1/3 cup plus 1 tablespoon fat-free milk

1. In a Dutch oven or large saucepan, cook the bacon over medium heat until crisp. Remove to paper towels; drain, reserving 2 teaspoons drippings.

2. Cook turkey in the drippings until no longer pink. Add the carrots, 1-3/4 cups of water, broth, onions, cel-

ery, rosemary and bay leaf. Bring to a boil. Reduce heat; cover and simmer for 20-30 minutes or until vegetables are tender.

3. Combine flour and remaining water until smooth; stir into turkey mixture. Bring to a boil; cook and stir for 2 minutes or until thickened. Discard bay leaf. Stir in the salt, pepper and reserved bacon.

4. In a large bowl, combine biscuit mix and milk. Drop batter in six mounds onto simmering stew. Cover and simmer for 15 minutes or until a toothpick inserted in a dumpling comes out clean (do not lift the cover while simmering). **Yield:** 6 servings.

Nutrition Facts: 1 cup equals 299 calories, 6 g fat (2 g saturated fat), 76 mg cholesterol, 787 mg sodium, 26 g carbohydrate, 2 g fiber, 34 g protein. **Diabetic Exchanges:** 4 very lean meat, 2 vegetable, 1 starch, 1 fat.

🏅 🏅 🏅
Country Potato Chowder

Sara Phillips, Topeka, Kansas

This chunky, down-home chowder is thick with potatoes, carrots, green beans and corn. My mother served it on chilly evenings with warm French bread. Any leftovers taste just as good and make a great lazy-day lunch.

- 6 bacon strips, diced
- 1 medium onion, chopped
- 3 celery ribs, chopped
- 1/4 cup all-purpose flour
- 1 quart half-and-half cream
- 4 medium potatoes, peeled and cut into 1/2-inch cubes
- 2 cans (10-3/4 ounces *each*) condensed cream of celery soup, undiluted
- 2 tablespoons dried parsley flakes
- 1 tablespoon Worcestershire sauce
- 1 teaspoon seasoned salt
- 1/2 teaspoon pepper
- 1 cup sliced carrots
- 1 cup fresh *or* frozen green beans, cut into 2-inch pieces
- 1 can (14-3/4 ounces) cream-style corn

1. In a Dutch oven or large soup kettle, cook bacon over medium heat until crisp; remove with a slotted spoon to paper towels. Drain, reserving 2 tablespoons drippings.

2. In the drippings, saute onion and celery until tender. Sprinkle with flour and stir until blended. Gradually add cream. Stir in the potatoes, soup, parsley, Worcestershire sauce, seasoned salt and pepper. Bring to a boil; cook and stir for 1 minute. Reduce heat; cover and simmer for 25 minutes, stirring occasionally.

3. Add the carrots and beans. Cover and simmer 15 minutes longer or until the vegetables are tender. Stir in corn and reserved bacon; heat through. **Yield:** 12 servings.

🎀🎀🎀
Split Pea Vegetable Soup

Maureen Ylitalo, Wahnapitae, Ontario

This home-style recipe originated with the "master chef" of our family—my father-in-law. The soup freezes well, so I often simmer up a double batch.

1-1/2 cups dried split peas, rinsed
2-1/2 quarts water
   7 to 8 whole allspice, tied in a cheesecloth bag
   2 teaspoons salt
1/2 teaspoon pepper
   6 large potatoes, peeled and cut into 1/2-inch cubes
   6 carrots, chopped
   2 medium onions, chopped
   2 cups cubed fully cooked ham
1/2 medium head cabbage, shredded

1. In a Dutch oven or large soup kettle, combine peas, water, allspice, salt and pepper; bring to a boil. Reduce heat; cover and simmer for 1 hour.

2. Stir in potatoes, carrots, onions, ham and cabbage; return to a boil. Reduce heat; cover and simmer for about 30 minutes or until vegetables are tender, stirring occasionally. Discard allspice. **Yield:** 16-20 servings (about 5 quarts).

🎀🎀🎀
Veggie Black Bean Stew

Marilyn Waters, Outing, Minnesota

You'll never miss the meat in this flavorful stew. Cilantro, honey and garlic nicely accent the beans and veggies.

✓ Uses less fat, sugar or salt. Includes Nutrition Facts and Diabetic Exchanges.

   2 large onions, chopped
1/2 cup *each* chopped celery, carrot and sweet red pepper

   2 tablespoons minced garlic
1/4 cup dry sherry *or* reduced-sodium chicken broth
   1 tablespoon olive oil
   3 cans (15 ounces *each*) black beans, rinsed and drained
   1 can (14-1/2 ounces) reduced-sodium chicken broth
   1 can (14-1/2 ounces) diced tomatoes, undrained
   2 tablespoons tomato paste
   2 tablespoons honey
   4 teaspoons chili powder
   2 teaspoons ground cumin
1/2 teaspoon dried oregano
1/4 cup minced fresh cilantro
   5 tablespoons shredded Monterey Jack cheese
   5 tablespoons reduced-fat sour cream
   2 tablespoons chopped green onion

1. In a Dutch oven or large saucepan, saute the onions, celery, carrot, red pepper and garlic in sherry or broth and oil until tender. Add the beans, can of broth, tomatoes, tomato paste, honey, chili powder, cumin and oregano. Bring to a boil. Reduce heat; cover and simmer for 40 minutes.

2. Stir in the cilantro; simmer 5-15 minutes longer or until stew is thickened. Garnish with cheese, sour cream and green onion. **Yield:** 5 servings.

Nutrition Facts: 1-1/2 cups equals 335 calories, 8 g fat (3 g saturated fat), 14 mg cholesterol, 1,482 mg sodium, 62 g carbohydrate, 17 g fiber, 17 g protein. **Diabetic Exchanges:** 3 vegetable, 2-1/2 starch, 2 very lean meat, 1 fat.

Mexican Pork Stew

Mickey Terry, Del Valle, Texas

This thick and zesty stew is terrific with corn bread on chilly days. I also like to spoon leftovers into corn tortillas with a little salsa and reduced-fat sour cream for a satisfying snack.

✓ Uses less fat, sugar or salt. Includes Nutrition Facts and Diabetic Exchanges.

- 1 pound boneless pork loin roast, cut into 3/4-inch cubes
- 3 teaspoons olive oil
- 1 large onion, chopped
- 2 celery ribs, chopped
- 1 jalapeno pepper, seeded and chopped
- 1 garlic clove, minced
- 1-1/2 cups water
- 1 tablespoon chili powder
- 2 teaspoons brown sugar
- 1 teaspoon ground cumin
- 1/2 teaspoon salt
- 1/4 teaspoon pepper
- 1 can (6 ounces) tomato paste
- 1 can (16 ounces) kidney beans, rinsed and drained
- 1 can (15 ounces) pinto beans, rinsed and drained
- 1 can (14-1/2 ounces) diced tomatoes, undrained
- 2 teaspoons minced fresh cilantro

1. In a Dutch oven or large soup kettle over medium-high heat, brown meat on all sides in 1 teaspoon oil; drain. Remove meat and keep warm.

2. In the same pan, saute the onion, celery, jalapeno and garlic in remaining oil until tender. Stir in the water, chili powder, brown sugar, cumin, salt and pepper. Return meat to pan. Bring to a boil. Reduce heat; cover and simmer for 30 minutes.

3. Stir in the tomato paste, beans and tomatoes. Return to a boil. Reduce heat; cover and simmer 20 minutes longer or until meat is tender and beans are heated through. Sprinkle with cilantro. **Yield:** 5 servings.

Nutrition Facts: 1-1/2 cups equals 377 calories, 9 g fat (2 g saturated fat), 50 mg cholesterol, 991 mg sodium, 43 g carbohydrate, 13 g fiber, 32 g protein. **Diabetic Exchanges:** 4 lean meat, 2 starch, 1 vegetable.

Editor's Note: When cutting or seeding hot peppers, use rubber or plastic gloves to protect your hands. Avoid touching your face.

Enchilada Chicken Soup

Cristin Fischer, Bellevue, Nebraska

Canned soups, prepared enchilada sauce and a few other convenience items make this recipe one of my fast-to-fix favorites. Use mild green chilies if they suit your taste, or try a spicier variety if you prefer more of a kick.

- 1 can (11 ounces) condensed fiesta nacho cheese soup, undiluted
- 1 can (10-3/4 ounces) condensed cream of chicken soup, undiluted
- 2-2/3 cups milk
- 1 can (10 ounces) chunk white chicken, drained
- 1 can (10 ounces) enchilada sauce
- 1 can (4 ounces) chopped green chilies

Sour cream

In a large saucepan, combine the soups, milk, chicken, enchilada sauce and chilies; mix well. Cook until heated through. Serve with sour cream. **Yield:** 7 servings.

🎗️ 🎗️ 🎗️

Mediterranean Seafood Stew

Virginia Anthony, Blowing Rock, North Carolina

With Mediterranean flavors and three kinds of seafood, this dish is special enough for company. Dollop each bowlful with garlic-flavored mayonnaise for the perfect finish.

✓ Uses less fat, sugar or salt. Includes Nutrition Facts and Diabetic Exchanges.

  1 **medium onion, finely chopped**
1-1/2 **teaspoons minced garlic, *divided***
  1 **tablespoon olive oil**
1/2 **pound plum tomatoes, seeded and diced**
  1 **teaspoon grated lemon peel**
1/4 **teaspoon crushed red pepper flakes**
  1 **cup clam juice**
1/3 **cup white wine *or* additional clam juice**
  1 **tablespoon tomato paste**
1/2 **teaspoon salt**
  1 **pound orange roughy *or* red snapper fillets, cut into 1-inch cubes**
  1 **pound uncooked large shrimp, peeled and deveined**
1/2 **pound sea scallops**
1/3 **cup minced fresh parsley**
1/3 **cup reduced-fat mayonnaise**

1. In a Dutch oven or large saucepan, saute onion and 1/2 teaspoon garlic in oil until tender. Add the tomatoes, lemon peel and pepper flakes; cook and stir for 2 minutes. Add the clam juice, wine or additional clam juice, tomato paste and salt. Bring to a boil. Reduce heat; cover and simmer for 10 minutes or until heated through.

2. Add the fish, shrimp, scallops and parsley. Cover and cook for 8-10 minutes or until fish flakes easily with a fork, the shrimp turn pink and scallops are opaque. Combine mayonnaise and remaining garlic; dollop onto each serving. **Yield:** 6 servings.

Nutrition Facts: 1 cup stew with 2 teaspoons mayonnaise topping equals 221 calories, 8 g fat (1 g saturated fat), 123 mg cholesterol, 607 mg sodium, 7 g carbohydrate, 1 g fiber, 28 g protein. **Diabetic Exchanges:** 4 very lean meat, 1 vegetable, 1 fat.

🎗 🎗 🎗
Raspberry-Cranberry Soup

(Also pictured on page 46)

Susan Stull, Chillicothe, Missouri

Served hot, this colorful and tangy soup helps beat the winter "blahs." But it's also refreshing served cold on a sunny summer day. Either way, people scrape their bowls clean.

- 2 cups fresh *or* frozen cranberries
- 2 cups apple juice
- 1 cup fresh *or* frozen unsweetened raspberries, thawed
- 1/2 to 1 cup sugar
- 1 tablespoon lemon juice
- 1/4 teaspoon ground cinnamon
- 2 cups half-and-half cream, *divided*
- 1 tablespoon cornstarch

Whipped cream, additional raspberries and mint, optional

1. In a large saucepan, bring cranberries and apple juice to a boil. Reduce heat and simmer, uncovered, for 10 minutes. Press through a sieve; return to the pan. Also press the raspberries through the sieve; discard skins and seeds. Add to cranberry mixture; bring to a boil. Add sugar, lemon juice and cinnamon; remove from the heat.

2. Cool 4 minutes. Stir 1 cup into 1-1/2 cups cream. Return all to pan; bring to a gentle boil. Mix cornstarch with remaining cream until smooth; gradually stir into soup. Cook and stir for 2 minutes or until thickened. Serve hot or chilled. Serve with whipped cream, raspberries and mint if desired. **Yield:** 4 servings.

🎗 🎗 🎗
Pork and Winter Squash Stew

Evelyn Plyler, Apple Valley, California

Here in the high desert area of California, we do get snow. This warm-you-up stew with noodles is a wintertime favorite.

 Uses less fat, sugar or salt. Includes Nutrition Facts and Diabetic Exchanges.

- 2 pounds lean boneless pork, cut into 1-inch cubes
- 2 tablespoons vegetable oil, *divided*
- 2 cups chopped onion
- 2 garlic cloves, minced
- 3 cups sliced fresh mushrooms
- 2-1/2 cups sliced carrots
- 2 cans (14-1/2 ounces *each*) Italian stewed tomatoes
- 2 teaspoons dried thyme
- 1/2 teaspoon pepper
- 1-1/2 teaspoons salt, optional
- 4 cups cubed peeled butternut squash

Hot cooked noodles, optional

1. In a Dutch oven or large saucepan, brown pork in 1 tablespoon of oil. Remove from pan; drain and set aside.

2. Heat remaining oil in the same pan over medium heat. Saute onion and garlic for 3 minutes. Return pork to pan. Add the mushrooms, carrots, tomatoes and seasonings; bring to a boil. Reduce heat; cover and simmer for 1 hour.

3. Add squash; simmer, uncovered, for 30 minutes or until meat and vegetables are tender. Serve over noodles if desired. **Yield:** 8 servings.

Nutrition Facts: 1/8 recipe (calculated without added salt or noodles) equals 298 calories, 14 g fat (0 saturated fat), 60 mg cholesterol, 393 mg sodium, 26 g carbohydrate, 0 fiber, 22 g protein. **Diabetic Exchanges:** 2 meat, 2 vegetable, 1 starch, 1 fat.

🎀🎀🎀
Hearty Italian Chili

Chloe Buckner, Edinburg, Pennsylvania

As a child, I was my grandmother's constant helper in the kitchen. And, like her, I can't seem to follow a recipe without changing it! I came up with this Italian-flavored chili when I got bored with the usual version.

- 1 pound ground beef
- 1/2 pound bulk Italian sausage
- 1 medium onion, chopped
- 1/2 cup chopped green pepper
- 1 can *or* jar (26-1/2 to 30 ounces) spaghetti sauce
- 1 can (16 ounces) kidney beans, rinsed and drained
- 1 can (14-1/2 ounces) diced tomatoes, undrained
- 1 jar (4-1/2 ounces) sliced mushrooms, drained
- 1 cup water
- 1/3 cup halved sliced pepperoni
- 5 teaspoons chili powder
- 1/2 teaspoon salt

Pinch pepper

In a large saucepan, cook beef, sausage, onion and green pepper over medium heat until the meat is no longer pink; drain. Add remaining ingredients; bring to a boil. Reduce heat; simmer, uncovered, for 30 minutes. **Yield:** 6-8 servings (2-1/4 quarts).

🎀🎀🎀
Sausage Chicken Soup

Helen MacDonald, Lazo, British Columbia

I've been ladling up this meaty soup for years, and my husband still is thrilled whenever I put it on the table. Every bowl is loaded with slices of smoked sausage, chunks of chicken, fresh peppers and potatoes. Spice it up or tone it down as you like with your favorite picante sauce.

- 3/4 pound boneless skinless chicken breasts
- 2 medium potatoes, peeled and cut into 1/4-inch cubes
- 1 can (14-1/2 ounces) chicken broth
- 1 medium onion, diced
- 1 medium sweet red pepper, diced
- 1 medium green pepper, diced
- 1 garlic clove, minced
- 3/4 cup picante sauce
- 3 tablespoons all-purpose flour
- 3 tablespoons water
- 1/2 pound smoked sausage, diced

Sliced habanero peppers, optional

1. Place chicken in a greased microwave-safe dish. Cover and microwave on high for 5-7 minutes or until juices run clear, turning every 2 minutes. Cut into cubes; set aside.

2. Place potatoes and broth in a 2-1/2-qt. microwave-safe bowl. Cover and microwave on high for 5 minutes. Add the onions, peppers and garlic; cook 5 minutes longer or until potatoes are tender. Stir in the picante sauce.

3. In a small bowl, combine the flour and water until smooth. Add to the potato mixture. Cover and cook on high for 3 minutes or until thickened. Add chicken and sausage; cook 1-2 minutes longer or until heated through. Sprinkle with habaneros if desired. **Yield:** 6 servings.

Editor's Note: This recipe was tested with an 850-watt microwave.

8 medium fresh tomatoes (about 4 pounds),
  peeled and cut into sixths
1-1/2 cups tomato juice
  4 small zucchini, sliced into 1/4-inch pieces
2-1/2 teaspoons Italian seasoning
1-1/2 to 2 teaspoons salt
  1 teaspoon sugar
  1/2 teaspoon garlic salt
  1/2 teaspoon pepper
  3 cups canned whole kernel corn, drained
  2 medium green peppers, sliced into 1-inch
    pieces
  1/4 cup cornstarch
  1/4 cup water
Shredded part-skim mozzarella cheese

🎗🎗🎗
Tomato Zucchini Stew

(Also pictured on page 47)

Helen Miller, Hickory Hills, Illinois

Filled with Italian sausage and sprinkled with mozzarella, this stew is "famous" among my friends and family. I make it for potlucks and other get-togethers.

1-1/4 pounds bulk Italian sausage
1-1/2 cups sliced celery (3/4-inch pieces)

1. In a Dutch oven or large saucepan, crumble sausage and cook over medium heat until no longer pink; drain. Add celery and cook for 15 minutes; drain.

2. Add tomatoes, tomato juice, zucchini and seasonings; bring to a boil. Reduce heat; cover and simmer for 20 minutes. Add corn and peppers; cover and simmer for 15 minutes.

3. Combine cornstarch and water; stir into stew. Bring to a boil; cook and stir until mixture thickens. Sprinkle with cheese. **Yield:** 6-8 servings.

🎗🎗🎗
Kielbasa Cabbage Stew

Valerie Burrows, Shelby, Michigan

If you like German potato salad, you'll love this sweet-and-sour stew. Caraway seeds, smoky kielbasa, tender potatoes and shredded cabbage make it a hearty change of pace at dinner.

 Uses less fat, sugar or salt. Includes Nutrition Facts and Diabetic Exchanges.

1/2 pound smoked turkey kielbasa *or* Polish
  sausage, sliced
  1 pound potatoes, peeled and cubed
  2 cups shredded cabbage
  1 large onion, chopped
  1 can (14-1/2 ounces) reduced-sodium chicken
    broth
3/4 cup water, *divided*
  2 tablespoons sugar
  1 teaspoon caraway seeds
1/4 teaspoon pepper
  1 can (16 ounces) kidney beans, rinsed and
    drained
  3 tablespoons cider vinegar
  2 tablespoons all-purpose flour

1. In a large saucepan or nonstick skillet, brown sausage over medium heat. Add the potatoes, cabbage, onion, broth, 1/2 cup water, sugar, caraway and pepper. Bring to a boil. Reduce heat; cover and simmer for 15-18 minutes or until potatoes are tender, stirring occasionally.

2. Add beans and vinegar; cover and simmer 5-10 minutes longer. Combine flour and remaining water until smooth; stir into stew. Bring to a boil; cook and stir for 2 minutes or until thickened. **Yield:** 4 servings.

Nutrition Facts: 1-3/4 cups equals 322 calories, 3 g fat (1 g saturated fat), 25 mg cholesterol, 1,143 mg sodium, 57 g carbohydrate, 7 g fiber, 17 g protein. **Diabetic Exchanges:** 3 starch, 2 lean meat, 1 vegetable.

Southwest Sausage Bake, p. 68

Buttermilk Pecan Waffles, p. 76

Cherry Kringle, p. 82

Breakfast & Brunch

You'll want to skip the snooze button when these taste-tempting recipes are on the morning menu. From home-style casseroles to golden rolls, they'll get your day off to a scrumptious start.

Breakfast Upside-Down Cake, p. 80

🎗🎗🎗 Cheddar English Muffins

Marge Goral, Ridgefield, Connecticut

These chewy English muffins have a scrumptious, mild cheese flavor that intensifies when they're split and toasted. My family really enjoys them for breakfast or brunch.

✓ Uses less fat, sugar or salt. Includes Nutrition Facts and Diabetic Exchanges.

   3 to 3-1/4 cups bread flour
   1 tablespoon sugar
   1 package (1/4 ounce) active dry yeast
   1 teaspoon salt
  3/4 cup warm water (120° to 130°)
   2 tablespoons canola oil
   1 *egg*
   1 tablespoon cider vinegar
 1/2 cup shredded cheddar cheese
   4 tablespoons cornmeal, *divided*

1. In a large mixing bowl, combine 2 cups flour, sugar, yeast and salt. Add water and oil; beat on medium speed for 2 minutes. Add egg and vinegar; beat on high for 2 minutes. Stir in cheese and enough remaining flour to form a stiff dough.

2. Turn onto a floured surface; knead until dough is smooth and no longer sticky, about 2 minutes.

3. Roll dough to about 1/2-in. thickness. Cut with a 3-in. round cutter. Roll scraps if desired. Coat baking sheets with nonstick cooking spray and sprinkle with 2 tablespoons cornmeal. Cover and let rise until doubled, about 1 hour.

4. Heat an ungreased griddle or electric skillet to 325°. Cook muffins for 20-25 minutes or until golden brown, turning every 5 minutes. Remove to wire racks to cool. Split with a fork and toast if desired. **Yield:** about 16 muffins.

Nutrition Facts: 1 muffin equals 128 calories, 3 g fat (1 g saturated fat), 17 mg cholesterol, 173 mg sodium, 21 g carbohydrate, 1 g fiber, 5 g protein. **Diabetic Exchanges:** 1-1/2 starch, 1/2 fat.

🎗🎗🎗 Southwest Sausage Bake

(Also pictured on page 66)

Barbara Waddel, Lincoln, Nebraska

Not only is this layered tortilla dish delicious, but it's a real time-saver because you assemble it the night before. I like to serve the casserole with sour cream and salsa.

   6 flour tortillas (10 inches), cut into 1/2-inch strips
   4 cans (4 ounces *each*) chopped green chilies, drained
   1 pound bulk pork sausage, cooked and drained
   2 cups (8 ounces) shredded Monterey Jack cheese
  10 eggs
 1/2 cup milk
 1/2 teaspoon *each* salt, garlic salt, onion salt, pepper and ground cumin
Paprika
   2 medium tomatoes, sliced
Sour cream and salsa

1. In a greased 13-in. x 9-in. x 2-in. baking dish, layer half of the tortilla strips, chilies, sausage and cheese. Repeat layers. In a bowl, beat the eggs, milk and seasonings; pour over cheese. Sprinkle with paprika. Cover and refrigerate overnight.

2. Remove from the refrigerator 30 minutes before baking. Bake, uncovered, at 350° for 50 minutes. Arrange tomato slices over the top. Bake 10-15 minutes longer or until a knife inserted near the center comes out clean. Let stand for 10 minutes before cutting. Serve with sour cream and salsa. **Yield:** 12 servings.

🎀🎀🎀 Breakfast Patties

Jeannine Stallings, East Helena, Montana

This homemade sausage is lean, holds together well and shrinks very little when cooked. It's an incredibly easy way to make breakfast special.

1/4 **cup water**
2 **teaspoons salt**
2 **teaspoons rubbed sage**
1 **teaspoon pepper**
1/2 **teaspoon ground nutmeg**
1/4 **teaspoon crushed red pepper flakes**
1/8 **teaspoon ground ginger**
2 **pounds ground pork**

1. In a large bowl, combine water and seasonings. Add pork and mix well. Shape into eight 4-in. patties.

2. In a large skillet, cook patties over medium heat for 5-6 minutes on each side or until no longer pink in the center and a meat thermometer reads 160°. **Yield:** 8 patties.

🎀🎀🎀 Raspberry Coffee Cake

Mary Bergman, Navarra, Spain

My husband, our three children and I are missionaries in northern Spain. Special treats like this swirled cake are truly a taste of home for us. With the creamy berry filling and sweet glaze, it's hard to stop at one slice.

1 **tablespoon active dry yeast**
1/3 **cup warm water (110° to 115°)**
1/2 **cup warm sour cream (110° to 115°)**
1/4 **cup butter, melted**
1/4 **cup sugar**
1 **teaspoon salt**
1 **egg**
2-1/4 to 2-1/2 **cups all-purpose flour**
FILLING:
1 **package (8 ounces) cream cheese, softened**
1 **egg**
1/2 **cup sugar**
1 **teaspoon vanilla extract**
1/8 **teaspoon salt**
1/2 **cup raspberry jam**
GLAZE:
1-1/4 **cups confectioners' sugar**
1 **teaspoon vanilla extract**
2 **tablespoons milk**

1. In a large bowl, dissolve yeast in warm water. Stir in sour cream, butter, sugar, salt and egg. Stir in enough flour to form a soft dough.

2. Turn onto a floured surface; knead 20 times or until smooth. Place in a greased bowl, turning once to grease top. Cover and let rise in a warm place until doubled, about 1-1/4 hours.

3. In a small mixing bowl, beat the cream cheese, egg, sugar, vanilla and salt until smooth; set aside. Punch dough down. Turn onto a lightly floured surface; divide in half.

4. Roll each piece into a 12-in. x 8-in. rectangle. Spread filling to within 1/2 in. of edges. Spoon jam lengthwise over half of the filling. Roll up jelly-roll style, starting with the long side with the jam. Pinch seams to seal; tuck ends under.

5. Place loaves seam side down on a greased baking sheet. With a sharp knife, cut shallow slashes across the top of each. Cover and let rise until doubled, about 30 minutes.

6. Bake at 375° for 15-20 minutes or until golden brown. Remove from pan to a wire rack. Combine glaze ingredients; drizzle over warm coffee cakes. **Yield:** 2 loaves (10 slices each).

Frozen Banana Pineapple Cups

Alice Miller, Middlebury, Indiana

After you stir together this frosty medley, just pop it in the freezer for the next morning. In summer, our kids prefer this frozen treat over store-bought ones as a snack.

3 cups water
2-2/3 cups mashed ripe bananas (5 to 6 medium)
1-1/2 cups sugar
1 can (20 ounces) crushed pineapple, undrained
1 can (6 ounces) frozen orange juice concentrate, thawed

In a 2-qt. freezer container, combine all ingredients; mix well. Cover and freeze for 5 hours or overnight. Remove from the freezer 15 minutes before serving. **Yield:** 9-12 servings.

🎀🎀🎀
Candy Cane Coffee Cake
Linda Hollingsworth, Quitman, Mississippi

Dotted with dried apricots and maraschino cherries, this tender coffee cake looks festive and tastes that way, too. I love to serve it at Christmastime and even give it as a gift.

    2 packages (1/4 ounce *each*) active dry yeast
1/2 cup warm water (110° to 115°)
    2 cups warm sour cream (110° to 115°)
    6 tablespoons butter, *divided*
1/3 cup sugar
    2 eggs
    2 teaspoons salt
5-3/4 to 6-1/4 cups all-purpose flour
1-1/2 cups finely chopped dried apricots
1-1/2 cup finely chopped maraschino cherries
    2 cups confectioners' sugar
    2 tablespoons cold water
Additional cherries, halved

1. In a large mixing bowl, dissolve yeast in warm water. Beat in sour cream, 4 tablespoons butter, sugar, eggs, salt and 2 cups flour; beat until smooth. Stir in enough remaining flour to form a soft dough.

2. Turn onto a floured surface; knead until smooth and elastic, about 6-8 minutes. Place in a greased bowl, turning once to grease top. Cover and let rise in a warm place until doubled, about 1 hour.

3. Punch dough down. Turn onto a lightly floured surface; divide into thirds. Roll each portion into a 14-in. x 7-in. rectangle on a greased baking sheet.

4. Combine apricots and cherries; spoon down the center of each rectangle. On each long side, cut 3/4-in.-wide strips about 2 in. into center. Starting at one end, fold alternating strips at an angle across filling. Pinch ends to seal. Curve top.

5. Bake at 375° for 18-20 minutes or until golden brown. Meanwhile, melt remaining butter; brush over warm coffee cakes.

6. Combine confectioners' sugar and cold water until smooth; drizzle over the tops. Arrange cherries on top of each coffee cake. **Yield:** 3 loaves.

🎀🎀🎀
Maple Apple Topping
Ruth Harrow, Alexandria, New Hampshire

I discovered this sweet, nutty topping when I had an abundance of apples to use up. My family enjoys it over waffles, but it's also wonderful over slices of purchased pound cake or scoops of vanilla ice cream.

1/2 cup butter, cubed
    3 large tart apples, peeled and sliced
1-1/2 cups maple syrup
    1 teaspoon ground cinnamon
1/2 cup chopped nuts

In a large skillet, melt butter; add the apples, syrup and cinnamon. Cook and stir over medium-low heat until apples are tender. Stir in nuts. Serve over waffles or pancakes. **Yield:** 8 servings.

🎗🎗🎗 Rhubarb Sticky Buns

Amy Graef, Tacoma, Washington

I have numerous rhubarb plants in the backyard, so I'm always interested in ways to use up the harvest. My husband and sons are crazy about these sticky buns. I discovered the recipe in an old file I purchased at a rummage sale.

1/4 cup cold butter
1/2 cup packed brown sugar
  1 cup chopped fresh *or* frozen rhubarb, thawed
BATTER:
1/3 cup butter, softened
1/3 cup sugar
  1 egg
1-1/2 cups all-purpose flour
  2 teaspoons baking powder
1/2 teaspoon salt
1/4 teaspoon ground nutmeg
1/2 cup milk

1. In a small bowl, cut butter into brown sugar until crumbly. Stir in rhubarb. Spoon evenly into 12 well-greased muffin cups; set aside.

2. In a large mixing bowl, cream butter and sugar. Beat in egg. Combine the flour, baking powder, salt and nutmeg; add to creamed mixture alternately with milk.

3. Spoon over rhubarb mixture, filling cups three-fourths full. Bake at 350° for 15-20 minutes or until a toothpick comes out clean. Cool for 5 minutes before inverting onto a serving plate. Serve warm. **Yield:** 1 dozen.

Editor's Note: If using frozen rhubarb, measure rhubarb while still frozen, then thaw completely. Drain in a colander, but do not press liquid out.

🎗🎗🎗 Meaty Apple Skillet

Sharon Berry, Henderson, Nevada

Cinnamon, nutmeg and apple slices combine with four different meats in this robust, down-home specialty. I slice and cook the meat the day before to save time in the morning.

  1 large tart apple, peeled and thinly sliced
  2 tablespoons butter
  1 teaspoon ground cinnamon
1/8 teaspoon ground nutmeg
  2 teaspoons cornstarch
2/3 cup cranberry-apple juice
  1 pound smoked kielbasa *or* Polish sausage
3/4 pound bulk pork sausage, cooked and drained
3/4 pound pork sausage links, cooked and sliced
1-1/2 cups cubed fully cooked ham

1. In a skillet, saute apple slices in butter; sprinkle with cinnamon and nutmeg. Cover and cook for 5 minutes or until apples are tender.

2. Combine cornstarch and juice until smooth; stir into apple mixture. Bring to a boil; cook and stir for 2 minutes or until thickened. Add the sausage and ham; heat through. **Yield:** 12-16 servings.

Onion Pie

Marian Benthin, Apalachin, New York

My mother got this recipe over 30 years ago and said it originated in a Pennsylvania Dutch kitchen. The simple but delicious pie is a sure hit with onion lovers.

1-1/3 cups biscuit/baking mix
1 teaspoon rubbed sage
1/2 teaspoon salt
4 to 5 tablespoons milk
FILLING:
5 cups thinly sliced onions (about 5 medium)
2 tablespoons vegetable oil
1/2 teaspoon salt
1 egg
1 cup half-and-half cream

1. In a large bowl, combine the biscuit mix, sage and salt. Add enough milk until mixture holds together. Press onto the bottom and up the sides of a 9-in. pie plate; set aside.

2. In a large skillet, saute onions in oil until tender. Sprinkle with salt. Spoon into crust. In a bowl, beat egg and cream; pour over onions.

3. Bake, uncovered, at 375° for 15 minutes. Reduce heat to 325°. Bake 25-30 minutes longer or until a knife inserted near the center comes out clean. **Yield:** 6-8 servings.

Cheddar Salmon Quiche

Jane Horn, Bellevue, Ohio

My mother-in-law shared this recipe, which we enjoy frequently during Lent. The cheesy quiche dresses up convenient canned salmon in a very satisfying way.

1 cup all-purpose flour
1/4 teaspoon salt
3 tablespoons cold butter
3 tablespoons shortening
1/4 cup milk
FILLING:
1 can (14-3/4 ounces) salmon, drained, bones and skin removed
1 cup (4 ounces) shredded cheddar cheese
1/4 cup chopped green pepper
1/4 cup chopped onion
1 tablespoon all-purpose flour
1/2 teaspoon salt
1/8 teaspoon pepper
3 eggs
1-1/4 cups milk

1. In a large bowl, combine the flour and salt; cut in butter and shortening until crumbly. Stir in milk.

2. On a floured surface, roll dough into a 10-in. circle. Transfer to an ungreased 9-in. pie plate or quiche dish. Trim and flute edges. Bake at 350° for 10 minutes.

3. In a large bowl, combine salmon, cheese, green pepper, onion, flour, salt and pepper; spoon into crust. Combine the eggs and milk; pour over salmon mixture.

4. Bake for 50-55 minutes or until a knife inserted near the center comes out clean. Let stand for 10 minutes before cutting. **Yield:** 6 servings.

🎗🎗🎗
Ham 'n' Egg Sandwich

DeeDee Newton, Toronto, Ontario

Whenever the whole family gets together for a holiday or long weekend, they request this all-in-one breakfast sandwich. I stack ham, tomato, scrambled eggs, onion and cheese inside a loaf of French bread, then simply pop it in the oven.

- 1 unsliced loaf (1 pound) French bread
- 4 tablespoons butter, softened, *divided*
- 2 tablespoons mayonnaise
- 8 thin slices deli ham
- 1 large tomato, sliced
- 1 small onion, thinly sliced
- 8 eggs, lightly beaten
- 8 slices cheddar cheese

1. Cut bread in half lengthwise; carefully hollow out top and bottom, leaving 1/2-in. shells (discard removed bread or save for another use). Spread 3 tablespoons of butter and all of the mayonnaise inside bread shells. Line bottom bread shell with ham; top with tomato and onion.

2. In a large skillet, melt remaining butter; add eggs. Cook over medium heat, stirring occasionally until edges are almost set.

3. Spoon into bottom bread shell; top with cheese. Cover with bread top. Wrap in greased foil. Bake at 375° for 15-20 minutes or until heated through. Cut into serving-size pieces. **Yield:** 6-8 servings.

🎗🎗🎗
Green Bean Quiche

Lee Campbell, Bartow, Florida

This tomato-topped quiche is so delicious that I'll serve it any time of day. Each fresh-tasting slice is filled with green beans and mushrooms.

- 1 package (10 ounces) frozen cut green beans
- 1/2 cup water
- 1/2 cup chopped onion
- 2 tablespoons butter
- 1/2 cup sliced fresh mushrooms
- 1/4 cup diced green pepper
- 1/2 cup mayonnaise
- 1/4 cup sour cream
- 1/4 teaspoon salt
- 1/4 cup crushed saltines (about 8 crackers)
- 6 eggs, lightly beaten
- 1 medium tomato, seeded and chopped
- 3/4 cup shredded sharp cheddar cheese

1. Place beans in a saucepan and cover with water; bring to a boil. Reduce heat. Cover and simmer for 6-8 minutes or until crisp-tender; drain and set aside.

2. In a small skillet, saute onion in butter until tender. Add mushrooms and green pepper; saute until tender.

3. In a large bowl, combine the mayonnaise, sour cream and salt; stir in the beans, mushroom mixture and cracker crumbs. Gradually stir in eggs. Pour into a greased deep-dish 9-in. pie plate. Sprinkle with tomato and cheese.

4. Bake at 350° for 25-30 minutes or until a knife inserted near the center comes out clean. Let stand for 5-10 minutes before cutting. **Yield:** 6 servings.

Editor's Note: Reduced-fat or fat-free mayonnaise is not recommended for this recipe.

Carrot Pancakes

Denise Rushing, Greenwood, Arkansas

These rave-winning flapjacks have the sweet flavor of carrot cake and a rich cream cheese topping. To save time, grate the carrots in your food processor.

1-1/4 cups all-purpose flour
  2 tablespoons finely chopped pecans
  2 teaspoons baking powder
  1 teaspoon ground cinnamon
1/4 teaspoon salt
1/4 teaspoon ground ginger
  1 egg, lightly beaten
1/3 cup packed brown sugar
  1 cup milk
  1 cup grated carrots
  1 teaspoon vanilla extract

CREAM CHEESE SPREAD:
  4 ounces cream cheese, softened
1/4 cup confectioners' sugar
  2 tablespoons milk
1/2 teaspoon vanilla extract
Dash ground cinnamon

1. In a large bowl, combine the first six ingredients. Combine the egg, brown sugar, milk, carrots and vanilla; mix well. Stir into the dry ingredients just until moistened.

2. Pour batter by 1/4 cupfuls onto a greased hot griddle. Turn when bubbles form on top of pancake; cook until second side is golden brown.

3. Meanwhile, place the cream cheese, confectioners' sugar, milk and vanilla in a blender or food processor; cover and process until smooth. Transfer to a bowl; sprinkle with cinnamon. Serve with pancakes. **Yield:** 4 servings.

Buttermilk Pecan Waffles

(Also pictured on page 66)

Edna Hoffman, Hebron, Indiana

I like cooking with buttermilk, and I whip up these golden waffles often. They're as easy to prepare as ordinary waffles.

        2 cups all-purpose flour
        1 tablespoon baking powder
        1 teaspoon baking soda
    1/2 teaspoon salt
        4 eggs
        2 cups buttermilk
    1/2 cup butter, melted
        3 tablespoons chopped pecans

1. In a large bowl, combine the flour, baking powder, baking soda and salt; set aside.

2. In a large mixing bowl, beat eggs until light. Add buttermilk; mix well. Add dry ingredients and beat until batter is smooth. Stir in butter.

3. Pour about 3/4 cup batter onto a lightly greased preheated waffle iron. Sprinkle with a few pecans. Bake according to manufacturer's directions until golden brown. Repeat until batter and pecans are gone. **Yield:** 7 waffles (about 8 inches each).

Creamy Rhubarb Crepes

Stasha Wampler, Gate City, Virginia

This delightful idea for rhubarb brings a taste of spring to breakfast. I adapted the crepe recipe, which originally called for strawberry jelly, from one I loved as a child. My husband declared it a "winner" and even came up with the name.

        3 eggs
        1 cup milk
        5 tablespoons butter, melted
    1/4 cup sugar
    1/4 teaspoon salt
        1 cup all-purpose flour
Additional butter

SAUCE/FILLING:

        1 cup sugar
        1 tablespoon cornstarch
    1/4 teaspoon ground cinnamon
        2 cups thinly sliced fresh or frozen rhubarb,
          thawed
        1 package (8 ounces) cream cheese, softened
Confectioners' sugar

1. In a large bowl, whisk eggs, milk, melted butter, sugar and salt. Beat in flour until smooth; let stand for 30 minutes.

2. Melt 1/2 teaspoon butter in an 8-in. nonstick skillet. Pour 1/4 cup batter into the center of skillet; lift and turn pan to cover bottom. Cook until lightly browned; turn and brown the other side. Remove to a wire rack; cover with paper towel. Repeat with remaining batter, adding butter to skillet as needed.

3. Meanwhile, for sauce, combine the sugar, cornstarch and cinnamon in a saucepan. Stir in rhubarb. Bring to a boil over medium heat; cook and stir for 2 minutes or until slightly thickened and rhubarb is tender. Remove from the heat; cool slightly.

4. For filling, in a mixing bowl, beat cream cheese and 1/4 cup of the rhubarb sauce until smooth and creamy. Place a rounded tablespoonful on each crepe; fold in half and in half again, forming a triangle. Dust with confectioners' sugar. Serve with remaining sauce. **Yield:** 10 crepes.

Editor's Note: If using frozen rhubarb, measure rhubarb while still frozen, then thaw completely. Drain in a colander, but do not press liquid out.

Apple Sausage Breakfast Ring

Cherie Sechrist, Red Lion, Pennsylvania

When I have weekend guests, I rely on this all-in-one breakfast. I can make the ring the night before, refrigerate it and pop it in the oven in the morning. While it bakes, I prepare the scrambled eggs that go in the center.

- 2 pounds lean bulk pork sausage
- 2 eggs, lightly beaten
- 1-1/2 cups crushed butter-flavored crackers
- 1 cup grated apple, peeled
- 1/2 cup minced onion
- 1/4 cup milk
- Scrambled eggs

1. Line a 2-1/2-qt. ring mold with plastic wrap or waxed paper. Combine first six ingredients; mix well and press firmly into mold. Chill several hours or overnight.

2. Unmold, removing plastic/paper, onto a baking sheet with raised edges. Bake at 350° for 1 hour.

3. Transfer onto a serving platter; fill center of ring with scrambled eggs. **Yield:** 8 servings.

Make-Ahead Scrambled Eggs

Diane Sackfield, Kingston, Ontario

This overnight egg dish is so convenient for busy days. I've served it for breakfast and also as part of a full brunch buffet alongside biscuits, bagels and salads.

- 5 tablespoons butter, *divided*
- 1/4 cup all-purpose flour
- 2 cups milk
- 2 cups (8 ounces) shredded cheddar cheese
- 1 cup sliced fresh mushrooms
- 1/4 cup finely chopped onion
- 12 eggs, beaten
- 1 teaspoon salt
- 1 package (10 ounces) frozen chopped broccoli, cooked and drained
- 1 cup soft bread crumbs

1. In a saucepan, melt 2 tablespoons butter. Add flour; cook and stir until the mixture begins to bubble. Gradually stir in milk; bring to boil. Cook and stir for 2 minutes. Remove from the heat.

2. Stir in cheese until melted; set aside. In a large skillet, saute mushrooms and onion in 2 tablespoons butter until tender. Add eggs and salt; cook and stir until the eggs are completely set. Add the cheese sauce and broccoli; mix well.

3. Pour into a greased 11-in. x 7-in. x 2-in. baking dish. Melt the remaining butter and toss with bread crumbs. Sprinkle over egg mixture. Cover and refrigerate overnight.

4. Remove from the refrigerator 30 minutes before baking. Bake, uncovered, at 350° for 25-30 minutes or until top is golden brown. **Yield:** 6-8 servings.

🎗🎗🎗 Coffee Cake Muffins

Margaret McNeil, Memphis, Tennessee

I combine the dry ingredients in this recipe the night before. In the morning, I add the remaining items, fill the muffin cups and pop them in the oven. Brown sugar, cinnamon and pecans give these goodies their coffee cake-like flavor.

1/4 cup packed brown sugar
1/4 cup chopped pecans
1 teaspoon ground cinnamon
1-1/2 cups all-purpose flour
1/2 cup sugar
2 teaspoons baking powder
1/4 teaspoon baking soda
1/4 teaspoon salt
1 egg
3/4 cup milk
1/3 cup vegetable oil
GLAZE:
1/2 cup confectioners' sugar
1 tablespoon milk
1 teaspoon vanilla extract

1. In a small bowl, combine the brown sugar, pecans and cinnamon; set aside.

2. In a large bowl, combine the flour, sugar, baking powder, baking soda and salt. In another bowl, beat the egg, milk and oil; stir into dry ingredients just until moistened.

3. Spoon 1 tablespoon of batter into paper-lined muffin cups. Top each with 1 teaspoon nut mixture and about 2 tablespoons batter. Sprinkle with the remaining nut mixture.

4. Bake at 400° for 22-24 minutes or until a toothpick comes out clean. Cool for 5 minutes before removing from pan to a wire rack.

5. Combine glaze ingredients; spoon over muffins. **Yield:** 1 dozen.

🎗🎗🎗 Hash Brown Casserole

Jan Huntington, Painesville, Ohio

I first served this cheesy bake years ago at a brunch for my husband's birthday. The casserole was such a hit that it became a mainstay at our family get-togethers. It also makes a delicious supper alongside fruit salad and crusty bread.

12 eggs
1 can (12 ounces) evaporated milk
1 teaspoon salt
1/2 teaspoon pepper
1/8 teaspoon cayenne pepper, optional
1 package (30 ounces) frozen shredded hash brown potatoes, thawed
2 cups (8 ounces) shredded cheddar cheese
1 large onion, chopped
1 medium green pepper, chopped
1 cup cubed fully cooked ham

1. In a large bowl, combine the eggs, milk, salt, pepper and cayenne if desired. Stir in the potatoes, cheese, onion, green pepper and ham.

2. Pour into a greased 13-in. x 9-in. x 2-in. baking dish. Bake, uncovered, at 350° for 45-50 minutes or until a knife inserted near the center comes out clean. **Yield:** 12-15 servings.

🎗️ 🎗️ 🎗️
Asparagus Omelets

Becky Roth, Kawkawlin, Michigan

My husband and I created this recipe when trying to use up leftover asparagus and hollandaise sauce. They give the omelets irresistible flavor, and bacon bits provide a nice crunch.

- **1 envelope hollandaise sauce mix**
- **1 cup milk**
- **1/4 cup butter, softened**
- **8 bacon strips, diced**
- **1/2 pound fresh mushrooms, sliced**
- **1 pound asparagus, trimmed and cut into 1-inch pieces**
- **3 tablespoons water**
- **12 eggs, lightly beaten**
- **1 cup (4 ounces) shredded part-skim mozzarella cheese**

1. In a large saucepan, prepare the hollandaise sauce mix with milk and butter according to package directions; keep warm.

2. In a large skillet, cook bacon over medium heat until crisp; remove to paper towels. In the drippings, saute mushrooms until tender; set aside.

3. Place asparagus and water in a microwave-safe bowl. Cover and microwave on high for 4-5 minutes or until crisp-tender; drain and keep warm.

4. Heat an 8-in. skillet coated with nonstick cooking spray over medium-low heat; add 3/4 cup beaten eggs (3 eggs). As eggs set, lift edges, letting uncooked portion flow underneath. Sprinkle with a fourth of the asparagus, 1/4 cup cheese and a fourth of the mushrooms.

5. Fold omelet in half. Cover for 1-2 minutes or until the cheese is melted. Repeat for remaining omelets. Top with hollandaise sauce and bacon. **Yield:** 4 omelets.

✿ ✿ ✿
Breakfast Upside-Down Cake
(Also pictured on page 67)

Stacy Walker, Winsor Heights, Iowa

This moist, golden treat quickly became my husband's favorite. Because it calls for a boxed muffin mix and canned pineapple, I never have a problem finding time to prepare it. Plus, it looks pretty enough to serve company.

- 1 package (18.9 ounces) blueberry muffin mix
- 1 package (1/4 ounce) quick-rise yeast
- 1 can (8 ounces) pineapple slices
- 1 egg, lightly beaten
- 1/3 cup packed brown sugar
- 1/4 cup butter, melted
- 4 maraschino cherries, halved

Fresh blueberries, optional

1. Rinse and drain blueberries from muffin mix; set aside. Place muffin mix and yeast in a large bowl; set aside.

2. Drain pineapple, reserving the juice in a measuring cup. Set pineapple aside. Add enough water to juice to measure 2/3 cup.

3. Pour into saucepan; heat to 120°-130°. Add to muffin mix; stir just until moistened. Beat in the egg. Cover and let rest for 10 minutes.

4. Combine brown sugar and butter; pour into a greased 9-in. round baking pan. Cut each pineapple slice in half; arrange over brown sugar mixture. Tuck cherries into pineapple.

5. Spoon half of batter over pineapple. Sprinkle with reserved blueberries. Spread with remaining batter.

6. Bake at 350° for 40-45 minutes or until a toothpick inserted into cake comes out clean. Immediately invert onto a serving plate. Cool completely. Garnish with fresh blueberries if desired. **Yield:** 8 servings.

✿ ✿ ✿
Ham 'n' Cheese Strata

Marilyn Kroeker, Steinbach, Manitoba

A comforting combination of popular breakfast ingredients, this layered casserole is a guaranteed hit at morning potlucks. My family wouldn't mind if I made this every weekend!

- 12 slices white bread, crusts removed
- 1 pound fully cooked ham, diced
- 2 cups (8 ounces) shredded cheddar cheese
- 6 eggs
- 3 cups milk
- 2 teaspoons Worcestershire sauce
- 1 teaspoon ground mustard
- 1/2 teaspoon salt
- 1/4 teaspoon pepper

Dash cayenne pepper

- 1/4 cup finely chopped onion
- 1/4 cup finely chopped green pepper
- 1/4 cup butter, melted
- 1 cup crushed cornflakes

1. Arrange six slices of bread in the bottom of a greased 13-in. x 9-in. x 2-in. baking dish. Top with ham and cheese. Cover with remaining bread.

2. In a bowl, beat eggs, milk, Worcestershire sauce, mustard, salt, pepper and cayenne. Stir in onion and green pepper; pour over all. Cover and refrigerate overnight.

3. Remove from the refrigerator 30 minutes before baking. Pour butter over bread; sprinkle with cornflakes. Bake, uncovered, at 350° for 50-60 minutes or until a knife inserted near the center comes out clean. Let stand 10 minutes before serving. **Yield:** 8-10 servings.

Blintz Pancakes

Dianna Digoy, San Diego, California

Blending sour cream and cottage cheese into the batter of these pancakes provides them with their old-fashioned flavor. Pour on some berry syrup, and you'll turn an ordinary morning into an extraordinary one.

✓ Uses less fat, sugar or salt. Includes Nutrition Facts and Diabetic Exchanges.

 1 cup all-purpose flour
 1 tablespoon sugar
 1/2 teaspoon salt
 1 cup (8 ounces) sour cream
 1 cup (8 ounces) small-curd cottage cheese
 4 eggs, lightly beaten
Strawberry or blueberry syrup
Sliced fresh strawberries, optional

1. In a bowl, combine the flour, sugar and salt; mix well. Add the sour cream, cottage cheese and eggs; mix just until combined.

2. Spoon 1/4 cupfuls of batter onto a greased hot griddle. Turn when edges are set; cook until the second side is golden brown. Serve with syrup and strawberries if desired. **Yield:** 12 pancakes.

Nutrition Facts: Two pancakes (prepared with reduced-fat sour cream, fat-free cottage cheese and 1 cup egg substitute; calculated without syrup or strawberries) equals 184 calories, 4 g fat (3 g saturated fat), 17 mg cholesterol, 429 mg sodium, 23 g carbohydrate, 1 g fiber, 14 g protein. **Diabetic Exchanges:** 1-1/2 starch, 1 lean meat.

Bacon and Eggs Casserole

Deanna Durward-Orr, Windsor, Ontario

This is a top choice of mine for after-church brunches because it requires so little time and is a real crowd-pleaser. I serve the egg bake with a fruit salad, muffins and croissants.

 4 bacon strips
 18 eggs
 1 cup milk
 1 cup (4 ounces) shredded cheddar cheese
 1 cup (8 ounces) sour cream
 1/4 cup sliced green onions
 1 to 1-1/2 teaspoons salt
 1/2 teaspoon pepper

1. In a large skillet, cook bacon over medium heat until crisp. Remove to paper towel to drain.

2. In a large bowl, beat eggs. Add milk, cheese, sour cream, onions, salt and pepper.

3. Pour into a greased 13-in. x 9-in. x 2-in. baking dish. Crumble bacon and sprinkle on top. Bake, uncovered, at 325° for 40-45 minutes or until knife inserted near the center comes out clean. Let stand for 5 minutes. **Yield:** 8-10 servings.

🎗️🎗️🎗️
Cherry Kringle
(Also pictured on page 66)

Mary Christianson, Carmel, Indiana

The soft dough in this recipe is easy to work with and yields four loaves that freeze well. The cherry center is luscious!

- 1 package (1/4 ounce) active dry yeast
- 1 cup warm milk (110° to 115°)
- 4 cups bread flour
- 2 tablespoons sugar
- 1 teaspoon salt
- 1/2 cup cold butter
- 1/2 cup shortening
- 2 eggs, lightly beaten
- 4 cups cherry pie filling

ICING:

- 2 cups confectioners' sugar
- 2 to 3 tablespoons milk

1. In a large mixing bowl, dissolve yeast in warm milk. In another bowl, combine the flour, sugar and salt; cut in butter and shortening until crumbly. Add to yeast mixture. Add eggs; beat to form a very soft dough (do not knead the dough). Cover and refrigerate for at least 8 hours.

2. Turn dough onto a lightly floured surface; divide into fourths. Roll each portion into a 14-in. x 11-in. rectangle; spread cherry pie filling down the center third of each rectangle. Starting at a long side, fold a third of the dough over filling; fold other third over top. Pinch to seal. Pinch ends and tuck under. Place 2 in. apart on greased baking sheets.

3. Bake at 350° for 25 minutes or until golden brown. Remove from pans to wire racks to cool completely. Combine icing ingredients; drizzle over kringles. **Yield:** 4 loaves.

Kringle Creativity

Because the Cherry Kringle recipe on this page yields four loaves, you may want to prepare a few with pie fillings of different flavors for variety. For example, you could try apple, peach or raspberry. If you won't be serving all of the loaves at the same time, freeze the extras in airtight containers or resealable plastic bags.

🎀🎀🎀 Jelly Doughnuts

Kathy Westendorf, Westgate, Iowa

With these lighter-than-air treats, there's no need to go to the bakery when you're craving jelly doughnuts. I've been making them for more than 25 years, and they disappear almost as fast as I can prepare them.

       2 packages (1/4 ounce *each*) active dry yeast
     1/2 cup warm water (110° to 115°)
     1/2 cup warm milk (110° to 115°)
     1/3 cup butter, softened
   1-1/3 cups sugar, *divided*
       3 egg yolks
       1 teaspoon salt
   3-3/4 cups all-purpose flour
       3 tablespoons jelly *or* jam
       1 egg white, beaten
Oil for deep-fat frying

1. In a large mixing bowl, dissolve yeast in warm water. Add milk, butter, 1/3 cup sugar, egg yolks and salt; mix well. Stir in enough flour to form a soft dough (do not knead).

2. Place in a greased bowl, turning once to grease top. Cover and let rise in a warm place until doubled, about 1-1/2 hours.

3. Punch dough down. Turn onto a lightly floured surface; knead about 10 times. Divide dough in half.

4. Roll each portion to 1/4-in. thickness; cut with a floured 2-1/2-in. round cutter. Place about 1/2 teaspoon jelly in the center of half of the circles; brush edges with egg white. Top with remaining circles; press edges to seal tightly.

5. Place on greased baking sheet. Cover and let rise until doubled, about 1 hour.

6. In an electric skillet, heat oil to 375°. Fry doughnuts, a few at a time, for 1-2 minutes on each side or until golden brown. Drain on paper towels. Roll doughnuts in remaining sugar while warm. **Yield:** 16 doughnuts.

🎀🎀🎀 Bacon Swiss Squares

Agarita Vaughan, Fairbury, Illinois

Not only does this cheesy breakfast pizza come together quickly with biscuit mix, but it's a cinch to double the recipe when I'm cooking for a crowd. The combination of eggs, bacon and Swiss cheese keeps guests coming back for more.

       2 cups biscuit/baking mix
     1/2 cup cold water
       8 ounces sliced Swiss cheese
       1 pound sliced bacon, cooked and crumbled
       4 eggs, lightly beaten
     1/4 cup milk
     1/2 teaspoon onion powder

1. In a large bowl, combine the biscuit mix and water; stir 20 strokes. Turn onto a floured surface; knead 10 times. Roll into a 14-in. x 10-in. rectangle.

2. Place on the bottom and 1/2 in. up the sides of a greased 13-in. x 9-in. x 2-in. baking dish. Arrange cheese over dough. Sprinkle with bacon. In a large bowl, whisk eggs, milk and onion powder; pour over bacon.

3. Bake at 425° for 15-18 minutes or until a knife inserted near the center comes out clean. Cut into squares; serve immediately. **Yield:** 12 servings.

1 cup packed brown sugar
1/2 cup butter, cubed
2 tablespoons light corn syrup
2 large tart apples, peeled and sliced 1/4 inch thick
3 eggs
1 cup milk
1 teaspoon vanilla extract
9 slices day-old French bread (3/4 inch thick)

SYRUP:
1 cup applesauce
1 jar (10 ounces) apple jelly
1/2 teaspoon ground cinnamon
1/8 teaspoon ground cloves

1. In a small saucepan, cook brown sugar, butter and syrup until thick, about 5-7 minutes. Pour into an ungreased 13-in. x 9-in. x 2-in. baking pan; arrange apples on top.

2. In a large mixing bowl, beat eggs, milk and vanilla. Dip bread slices into the egg mixture for 1 minute; place over apples. Cover and refrigerate overnight.

3. Remove from the refrigerator 30 minutes before baking. Bake, uncovered, at 350° for 35-40 minutes.

4. Meanwhile, combine syrup ingredients in a medium saucepan; cook and stir until hot. Serve with French toast. **Yield:** 9 servings.

🎗 🎗 🎗

Overnight Apple French Toast

Debra Blazer, Hegins, Pennsylvania

Sliced apples, apple jelly and applesauce all give orchard-fresh flavor to this oven-baked dish. With a wonderful homemade syrup, it makes a warm, comforting breakfast anytime.

🎗 🎗 🎗

Farmer's Casserole

Nancy Schmidt, Center, Colorado

We have a lot of visitors to our house, and this casserole is the perfect crowd-pleaser. You can put it together the night before, let the flavors blend and then bake it in the morning. It's also versatile...elegant enough for a ladies' brunch but hearty enough to satisfy man-sized appetites.

3 cups frozen shredded hash brown potatoes
3/4 cup shredded Monterey Jack cheese
1 cup diced fully cooked ham
1/4 cup chopped green onions
4 eggs
1 can (12 ounces) evaporated milk
1/4 teaspoon pepper
1/8 teaspoon salt

1. Place potatoes in an 8-in. square baking dish. Sprinkle with cheese, ham and onions. Beat eggs, milk, pepper and salt; pour over all. Cover and refrigerate for several hours or overnight.

2. Remove from refrigerator 30 minutes before baking. Bake, uncovered, at 350° for 55-60 minutes or until a knife inserted near the center comes out clean. **Yield:** 6 servings.

🎀🎀🎀
Cheesy Egg Puffs

Amy Soto, Winfield, Kansas

My father loves to entertain, and these buttery delights are one of his favorite brunch items. They're great reheated in the microwave, so Dad always stashes a few aside for me to take home after the party.

    1/2 pound fresh mushrooms, sliced
      4 green onions, chopped
      1 tablespoon plus 1/2 cup butter, cubed, *divided*
    1/2 cup all-purpose flour
      1 teaspoon baking powder
    1/2 teaspoon salt
     10 eggs, lightly beaten
      4 cups (16 ounces) shredded Monterey Jack cheese
      2 cups (16 ounces) small-curd cottage cheese

1. In a skillet, saute the mushrooms and onions in 1 tablespoon butter until tender. In a large bowl, combine the flour, baking powder and salt.

2. In another bowl, combine eggs, Monterey Jack cheese and cottage cheese. Melt remaining butter; add to egg mixture. Stir into dry ingredients along with mushroom mixture.

3. Fill greased muffin cups three-fourths full. Bake at 350° for 35-40 minutes or until a knife inserted near the center comes out clean. Carefully run the knife around the edge of the muffin cups before removing. **Yield:** 2-1/2 dozen.

🎀🎀🎀
Broccoli Ham Quiche

Sue Armstrong, Norman, Oklahoma

This is a terrific way for overnight guests to start off the day. Chock-full of cheese, ham and broccoli, the quiche has an easy crust made of frozen hash browns. And because it cooks in the microwave, it doesn't heat up the kitchen.

      2 cups frozen shredded hash brown potatoes
      1 cup (4 ounces) shredded cheddar cheese
      1 cup diced fully cooked ham
    1/2 cup chopped fresh broccoli
      4 eggs
    1/2 cup milk
      1 teaspoon dried minced onion
    1/2 teaspoon garlic powder
    1/2 teaspoon salt
    1/2 teaspoon pepper

1. Place hash browns in a greased 9-in. microwave-safe pie plate. Microwave, uncovered, on high for 4 minutes or until thawed. Press onto the bottom and halfway up the sides of the plate. Microwave, uncovered, on high for 3 minutes. Sprinkle with cheese, ham and broccoli.

2. In a large bowl, beat the eggs, milk and seasonings; pour over ham mixture. Cover with waxed paper. Microwave at 70% power for 10-12 minutes or until set. Let stand for 5 minutes before cutting. **Yield:** 4-6 servings.

Editor's Note: This recipe was tested with an 850-watt microwave.

Main Dishes

With this extra-big chapter of enticing entrees—71 in all—you have a bonanza of mouth-watering main courses for every occasion, from busy weeknights to holidays.

Italian Pot Roast, p. 98

Sweet 'n' Sour Halibut, p. 107

Chicken with Cheese Sauce, p. 118

Grilled Pineapple Pork Chops, p. 124

Apple Thyme Chicken

Peter Halferty, Corpus Christi, Texas

Apples and chicken may seem like an unusual combination, but they're wonderful when grilled to perfection for this delicious main dish.

✓ Uses less fat, sugar or salt. Includes Nutrition Facts and Diabetic Exchanges.

6 tablespoons apple juice
6 tablespoons lemon juice
4-1/2 teaspoons cider vinegar
4-1/2 teaspoons canola oil
1-1/2 teaspoons dried thyme
4 boneless skinless chicken breast halves (4 ounces *each*)
2 medium apples, peeled and quartered
1 tablespoon honey
SAUCE:
2 teaspoons cornstarch
1/4 teaspoon dried thyme
3/4 cup apple juice

1. In a large bowl, combine the first five ingredients; mix well. Pour half of the marinade into a large resealable plastic bag; add chicken. Seal bag and turn to coat; refrigerate for at least 2 hours. Cover and refrigerate remaining marinade.

2. Coat grill rack with nonstick cooking spray before starting the grill. Drain and discard marinade from chicken. Dip apples in reserved marinade; set aside.

3. Combine the honey with the remaining marinade. Grill chicken, covered, over medium heat for 4-6 minutes on each side or until juices run clear, basting frequently with the honey marinade.

4. Grill apples, uncovered, for 3-5 minutes, basting and turning frequently or until lightly browned.

5. In a large saucepan, combine the cornstarch, thyme and apple juice until blended. Bring to a boil; cook and stir for 2 minutes or until thickened. Slice the grilled apples; stir into sauce. Serve with chicken. **Yield:** 4 servings.

Nutrition Facts: 1 chicken breast half with 1/4 cup sauce equals 266 calories, 3 g fat (1 g saturated fat), 66 mg cholesterol, 76 mg sodium, 22 g carbohydrate, 1 g fiber, 26 g protein. **Diabetic Exchanges:** 3 lean meat, 1-1/2 fruit.

Herbed Pork Rib Roast

Joyce Kramer, Donalsonville, Georgia

My husband came up with this recipe, and it's a specialty of the house. The simple seasoning also works well on pork chops, beef roast and chicken.

1 tablespoon garlic powder
1 tablespoon onion powder
1 tablespoon dried marjoram
1 tablespoon dried parsley flakes
1 to 2 teaspoons cayenne pepper
1 bone-in pork rib roast (about 4 pounds)

1. In a small bowl, combine the garlic powder, onion powder, marjoram, parsley and cayenne. Rub over roast. Cover and refrigerate overnight.

2. Place roast bone side down in a shallow roasting pan. Bake, uncovered, at 350° for 1-1/2 to 1-3/4 hours or until a meat thermometer reads 160°. Let stand for 10 minutes before carving. **Yield:** 8 servings.

✿✿✿ Cheesy Crab Enchiladas

Kelly Mockler, Madison, Wisconsin

While I was in college, my roommates and I loved the taste of ranch dressing—it was our condiment of choice for almost everything. So I prepared these rich, delectable crab enchiladas using ranch dressing mix.

2 packages (8 ounces *each*) cream cheese, softened
1 envelope ranch salad dressing mix
3 tablespoons plus 1/4 cup milk, *divided*
1 small red onion, diced
2 garlic cloves, minced
2 tablespoons butter
1 pound fresh, frozen *or* canned crabmeat, flaked and cartilage removed
2 cans (2-1/2 ounces *each*) sliced ripe olives, drained
1 can (4 ounces) chopped green chilies
1/2 teaspoon pepper
1/4 teaspoon salt
2 cups (8 ounces) shredded Monterey Jack cheese, *divided*
8 flour tortillas (8 inches), warmed
1/2 cup shredded Colby cheese
Chopped green onions and tomatoes, shredded lettuce and additional sliced ripe olives, optional

1. In a large mixing bowl, combine cream cheese, dressing mix and 3 tablespoons milk until smooth. Set aside 3/4 cup for topping.

2. In a large skillet, saute onion and garlic in butter until tender. Stir in crab, olives, chilies, pepper and salt. Fold crab mixture and 1-1/2 cups Monterey Jack into remaining cream cheese mixture.

3. Spoon about 2/3 cup down the center of each tortilla. Roll up and place seam side down in a greased 13-in. x 9-in. x 2-in. baking dish. Combine the remaining milk and reserved cream cheese mixture until blended; pour over tortillas. Sprinkle with Colby and remaining Monterey Jack.

4. Cover and bake 350° for 25 minutes. Uncover; bake 5-10 minutes longer or until heated through. Serve with green onions, tomatoes, lettuce and olives if desired. **Yield:** 8 enchiladas.

✿✿✿ Vegetarian Linguine

Jane Bone, Cape Coral, Florida

Looking for a tasty alternative to meat-and-potatoes meals? Try this colorful, satisfying pasta dish created by my oldest son. It's a stick-to-your-ribs supper that takes advantage of fresh mushrooms, zucchini and other vegetables as well as basil and provolone cheese.

 Uses less fat, sugar or salt. Includes Nutrition Facts and Diabetic Exchanges.

6 ounces uncooked linguine
2 medium zucchini, thinly sliced
1/2 pound fresh mushrooms, sliced
2 green onions, chopped
1 garlic clove, minced
2 tablespoons butter
1 tablespoon olive oil
1 large tomato, chopped
2 teaspoons minced fresh basil
1/2 teaspoon salt
1/4 teaspoon pepper
4 ounces provolone cheese, shredded
3 tablespoons shredded Parmesan cheese

Cook linguine according to package directions. Meanwhile, in a large skillet, saute the zucchini, mushrooms, onions and garlic in butter and oil for 3-5 minutes. Add tomato, basil, salt and pepper; cover and simmer for 3 minutes. Drain linguine; add to vegetable mixture. Sprinkle with cheeses; toss to coat. **Yield:** 6 servings.

Nutrition Facts: 1-cup serving (prepared with reduced-fat provolone) equals 216 calories, 11 g fat (5 g saturated fat), 22 mg cholesterol, 416 mg sodium, 22 g carbohydrate, 3 g fiber, 12 g protein. **Diabetic Exchanges:** 1 starch, 1 lean meat, 1 vegetable, 1 fat.

Turkey Biscuit Potpie

Shirley Francey, St. Catharines, Ontario

My family's always happy when I serve this comforting dish loaded with chunks of turkey, potatoes, carrots and green beans. Topped with easy-to-make biscuits, it has down-home flavor that can't be beat.

✓ Uses less fat, sugar or salt. Includes Nutrition Facts and Diabetic Exchanges.

   1 **large onion, chopped**
   1 **garlic clove, minced**
1-1/2 **cups cubed peeled potatoes**
1-1/2 **cups sliced carrots**
   1 **cup frozen cut green beans, thawed**
   1 **cup reduced-sodium chicken broth**
4-1/2 **teaspoons all-purpose flour**
   1 **can (10-3/4 ounces) reduced-fat condensed cream of mushroom soup, undiluted**
   2 **cups cubed cooked turkey**
   2 **tablespoons minced fresh parsley**
1/2 **teaspoon dried basil**
1/2 **teaspoon dried thyme**
1/4 **teaspoon pepper**
BISCUITS:
   1 **cup all-purpose flour**
   2 **teaspoons baking powder**
1/2 **teaspoon dried oregano**
   2 **tablespoons butter**
   7 **tablespoons 1% milk**

1. In a large saucepan coated with nonstick cooking spray, cook onion and garlic over medium heat until tender. Add the potatoes, carrots, beans and broth; bring to a boil. Reduce heat; cover and simmer for 15-20 minutes or until potatoes are tender.

2. Remove from the heat. Combine the flour and mushroom soup; stir into vegetable mixture. Add the turkey and seasonings. Transfer to a 2-qt. baking dish coated with nonstick cooking spray.

3. In a large bowl, combine the flour, baking powder and oregano. Cut in the butter until evenly distributed. Stir in milk. Drop batter in six mounds onto hot turkey mixture.

4. Bake, uncovered, at 400° for 20-25 minutes or until a toothpick inserted in center of biscuits comes out clean and biscuits are golden brown. **Yield:** 6 servings.

Nutrition Facts: 1 serving equals 301 calories, 8 g fat (4 g saturated fat), 47 mg cholesterol, 616 mg sodium, 37 g carbohydrate, 3 g fiber, 19 g protein. **Diabetic Exchanges:** 2 starch, 2 very lean meat, 1 vegetable, 1 fat.

Potato Ham Skillet

Sharon Price, Urbana, Ohio

My mother prepared this cheesy stovetop dish when I was young, and now I make it for my own family. It's a great way to use ham or potatoes left over from last night's supper.

   4 **cups cubed cooked peeled potatoes**
   2 **cups cubed fully cooked ham**
1/2 **cup mayonnaise**
1/4 **teaspoon salt**
1/8 **teaspoon pepper**
   2 **cups (8 ounces *each*) shredded part-skim mozzarella cheese**

In a large skillet, combine the potatoes, ham, mayonnaise, salt and pepper. Cook and stir over medium–low heat until heated through. Stir in cheese until melted. **Yield:** 4 servings.

🎗🎗🎗
Pork Chops Creole

Josephine Bake, Litchfield, Illinois

A sure way to perk up pork chops is with this herbed creole sauce. With a sprinkle of green parsley, it makes a pretty presentation on the plate. Feel free to adjust the range of seasonings to suit your taste.

- 1/4 cup all-purpose flour
- 4 pounds boneless pork loin chops (3/4-inch thick and 4 ounces *each*)
- 5 tablespoons olive oil
- 1 large onion, thinly sliced
- 1/2 cup finely chopped green pepper
- 1 celery rib, finely chopped
- 2 garlic cloves, minced
- 2 cups stewed tomatoes
- 1/2 teaspoon salt
- 1/2 teaspoon sugar
- 1 to 1-1/2 teaspoons dried thyme
- 1/4 to 1/2 teaspoon pepper
- 1/4 to 1/2 teaspoon hot pepper sauce

Minced fresh parsley

1. Place flour in a large resealable plastic bag. Add the pork chops, one at a time, and shake to coat.

2. In a large skillet, brown pork chops, over medium-high heat, on both sides in oil. Remove chops and keep warm.

3. In the drippings, saute onion, green pepper, celery and garlic until vegetables are tender. Stir in the tomatoes, salt, sugar, thyme, pepper and hot pepper sauce.

4. Return pork chops to the pan. Bring to a boil. Reduce heat; cover and simmer for 10-15 minutes or until meat juices run clear. Serve sauce over pork chops; sprinkle with parsley. **Yield:** 4 servings.

🎗🎗🎗
Pineapple Chicken Lo Mein

Linda Stevens, Madison, Alabama

Perfect for busy weeknights, this speedy lo mein combines tender chicken and colorful veggies with a tangy sauce. Quick-cooking spaghetti and canned pineapple make this dish a cinch to throw together when time is short.

- 1 can (20 ounces) unsweetened pineapple chunks
- 1 pound boneless skinless chicken breasts, cut into 1-inch cubes
- 2 garlic cloves, minced
- 3/4 teaspoon ground ginger *or* 1 tablespoon minced fresh gingerroot
- 3 tablespoons vegetable oil, *divided*
- 2 medium carrots, julienned
- 1 medium green pepper, julienned
- 4 ounces spaghetti, cooked and drained
- 3 green onions, sliced
- 1 tablespoon cornstarch
- 1/3 cup soy sauce

1. Drain pineapple, reserving 1/3 cup juice (discard remaining juice or save for another use); set the pineapple aside.

2. In a large skillet over medium heat, cook the chicken, garlic and ginger in 2 tablespoons oil for 6 minutes. Add the carrots, green pepper and pineapple. Cover and cook for 2-3 minutes or until vegetables are crisp-tender and chicken juices run clear. Stir in spaghetti and onions.

3. In a small bowl, combine the cornstarch, soy sauce, reserved pineapple juice and remaining oil until smooth. Stir into chicken mixture. Bring to a boil; cook and stir for 2 minutes or until thickened. **Yield:** 4 servings.

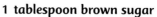
1 tablespoon brown sugar
2 teaspoons cornstarch
Dash ground allspice
1/2 cup cranberry juice
1 small apple, peeled and chopped
1/2 cup fresh *or* frozen cranberries
1 boneless fully cooked ham steak (1 pound)

1. In a microwave-safe bowl, combine the brown sugar, cornstarch and allspice. Stir in cranberry juice until smooth. Add apple and cranberries; mix well. Microwave, uncovered, on high for 3-5 minutes or until thickened, stirring every minute. Keep warm.

2. Place ham slice in a shallow 3-qt. microwave-safe dish. Cover and microwave at 70% power for 4-6 minutes or until heated through. Top with fruit mixture. **Yield:** 4 servings.

Editor's Note: This recipe was tested with an 850-watt microwave.

🎖 🎖 🎖
Cran-Apple Ham Slice

Jena Coffey, Rock Hill, Missouri

Cranberries, apple and a little brown sugar blend into a chunky accompaniment for this ham. The not-too-sweet sauce gets its pretty pink color from cranberry juice.

2 cups diced cooked turkey breast
1 cup (4 ounces) shredded reduced-fat Swiss cheese
1/2 cup dried cranberries
1/2 cup diced celery
1/2 cup fat-free mayonnaise
1/4 cup chopped walnuts
3 tablespoons minced fresh parsley
2 tablespoons honey mustard
1/2 teaspoon pepper
2 tubes (8 ounces *each*) refrigerated reduced-fat crescent rolls
1 egg white, lightly beaten

1. In a large bowl, combine the first nine ingredients. Coat a 14-in. pizza pan with nonstick cooking spray.

2. Separate the crescent roll dough into 16 triangles. Place the wide end of 1 triangle 3 in. from the edge of the prepared pan with the point overhanging edge of pan. Repeat with remaining triangles along outer edge of pan, overlapping the wide ends (dough will look like the rays of the sun when complete). Lightly press wide ends together.

3. Spoon turkey mixture over the wide ends of dough. Fold the points of the triangles over the filling and tuck under wide ends (filling will be visible). Brush with egg white. Bake at 375° for 20-25 minutes or until golden brown. **Yield:** 16 servings.

Editor's Note: As a substitute for 2 tablespoons honey mustard, combine 1 tablespoon Dijon mustard and 1 tablespoon honey.

Nutrition Facts: 1 serving equals 171 calories, 7 g fat (1 g saturated fat), 18 mg cholesterol, 373 mg sodium, 17 g carbohydrate, 1 g fiber, 10 g protein. **Diabetic Exchanges:** 1 starch, 1 lean meat, 1 fat.

🎖 🎖 🎖
Turkey Crescent Wreath

Jane Jones, Cedar, Minnesota

This savory wreath tastes as good as it looks! When hosting a get-together the day after Thanksgiving one year, I prepared it with leftover turkey. Everyone asked for a second slice.

✓ Uses less fat, sugar or salt. Includes Nutrition Facts and Diabetic Exchanges.

Savory Sausage and Peppers

Rickey Madden, Americus, Georgia

My mother gave me the recipe for this hearty kielbasa meal loaded with colorful pepper chunks. I like to use a soup mix that adds a hint of garlic, but you can substitute other varieties to suit your family's tastes.

- 1/2 pound smoked kielbasa *or* Polish sausage, cut into 1/2-inch slices
- 3 tablespoons olive oil
- 1 medium sweet red pepper, cut into 1-inch chunks
- 1 medium sweet yellow pepper, cut into 1-inch chunks
- 1 medium green pepper, cut into 1-inch chunks
- 1 medium onion, cut into small wedges
- 1 cup water
- 1 package (1.2 ounces) herb and garlic soup mix
- 1/8 teaspoon hot pepper sauce

Hot cooked rice

1. In a large skillet, brown sausage in oil over medium-high heat. Remove with a slotted spoon and keep warm. In the drippings, saute peppers and onion until crisp-tender.

2. In a large bowl, combine the water and contents of one soup mix envelope (save the second envelope for another use). Add soup mixture, hot pepper sauce and sausage to the vegetables. Reduce heat; cover and simmer for 5 minutes or until thickened. Serve with rice. **Yield:** 2-3 servings.

Oriental Pork Burgers

Deborah Messerly, Steamboat Rock, Iowa

My home state of Iowa is a leader in pork production. This burger recipe is a truly delicious and nutritious way to serve ground pork.

- 1 cup soft bread crumbs
- 1/3 cup finely chopped green onions
- 1/3 cup finely chopped green pepper
- 1 can (8 ounces) water chestnuts, drained and chopped
- 1 egg, lightly beaten
- 2 tablespoons soy sauce
- 1 garlic clove, minced
- 1 teaspoon salt
- 1/8 teaspoon ground ginger
- 2 pounds ground pork

SAUCE:
- 1 can (8 ounces) crushed pineapple, drained
- 2/3 cup ketchup
- 1/4 cup white vinegar
- 1/4 cup orange marmalade
- 2 tablespoons prepared mustard
- 8 hamburger buns, split and toasted

1. In a large bowl, combine the first nine ingredients. Crumble pork over mixture and mix well. Shape into eight patties. Cover and refrigerate for 1 hour.

2. Meanwhile, in a saucepan, combine the pineapple, ketchup, vinegar, marmalade and mustard. Cook and stir for 5 minutes or until marmalade is melted. Remove from the heat; set aside.

3. Grill patties, covered, over medium heat for 4-6 minutes on each side or until a meat thermometer reads 160°. Spoon 1 tablespoon of sauce onto each burger during the last 2 minutes of grilling. Serve on buns with remaining sauce. **Yield:** 8 servings.

1 package (16 ounces) fettuccine
1 pound uncooked medium shrimp, peeled and deveined
3 garlic cloves, minced
1/2 cup butter
1 package (8 ounces) cream cheese, cubed
1 cup milk
1/2 cup shredded Parmesan cheese
1 package (10 ounces) frozen broccoli florets
1/2 teaspoon salt
Dash pepper

1. Cook fettuccine according to package directions. Meanwhile, in a large skillet, saute shrimp and garlic in butter until shrimp turn pink. Remove and keep warm. In the same skillet, combine the cream cheese, milk and Parmesan cheese; cook until cheeses are melted and smooth.

2. Place 1 in. of water in a saucepan; add broccoli. Bring to a boil. Reduce heat; cover and simmer for 6-8 minutes or until tender. Drain. Stir the broccoli, shrimp, salt and pepper into cheese sauce; heat through. Drain fettuccine; top with shrimp mixture. **Yield:** 4 servings.

🎗 🎗 🎗
Broccoli Shrimp Alfredo

Rae Natoli, Kingston, New York

After enjoying fettuccine Alfredo at a restaurant, I tried to duplicate the recipe at home. I came up with this creamy dish, and my husband likes it even better than the restaurant's version.

🎗 🎗 🎗
Turkey Pepper Kabobs

Traci Goodman, Paducah, Kentucky

A summertime favorite at our house, these kabobs have a sweet basting sauce and chunks of pineapple. The recipe also works well with chicken instead of turkey.

✓ Uses less fat, sugar or salt. Includes Nutrition Facts and Diabetic Exchanges.

1 can (8 ounces) unsweetened pineapple chunks
1/4 cup packed brown sugar
2 tablespoons canola oil
2 tablespoons Worcestershire sauce
1 garlic clove, minced
1 teaspoon prepared mustard
1 pound turkey tenderloin, cut into 1-inch cubes
1 large sweet onion, cut into 3/4-inch pieces
1 large green pepper, cut into 1-inch pieces
1 large sweet red pepper, cut into 1-inch pieces

1. Drain pineapple, reserving 1/4 cup juice (discard remaining juice or save for another use). In a large bowl, combine the reserved pineapple juice, brown sugar, oil, Worcestershire sauce, garlic and mustard; mix well. Pour 1/3 cup into a large resealable plastic bag; add the turkey. Seal bag and turn to coat; refrigerate for 2-3 hours. Cover and refrigerate remaining marinade.

2. If grilling the kabobs, coat grill rack with nonstick cooking spray before starting the grill. Drain and discard marinade from turkey.

3. On eight metal or soaked wooden skewers, alternately thread vegetables, turkey and pineapple. Grill, uncovered, over medium heat or broil 4-6 in. from the heat for 4-5 minutes on each side or until meat is no longer pink, turning three times and basting frequently with reserved marinade. **Yield:** 4 servings.

Nutrition Facts: 2 kabobs equals 262 calories, 4 g fat (1 g saturated fat), 82 mg cholesterol, 110 mg sodium, 24 g carbohydrate, 3 g fiber, 31 g protein. **Diabetic Exchanges:** 4 very lean meat, 2 vegetable, 1 fruit.

🏅🏅🏅
Marinated Pork Chops

Ruth Reazin, Lyons, Kansas

My husband came across a variation of this recipe and shared it with me. Not only did it win raves at home, it received a blue ribbon at a fair.

> 1 can (12 ounces) cola
> 1/4 cup soy sauce
> 3/4 teaspoon garlic powder
> 3/4 teaspoon ground ginger
> 3/4 teaspoon ground mustard
> 1/2 teaspoon salt
> 1/2 teaspoon pepper
> 6 bone-in pork loin chops (3/4 inch thick and 8 ounces *each*)

1. In a 2-cup measuring cup, combine the first seven ingredients. Pour 1-1/2 cups into a large resealable plastic bag; add pork chops. Seal bag and turn to coat; refrigerate for 8 hours or overnight. Cover and refrigerate remaining marinade for basting.

2. Drain and discard marinade from pork. Grill, covered, over medium heat for 5-6 minutes on each side or until meat juices run clear, basting with reserved marinade. **Yield:** 6 servings.

🏅🏅🏅
Garlic Shrimp Stir-Fry

Irene Lalevee, River Vale, New Jersey

This taste-tempting entree is pretty enough to serve to company, and most of the preparation can be done in advance. Tender shrimp, colorful sweet peppers and crunchy snow peas give it a variety of interesting textures and flavors.

☑ Uses less fat, sugar or salt. Includes Nutrition Facts and Diabetic Exchanges.

> 4 garlic cloves, minced
> 2 tablespoons butter
> 1 pound uncooked medium shrimp, peeled and deveined
> 6 ounces fresh snow peas
> 1/2 cup julienned sweet red pepper
> 1/2 cup julienned sweet yellow pepper
> 3 tablespoons minced fresh basil *or* 1 tablespoon dried basil
> 3 tablespoons minced fresh parsley
> 1/2 teaspoon salt
> 1/4 teaspoon pepper
> 1/4 cup chicken broth
> Hot cooked rice

In a large skillet, saute garlic in butter until tender. Add the shrimp, peas, peppers, basil, parsley, salt and pepper. Stir-fry for 5 minutes or until shrimp turn pink and vegetables are crisp-tender. Add broth. Cook 1 minute longer or until heated through. Serve with rice. **Yield:** 4 servings.

Nutrition Facts: 1 cup stir-fry (calculated without rice) equals 205 calories, 8 g fat (4 g saturated fat), 188 mg cholesterol, 563 mg sodium, 8 g carbohydrate, 2 g fiber, 25 g protein. **Diabetic Exchanges:** 3 lean meat, 1 vegetable.

 🎗️🎗️🎗️

Garden Bounty Beef Kabobs

Christine Klessig, Amherst Junction, Wisconsin

These classic kabobs are a hearty way to use up your garden harvest. At our house, everyone fixes their own skewers for an all-in-one dinner.

Uses less fat, sugar or salt. Includes Nutrition Facts and Diabetic Exchanges.

   1/4 **cup reduced-sodium soy sauce**
     2 **tablespoons olive oil**
     1 **tablespoon molasses**
     3 **garlic cloves, minced**
     1 **teaspoon ground ginger**
     1 **teaspoon ground mustard**
     1 **pound boneless beef sirloin steak, cut into**
       1-inch cubes
     1 **large sweet onion, cut into 1-inch pieces**
     1 **large green *or* sweet red pepper, cut into 1-inch**
       pieces
     1 **medium zucchini, cut into 1-inch slices**
     1 **pint cherry tomatoes**
  1/2 **pound large fresh mushrooms**

DIPPING SAUCE:
     1 **cup (8 ounces) reduced-fat sour cream**
  1/4 **cup fat-free milk**
     3 **tablespoons dry onion soup mix**
     2 **tablespoons Dijon mustard**
  1/8 **teaspoon pepper**

1. In a large resealable plastic bag, combine the first six ingredients; add the beef. Seal bag and turn to coat; refrigerate for 1 hour.

2. If grilling the kabobs, coat grill rack with nonstick cooking spray before starting the grill. Drain and discard marinade.

3. On eight metal or soaked wooden skewers, alternately thread beef and vegetables. Grill, covered, over medium heat or broil 4-6 in. from the heat for 3-4 minutes on each side or until beef reaches desired doneness, turning three times.

4. In a small saucepan, combine the dipping sauce ingredients. Cook over low heat until heated through. Serve with kabobs. **Yield:** 4 servings.

Nutrition Facts: 2 kabobs with 5 tablespoons of sauce equals 369 calories, 15 g fat (7 g saturated fat), 97 mg cholesterol, 856 mg sodium, 24 g carbohydrate, 4 g fiber, 35 g protein. **Diabetic Exchanges:** 4 lean meat, 3 vegetable, 1 fat, 1/2 starch.

🎀🎀🎀 Seafood Lasagna

Elena Hansen, Ruidoso, New Mexico

This comforting main course is loaded with scallops, shrimp and crab. With a creamy sauce, too, it's a standout in my collection of seafood entree recipes.

- 1 green onion, finely chopped
- 2 tablespoons vegetable oil
- 2 tablespoons plus 1/2 cup butter, *divided*
- 1/2 cup chicken broth
- 1 bottle (8 ounces) clam juice
- 1 pound bay scallops
- 1 pound uncooked small shrimp, peeled and deveined
- 1 package (8 ounces) imitation crabmeat, chopped
- 1/4 teaspoon white pepper, *divided*
- 1/2 cup all-purpose flour
- 1-1/2 cups milk
- 1/2 teaspoon salt
- 1 cup heavy whipping cream
- 1/2 cup shredded Parmesan cheese, *divided*
- 9 lasagna noodles, cooked and drained

1. In a large skillet, saute onion in oil and 2 tablespoons butter until tender. Stir in broth and clam juice; bring to a boil. Add the scallops, shrimp, crab and 1/8 teaspoon pepper; return to a boil. Reduce heat; simmer, uncovered, for 4-5 minutes or until shrimp turn pink and scallops are firm and opaque, stirring gently. Drain, reserving cooking liquid; set seafood mixture aside.

2. In a saucepan, melt the remaining butter; stir in flour until smooth. Combine milk and reserved cooking liquid; gradually add to the saucepan. Add salt and remaining pepper. Bring to a boil; cook and stir for 2 minutes or until thickened. Remove from the heat; stir in cream and 1/4 cup Parmesan cheese. Stir 3/4 cup white sauce into the seafood mixture.

3. Spread 1/2 cup white sauce in a greased 13-in. x 9-in. x 2-in. baking dish. Top with three noodles; spread with half of the seafood mixture and 1-1/4 cups sauce. Repeat layers. Top with remaining noodles, sauce and Parmesan.

4. Bake, uncovered, at 350° for 35-40 minutes or until golden brown. Let stand for 15 minutes before cutting. **Yield:** 12 servings.

🎀🎀🎀 Dilly Pork Chops

Robin Hightower Parker, Church Hill, Tennessee

Everyone who tastes these tender chops loves them. In fact, they're so good that I often cook extra and freeze them for another busy night. The savory mixture of butter, mustard and dill is also great on chicken and fish.

- 6 boneless pork loin chops (1/2 inch thick)
- 1/4 cup butter, melted
- 1 tablespoon Dijon mustard
- 1 to 1-1/2 teaspoons dill weed
- 1 teaspoon Worcestershire sauce
- 1/8 teaspoon garlic powder

1. Prick pork chops with a fork. In a small bowl, combine the remaining ingredients; spoon over both sides of chops.

2. Place on a broiler pan; broil 4-6 in. from the heat for 4 minutes on each side or until juices run clear. **Yield:** 6 servings.

🎀 🎀 🎀
Pizza Rice Casserole

Christine Reimer, Niverville, Manitoba

Anyone who likes pizza and lasagna will love this Italian-style rice. Usually, I make two or three of the casseroles at one time and freeze some for future meals.

3/4 pound ground beef
1 medium onion, chopped
2 cans (8 ounces *each*) tomato sauce
1 teaspoon sugar
1 teaspoon salt
1 teaspoon dried parsley flakes
1/4 teaspoon garlic powder
1/4 teaspoon oregano
Dash pepper
2 cups cooked rice
1/2 cup small-curd cottage cheese
1/2 cup shredded part-skim mozzarella cheese

1. In a large skillet, cook beef and onion over medium heat until meat is no longer pink; drain. Add the tomato sauce, sugar, salt, parsley, garlic powder, oregano and pepper. Bring to a boil. Reduce heat; cover and simmer for 15 minutes.

2. Combine the rice and cottage cheese; spoon half into a greased 11-in. x 7-in. x 2-in. baking dish. Top with half of the meat mixture. Repeat layers. Sprinkle with mozzarella cheese.

3. Bake, uncovered, at 325° for 30-35 minutes or until heated through and bubbly. **Yield:** 4 servings.

🎀 🎀 🎀
Italian Pot Roast

(Also pictured on page 86)

Marilyn Riel, Swansea, Massachusetts

I received this recipe from my mother's friend when I was a newlywed. I was in a panic over what to serve to guests, and she suggested this flavorful pot roast. It was a big hit, and I've been serving it for the past 40 years.

1 boneless beef rump roast (3 to 3-1/2 pounds)
2 tablespoons vegetable oil
1 can (14-1/2 ounces) beef broth
1 can (6 ounces) tomato paste
1 can (4 ounces) mushroom stems and pieces, drained
1 medium onion, chopped
1 large carrot, chopped
1 celery rib, chopped
3 garlic cloves, minced
2 teaspoons Italian seasoning
2 teaspoons salt
1/8 teaspoon pepper
2 tablespoons all-purpose flour
1/4 cup cold water

1. In a Dutch oven, brown roast in oil on all sides over medium-high heat; drain. Combine the broth, tomato paste, mushrooms, onion, carrot, celery, garlic, Italian seasoning, salt and pepper; pour over roast. Bring to a boil. Reduce heat; cover and simmer for 3 to 3-1/4 hours or until the meat is tender.

2. Remove roast; keep warm. Pour pan drippings and loosened browned bits into a measuring cup. Skim fat; pour drippings into a saucepan. Combine flour and water until smooth; gradually stir into drippings. Bring to a boil; cook and stir for 2 minutes or until thickened. Slice roast; serve with gravy. **Yield:** 6-8 servings.

🎗🎗🎗 Pinwheel Flank Steaks

Nancy Tafoya, Fort Collins, Colorado

Here's a tempting, elegant-looking steak dish that's a breeze to make. Much of the preparation can be done in advance.

- 1-1/2 **pounds beef flank steak**
- 1/4 **cup olive oil**
- 2 **tablespoons red wine vinegar**
- 2 **teaspoons Worcestershire sauce**
- 2 **teaspoons Italian seasoning**
- 1-1/2 **teaspoons garlic powder**
- 1-1/2 **teaspoons pepper, *divided***
- 1 **teaspoon seasoned salt**
- 8 **bacon strips, cooked and crumbled**
- 2 **garlic cloves, minced**
- 1/4 **cup minced fresh parsley**
- 1/4 **cup finely chopped onion**
- 1/2 **teaspoon salt**

1. Flatten steak to 1/4-in. thickness. In a large resealable plastic bag, combine the oil, vinegar, Worcestershire sauce, Italian seasoning, garlic powder, 1 teaspoon pepper and seasoned salt; add the steak. Seal bag and turn to coat; refrigerate for 8 hours or overnight.

2. Drain and discard marinade. Combine the bacon, garlic, parsley, onion, salt and remaining pepper; sprinkle over steak to within 1 in. of edges. Roll up jelly-roll style, starting with a long side; tie with kitchen string at about 1-in. intervals. Cut into 1-1/4-in. rolls.

3. Coat grill rack with nonstick cooking spray before starting the grill. Grill steak rolls, uncovered, over medium heat for 10-12 minutes on each side or until meat reaches desired doneness (for medium-rare, a meat thermometer should read 145°; medium, 160°; well-done, 170°). Cut and remove string before serving. **Yield:** 6 servings.

🎗🎗🎗 Pork Chops with Apples

Marilou Robinson, Portland, Oregon

These moist, tender pork chops get delicious flavor from Dijon mustard, onions and apple slices. I think this entree is best with mashed sweet potatoes and a simple salad. For variation, try replacing the apples with pineapple rings.

- 4 **bone-in pork loin chops (3/4 inch thick and 7 ounces *each*)**
- 2 **tablespoons vegetable oil**
- 1/2 **teaspoon salt**
- 1/4 **teaspoon pepper**
- 2 **medium onions, thinly sliced**
- 1 **large green apple, cut into thin wedges**
- 1 **large red apple, cut into thin wedges**
- 2 **tablespoons Dijon mustard**
- 1 **tablespoon brown sugar**

1. In a large skillet, brown pork chops in oil on each side. Season with salt and pepper; remove and keep warm. In the same skillet, saute onions and apple wedges until crisp-tender.

2. Combine mustard and brown sugar; brush over chops. Return to the skillet; cook for 4 minutes or until meat juices run clear. **Yield:** 4 servings.

 🎀 🎀 🎀
Southwestern Skewers

Larry Smith, Youngstown, Ohio

Juicy pieces of chicken, cherry tomatoes, whole mushrooms and sweet peppers make these skewers filling. But it's the fresh garlic, chili powder, cumin and cayenne pepper that give them their zesty kick.

✓ Uses less fat, sugar or salt. Includes Nutrition Facts and Diabetic Exchanges.

- 1 bottle (8 ounces) reduced-fat Italian salad dressing
- 10 garlic cloves, minced
- 1 teaspoon white pepper
- 1 teaspoon chili powder
- 1 teaspoon ground cumin
- 1 teaspoon paprika
- 1/2 teaspoon cayenne pepper
- 1 medium green pepper, cut into 1-inch pieces
- 1 medium sweet red pepper, cut into 1-inch pieces
- 1 medium onion, cut into 1-inch pieces
- 8 large fresh mushrooms
- 8 cherry tomatoes
- 1 pound boneless skinless chicken breasts, cut into 1-inch cubes

1. In a large bowl, combine the first seven ingredients. Pour half into a large resealable plastic bag; add the vegetables. Seal bag and turn to coat. Pour remaining marinade into another large resealable plastic bag; add the chicken. Seal bag and turn to coat. Refrigerate vegetables and chicken for at least 2-3 hours.

2. If grilling the kabobs, coat grill rack with nonstick cooking spray before starting the grill. Drain chicken, discarding marinade. Drain vegetables, reserving marinade for basting.

3. On eight metal or soaked wooded skewers, alternately thread the chicken and vegetables. Grill, covered, over medium heat or broil 4-6 in. from the heat for 3-4 minutes on each side or until the chicken is no longer pink and the vegetables are tender, turning three times and basting frequently with the reserved marinade. **Yield:** 4 servings.

Nutrition Facts: 2 kabobs equals 231 calories, 7 g fat (1 g saturated fat), 63 mg cholesterol, 275 mg sodium, 15 g carbohydrate, 3 g fiber, 26 g protein. **Diabetic Exchanges:** 3 lean meat, 2 vegetable, 1 fat.

🎀🎀🎀
Fisherman's Crispy Coating

Tammi Freih, Lakewood, California

My father, Garfield Freih, is an avid fisherman and frequently acts as chef on the fishing trips he takes with his buddies. He came up with this pleasantly mild and crispy coating, which both friends and family enjoy.

       1 egg
       1 cup milk
       1 cup crisp rice cereal, crushed
     1/4 cup all-purpose flour
     1/4 cup cornmeal
 1-1/2 teaspoons lemon-pepper seasoning
     1/4 teaspoon seasoned salt
     1/8 teaspoon onion salt
     1/8 teaspoon garlic salt
       4 walleye *or* other whitefish fillets (1-3/4 to 2 pounds)
Oil for frying

1. In a shallow bowl, whisk together the egg and milk. In a large resealable plastic bag, combine the cereal, flour, cornmeal and seasonings. Dip the fish fillets into egg mixture, then coat with cereal mixture.

2. In a large skillet, heat 1/4 in. of oil over medium-high heat. Fry the fillets for 5-7 minutes on each side or until fish flakes easily with a fork. **Yield:** 4 servings.

🎀🎀🎀
Teriyaki Sirloin Steak

Nilah Lewis, Calgary, Alberta

Since a co-worker shared this recipe with me, I seldom make steak any other way. It's an excellent entree for folks like my husband who love meat, and it's earned me many compliments over the years.

   1/2 cup soy sauce
   1/4 cup vegetable oil
   1/4 cup packed brown sugar
     2 teaspoons ground mustard
     2 teaspoons ground ginger
     1 teaspoon garlic powder
     1 to 1-1/2 pounds boneless beef sirloin steak (3/4 inch thick)

1. In a large resealable plastic bag, combine the first six ingredients; add the steak. Seal bag and turn to coat; refrigerate for 8 hours or overnight.

2. Drain and discard marinade. Grill steak, covered, over medium heat for 5-8 minutes on each side or until meat reaches desired doneness (for medium-rare, a meat thermometer should read 145°; medium, 160°; well-done, 170°). **Yield:** 4-6 servings.

Shrimp Jambalaya

Marguerite Shaeffer, Sewell, New Jersey

This delightfully different jambalaya is lighter than many of the traditional sausage varieties. Plus, it's a great way to use up leftover ham. While you're cooking, the aroma will draw your family to the table.

- 1 cup cubed fully cooked ham
- 3/4 cup chopped onion
- 1 garlic clove, minced
- 2 tablespoons vegetable oil
- 2 cups chicken broth
- 1 can (14-1/2 ounces) stewed tomatoes
- 2 tablespoons minced fresh parsley
- 1/2 teaspoon salt
- 1/4 teaspoon dried thyme
- 1/8 teaspoon *each* cayenne pepper, chili powder and pepper
- 1 bay leaf
- 1 cup uncooked long grain rice
- 1 pound uncooked medium shrimp, peeled and deveined

In a large skillet, cook the ham, onion and garlic in oil until onion is tender. Stir in the broth, tomatoes, parsley and seasonings. Bring to a boil. Stir in rice. Reduce heat; cover and simmer for 15-20 minutes or until rice is tender. Add shrimp; cook 5 minutes longer or until shrimp turn pink. Discard bay leaf. **Yield:** 4 servings.

Marinated Turkey Tenderloins

Beth Wynne, Kill Devil Hills, North Carolina

Everyone loves this flavorful treatment for turkey tenderloins. Preparation is a breeze—just let them marinate overnight, then put them on the grill.

- 1 cup lemon-lime soda
- 1/4 cup soy sauce
- 2 tablespoons lemon juice
- 2 garlic cloves, minced
- 1 teaspoon prepared horseradish
- 1/2 teaspoon lemon-pepper seasoning
- 1/4 teaspoon curry powder
- 1/4 teaspoon ground ginger
- 1/4 teaspoon paprika
- 1/4 teaspoon crushed red pepper flakes
- 2 pounds turkey breast tenderloins

1. In a large bowl, combine the first 10 ingredients. Pour 1 cup into a large resealable plastic bag; add turkey. Seal bag and turn to coat; refrigerate 8 hours or overnight, turning occasionally. Cover and refrigerate remaining marinade for serving.

2. Drain and discard marinade from turkey. Grill, covered, over medium–hot heat for 20-25 minutes or until a meat thermometer reads 170°, turning every 6 minutes. Serve with reserved marinade. **Yield:** 8 servings.

Rosemary Chicken

Luke Armstead, Oregon City, Oregon

This recipe is terrific when you're cooking for one or two people. And, it can easily be doubled to feed more. Just add buttered beans and rolls for a complete meal.

✓ Uses less fat, sugar or salt. Includes Nutrition Facts and Diabetic Exchanges.

> 2 **boneless skinless chicken breast halves (4 ounces** *each***)**
> 2 **teaspoons canola oil**
> 1 **tablespoon lemon juice**
> 1 **teaspoon dried rosemary, crushed**
> 1/2 **teaspoon dried oregano**
> 1/4 **teaspoon pepper**

Flatten chicken to 1/4-in. thickness. In a nonstick skillet, cook chicken in oil over medium-high heat for 3-4 minutes on each side or until juices run clear. Sprinkle with lemon juice, rosemary, oregano and pepper. **Yield:** 2 servings.

Nutrition Facts: 1 serving equals 172 calories, 6 g fat (1 g saturated fat), 66 mg cholesterol, 74 mg sodium, 1 g carbohydrate, 1 g fiber, 26 g protein. **Diabetic Exchanges:** 3-1/2 very lean meat, 1 fat.

Dressed-Up Meatballs

Ivy Eresmas, Dade City, Florida

Frozen meatballs and purchased sweet-and-sour sauce make this dish a lifesaver when I'm racing against the clock. The sauce is dressed up with a hint of garlic and nicely coats the colorful mix of meatballs, carrots, green pepper and onion.

> 2 **pounds frozen fully cooked meatballs, thawed**
> 1 **small onion, sliced**
> 2 **medium carrots, julienned**
> 1 **small green pepper, julienned**
> 1 **garlic clove, minced**
> 1 **jar (10 ounces) sweet-and-sour sauce**
> 4-1/2 **teaspoons soy sauce**
> **Hot cooked rice**

1. Place the meatballs in a 3-qt. microwave-safe dish; top with the onion, carrots, green pepper and garlic. Combine the sweet-and-sour sauce and soy sauce; pour over meatballs.

2. Cover and microwave on high for 8-10 minutes or until vegetables are tender and meatballs are heated through, stirring twice. Serve over rice. **Yield:** 8 servings.

Editor's Note: This recipe was tested with an 850-watt microwave.

Round Steak with Dumplings

Sherri Odom, Plant City, Florida

My grandmother taught me how to make this old-fashioned, comforting dish. I like to serve it for special occasions.

  3/4 cup all-purpose flour
  1 tablespoon paprika
  3 pounds boneless beef top round steak, cut into serving-size pieces
  2 to 3 tablespoons vegetable oil
  1 medium onion, chopped
2-2/3 cups water
  2 cans (10-3/4 ounces *each*) condensed cream of chicken soup, undiluted
  1/2 teaspoon pepper
DUMPLINGS:
  3 cups all-purpose flour
  1/4 cup dried minced onion
  2 tablespoons baking powder
  1 tablespoon poppy seeds
1-1/2 teaspoons celery salt
1-1/2 teaspoons poultry seasoning
  3/4 teaspoon salt
1-1/2 cups milk

  6 tablespoons vegetable oil
  1 cup dry bread crumbs
  1/4 cup butter, melted

1. In a large resealable plastic bag, combine flour and paprika. Add beef, a few pieces at a time, and shake to coat.

2. In a Dutch oven over medium-high heat, brown steak in oil on both sides in batches, adding more oil if necessary. Remove and keep warm.

3. In the drippings, saute onion until tender. Stir in the water, soup and pepper. Bring to a boil. Return meat to pan. Cover and bake at 325° for 1-1/2 hours.

4. Meanwhile, for dumplings, combine the flour, minced onion, baking powder, poppy seeds, celery salt, poultry seasoning and salt in a bowl. Combine milk and oil; stir into dry ingredients just until moistened.

5. Increase oven temperature to 425°. In a large bowl, combine bread crumbs and butter. Drop dumpling batter by rounded tablespoonfuls into crumb mixture; roll to form dumplings. Place on top of simmering beef mixture.

6. Cover and bake 20-25 minutes longer or until a toothpick inserted in a dumpling comes out clean (do not lift the cover while baking). **Yield:** 10-12 servings.

★★★ Italian Steak Sandwiches

Maria Regakis, Somerville, Massachusetts

Created by my sister, these quick sandwiches use minced garlic and other seasonings to jazz up deli roast beef. Add some carrot sticks or a tomato salad for a fantastic lunch in minutes.

- 2 garlic cloves, minced
- 1/8 teaspoon crushed red pepper flakes
- 2 tablespoons olive oil
- 16 slices deli roast beef
- 1/2 cup beef broth
- 2 tablespoons red wine *or additional beef broth*
- 2 teaspoons dried parsley flakes
- 2 teaspoons dried basil
- 1/4 teaspoon salt
- 1/4 teaspoon dried oregano
- 1/8 teaspoon pepper
- 4 sandwich rolls, split
- 4 slices provolone cheese

In a large skillet, saute the garlic and pepper flakes in oil. Add the roast beef, beef broth, wine or additional beef broth and seasonings; heat through. Place beef slices on rolls; drizzle with the broth mixture. Top with cheese. **Yield:** 4 servings.

★★★ Catfish with Shrimp Salsa

Denise Wall, Ridgeway, South Carolina

This is one of my favorite recipes for catfish. Cajun seasoning, cumin and coriander spice up the fillets nicely, and the colorful salsa makes an excellent accompaniment.

- 2 tablespoons Cajun *or blackened seasoning*
- 1/2 teaspoon ground cumin
- 1/2 teaspoon ground coriander
- 4 catfish fillets (6 ounces *each*)
- 2 to 3 tablespoons vegetable oil

SALSA:
- 1 medium green pepper, diced
- 3/4 cup diced onion
- 1 celery rib, diced
- 1 jalapeno pepper, seeded and chopped
- 2 garlic cloves, minced
- 1 tablespoon butter
- 1-1/2 cups fresh *or frozen corn*
- 3 plum tomatoes, seeded and chopped
- 2 packages (5 ounces *each*) frozen cooked salad shrimp, thawed
- 1/2 teaspoon Cajun *or blackened seasoning*

Dash hot pepper sauce

1. In a small bowl, combine the Cajun seasoning, cumin and coriander; rub over catfish fillets. In a large skillet, fry fillets in oil over medium-high heat for 4-5 minutes on each side or until fish flakes easily with a fork. Remove and keep warm.

2. In the same skillet, saute the green pepper, onion, celery, jalapeno and garlic in butter until tender. Add the corn, tomatoes and shrimp; cook and stir for 4-5 minutes or until corn is tender. Stir in Cajun seasoning and hot pepper sauce. Serve with catfish fillets. **Yield:** 4 servings.

Editor's Note: When cutting or seeding hot peppers, use rubber or plastic gloves to protect your hands. Avoid touching your face.

5 cups frozen shredded hash brown potatoes, thawed
1 can (10-3/4 ounces) condensed cheddar cheese soup, undiluted
1 egg, lightly beaten
1/2 teaspoon salt
1/4 teaspoon pepper
2 pounds ground beef
1 medium onion, chopped
1 can (4 ounces) mushroom stems and pieces, drained
1 can (15 ounces) pizza sauce
4 cups (16 ounces) shredded pizza cheese blend, *divided*

1. In a large bowl, combine the potatoes, soup, egg, salt and pepper. Spread mixture into a greased 15-in. x 10-in. x 1-in. baking pan. Bake at 400° for 20-25 minutes or until lightly browned.

2. Meanwhile, in a large skillet over medium heat, cook beef, onion and mushrooms until meat is no longer pink; drain. Stir in pizza sauce; keep warm.

3. Sprinkle 2 cups cheese over hot crust. Spread mixture over the top; sprinkle with remaining cheese. Bake 5-10 minutes longer or until cheese is melted. **Yield:** 6-8 servings.

🎀 🎀 🎀
Beefy Hash Brown Pizza

Betty Warren, Maryville, Tennessee

Hash brown potatoes form the crust for this fun and different pizza. When my children were growing up, this dish was a popular Friday-night treat. Now my grandchildren ask for it whenever they spend Fridays with us.

1/2 pound fresh green beans, cut into 2-inch pieces
1/2 pound fresh wax beans, cut into 2-inch pieces
3 boneless skinless chicken breast halves (4 ounces *each*)
2 tablespoons vegetable oil
2 tablespoons plus 1-1/2 teaspoons cornstarch
3 tablespoons soy sauce
1 can (8 ounces) pineapple chunks
1 medium sweet red pepper, julienned
1 small onion, thinly sliced
1/4 teaspoon salt
1/4 teaspoon ground ginger
Hot cooked rice

1. Place beans in a saucepan and cover with water; bring to a boil. Cook, uncovered, for 3 minutes; drain and set aside. Flatten chicken to 1/4-in. thickness; cut into 1/2-in. strips. In a large skillet, stir-fry chicken in oil for 3-4 minutes or until no longer pink. Remove with a slotted spoon.

2. In a small bowl, combine cornstarch and soy sauce until smooth. Drain the pineapple, reserving juice; set pineapple aside. Stir the juice into the soy sauce mixture; set aside.

3. In the same skillet, stir-fry red pepper and onion for 5 minutes. Add the chicken, beans, pineapple, salt and ginger. Gradually stir in the soy sauce mixture. Bring to a boil; cook and stir for 2 minutes or until thickened. Serve with rice. **Yield:** 6 servings.

🎀 🎀 🎀
String Bean Chicken Skillet

Priscilla Gilbert, Indian Harbour Beach, Florida

I started to prepare a chicken stir-fry one day and discovered I was out of frozen snow peas. So I tossed in green beans instead and added a few leftover wax beans for color. I've been making the recipe that way ever since.

⚜⚜⚜ Turkey Sausage with Root Vegetables

Lisa Zeigler-Day, Forest Park, Illinois

I had a great stew recipe but rarely prepared it because it used sausage, which can be high in fat and sodium. Then I tried substituting low-fat turkey sausage. The made-over dish not only tastes good, it feels good—both hearty and healthy!

 Uses less fat, sugar or salt. Includes Nutrition Facts and Diabetic Exchanges.

- 1 package (14 ounces) reduced-fat smoked turkey Polish sausage, cut into 1/2-inch pieces
- 1 medium onion, chopped
- 1 cup cubed peeled rutabaga
- 1 cup sliced carrots
- 1 teaspoon canola oil
- 4 cups cubed peeled potatoes
- 1 can (14-3/4 ounces) reduced-sodium chicken broth
- 1 teaspoon dried thyme
- 1/4 teaspoon rubbed sage
- 1/4 teaspoon pepper
- 1 bay leaf
- 1/2 medium head cabbage, cut into 6 wedges
- 1 teaspoon all-purpose flour
- 1 tablespoon water
- 1 tablespoon minced fresh parsley
- 2 teaspoons cider vinegar

1. In a Dutch oven, cook the sausage, onion, rutabaga and carrots in oil for 5 minutes or until onion is tender. Add the potatoes, broth, thyme, sage, pepper and bay leaf. Bring to a boil. Place cabbage wedges on top. Reduce heat; cover and simmer for 20-25 minutes or until potatoes and cabbage are tender.

2. Carefully remove cabbage to a shallow serving bowl; keep warm. Discard bay leaf. Combine the flour and water until smooth; stir into sausage mixture. Bring to a boil; cook and stir for 2 minutes or until thickened. Stir in parsley and vinegar. Spoon over cabbage. **Yield:** 6 servings.

Nutrition Facts: 1-1/2 cups equals 231 calories, 3 g fat (1 g saturated fat), 23 mg cholesterol, 781 mg sodium, 39 g carbohydrate, 6 g fiber, 13 g protein. **Diabetic Exchanges:** 2 starch, 1 lean meat, 1 vegetable.

⚜⚜⚜ Sweet 'n' Sour Halibut

(Pictured on page 87)

Willa Gilio, Cayucos, California

We live on the West Coast and catch a lot of halibut off our fishing boat. Cooked in a sweet-and-sour sauce along with pineapple, green pepper and tomatoes, this fish is a favorite.

- 1 cup packed brown sugar
- 1 cup cider vinegar
- 1 cup apricot nectar
- 1/2 cup ketchup
- 1 teaspoon Worcestershire sauce
- 1 cup cubed green pepper
- 3 tablespoons all-purpose flour
- 4 tablespoons cold water, *divided*
- 1 tablespoon soy sauce

Dash *each* salt and pepper
- 1-1/2 pounds halibut steaks, cut into 1-inch pieces
- 1 tablespoon cornstarch
- 2 medium tomatoes, seeded and cubed
- 2 cups pineapple chunks

Hot cooked linguine *or* rice

1. In a large saucepan, combine the first five ingredients; bring to a boil. Reduce heat; simmer, uncovered, for 30 minutes. Add the green pepper; cook 5 minutes longer; set aside.

2. In a large bowl, combine the flour, 3 tablespoons water, soy sauce, salt and pepper. Add halibut; toss gently to coat. Transfer to a broiler pan. Broil 4 in. from the heat for 5-6 minutes or until fish flakes easily with a fork. Set aside and keep warm.

3. Combine cornstarch and remaining water until smooth; stir into green pepper mixture. Bring to a boil; cook and stir for 2 minutes or until thickened. Reduce heat to medium; add tomatoes and pineapple. Cook and stir for 4-5 minutes or until heated through. Serve with halibut and linguine or rice. **Yield:** 6 servings.

1 medium onion, chopped
1 celery rib, chopped
2 tablespoons butter
2 cups milk
1-1/4 cups uncooked instant rice
2 cups diced cooked turkey
1 can (10-3/4 ounces) condensed cream of mushroom soup, undiluted
1 cup seasoned stuffing cubes
1 can (4 ounces) chopped green chilies, drained
1 cup (4 ounces) shredded cheddar cheese, *divided*

1. In a 2-qt. microwave-safe dish, combine the onion, celery and butter. Cover and microwave on high for 2-3 minutes or until butter is melted. Stir in milk. Cover and cook on high for 4-6 minutes or until milk is steaming (do not boil). Stir in rice. Cover and let stand for 2 minutes.

2. Add the turkey, soup, croutons, chilies and 1/2 cup cheese. Cover and microwave on high for 5-7 minutes or until heated through, stirring once. Sprinkle with remaining cheese. Cover and let stand for 5 minutes. **Yield:** 6-8 servings.

Editor's Note: This recipe was tested with an 850-watt microwave.

🎗 🎗 🎗
Turkey Rice Casserole

Tamy Baker, Kearney, Nebraska

The recipe for this creamy and comforting bake came from my aunt and is perfect when you have leftover turkey. But I enjoy the casserole so much that I don't wait for leftovers to make it! The green chilies add a bit of a kick.

🎗 🎗 🎗
Creamy Chicken and Broccoli

Tamara Kalsbeek, Grand Rapids, Michigan

My family likes the taste of chicken cordon bleu, but I don't like spending a lot of time in the kitchen. This skillet sensation, with the addition of broccoli, gives my gang the flavors they crave with only a fraction of the work.

1 pound boneless skinless chicken breasts, cut into 1-inch cubes
1 small onion, chopped
2 tablespoons butter
1 can (10-3/4 ounces) condensed cream of mushroom soup, undiluted
2/3 cup mayonnaise
1/2 cup sour cream
2 tablespoons white wine *or* chicken broth
1/8 teaspoon garlic powder
Salt and pepper to taste
1 cup cubed fully cooked ham
1 package (10 ounces) frozen broccoli florets, thawed
3 bacon strips, cooked and crumbled
Hot cooked pasta *or* rice
1 cup (4 ounces) shredded Swiss cheese, optional

1. In a large skillet, saute chicken and onion in butter until meat is no longer pink.

2. Meanwhile, in a large bowl, combine the soup, mayonnaise, sour cream, wine or broth, garlic powder, salt and pepper. Add to the chicken mixture.

3. Stir in the ham, broccoli and bacon; cover and cook until heated through. Serve over pasta; sprinkle with cheese if desired. **Yield:** 4 servings.

Editor's Note: Reduced-fat or fat-free mayonnaise is not recommended for this recipe.

Beef 'n' Potato Pie

Thelma Musselman, Forest, Ohio

I began entering recipes at fairs during the 1970s. This savory, meat-and-potatoes pie with a pastry crust is one that received a Grand Champion ribbon.

- 2 cups all-purpose flour
- 1 teaspoon salt
- 1/2 teaspoon onion powder
- 3/4 cup butter-flavored shortening
- 1/4 cup cold water

FILLING:
- 1/4 cup chopped green pepper
- 1/4 cup chopped sweet red pepper
- 1 small onion, chopped
- 4 teaspoons vegetable oil, *divided*
- 3 cups cubed cooked beef roast
- 1 can (10-3/4 ounces) condensed beefy mushroom soup, undiluted
- 1 can (4 ounces) mushroom stems and pieces, drained
- 1 teaspoon Worcestershire sauce
- 1/4 teaspoon garlic powder

Dash pepper

- 1 tablespoon cornstarch
- 1 tablespoon water
- 2 cups sliced cooked peeled potatoes
- 1 egg, lightly beaten

1. In a large bowl, combine flour, salt and onion powder; cut in shortening until crumbly. Gradually add water, tossing with a fork until dough forms a ball.

2. Divide dough in half. Roll out one piece to fit a 9-in. pie plate. Line pie plate with bottom pastry; trim even with edge.

3. In a large skillet, saute the peppers and onion in 1 tablespoon oil. Add the beef, soup, mushrooms, Worcestershire sauce, garlic powder and pepper. Bring to a boil. Combine cornstarch and water until smooth; stir into skillet. Bring to a boil; cook and stir for 2 minutes or until thickened. Cool.

4. Spoon into crust. Top with potatoes. Brush remaining oil over potatoes. Roll out remaining pastry to fit top of pie; place over filling. Trim, seal and flute edges. Cut slits in pastry. Brush with egg.

5. Bake at 375° for 45 minutes. Cover edges loosely with foil. Bake 10 minutes longer or until golden brown. **Yield:** 6-8 servings.

★ ★ ★
Oriental Steak Skewers

Gina Hatchell, Mickleton, New Jersey

I'm always on the lookout for lighter meals that will satisfy my family, and these steak-and-veggie kabobs really fill the bill. Served with a creamy mustard sauce, the colorful bundles are special enough for company.

☑ Uses less fat, sugar or salt. Includes Nutrition Facts and Diabetic Exchanges.

>   1 pound boneless beef sirloin tip roast
>   1/3 cup reduced-sodium soy sauce
>   1/4 cup sugar
>   1/2 teaspoon ground ginger
>   1 cup water
>   4 medium carrots, julienned
>   1/2 pound fresh green beans, trimmed
>   1 large sweet red pepper, julienned
>   1/2 cup reduced-fat sour cream
>   2 tablespoon Dijon mustard
> 1-1/4 teaspoons prepared horseradish

1. Cut beef widthwise into 16 slices, 1/4 in. thick. In a large resealable plastic bag, combine the soy sauce, sugar and ginger; add beef. Seal bag and turn to coat; refrigerate for 4 hours.

2. In a large saucepan, bring water and carrots to a boil. Reduce heat; cover and simmer for 3 minutes. Add the beans and red pepper; cover and simmer for 3-5 minutes or until vegetables are crisp-tender. Drain and immediately place vegetables in ice water. Drain and pat dry.

3. Drain and discard marinade from beef. Arrange three beans, one carrot strip and one pepper strip down the center of each beef slice; roll up. For each kabob, use metal or soaked wooden skewers and thread two bundles on two parallel skewers.

4. If grilling the kabobs, coat grill rack with nonstick cooking spray before starting the grill. Grill kabobs, covered, over medium heat or broil 4-6 in. from the heat for 2-3 minutes on each side or until beef reaches desired doneness, turning once.

5. In a small bowl, combine the sour cream, mustard and horseradish. Serve with kabobs. **Yield:** 4 servings.

Nutrition Facts: 4 bundles with 2 tablespoons sauce equals 304 calories, 10 g fat (5 g saturated fat), 87 mg cholesterol, 542 mg sodium, 21 g carbohydrate, 5 g fiber, 31 g protein. **Diabetic Exchanges:** 4 lean meat, 3 vegetable, 1/2 fat.

🎗🎗🎗
Cranberry Salsa Chicken

Amy VanGuilder Dik, Minneapolis, Minnesota

This is a dish I made for my husband before we were married, and he absolutely loved it. Now I prepare it for dinner parties. Everyone likes it, and no one guesses they're eating healthy.

✓ Uses less fat, sugar or salt. Includes Nutrition Facts and Diabetic Exchanges.

     4 boneless skinless chicken breast halves
       (4 ounces *each*)
     1 tablespoon olive oil
     1 jar (16 ounces) chunky salsa
     1 cup dried cranberries
   1/4 cup water
     1 tablespoon honey
     2 garlic cloves, minced
   3/4 teaspoon ground cinnamon
   1/2 teaspoon ground cumin
     2 cups hot cooked couscous
   1/4 cup slivered almonds, toasted

1. In a large nonstick skillet, saute chicken in oil until browned on both sides.

2. In a small bowl, combine the salsa, cranberries, water, honey, garlic, cinnamon and cumin; mix well. Pour over chicken. Cover and cook over medium-low heat for 10-15 minutes or until chicken juices run clear. Serve over couscous. Sprinkle with almonds. **Yield:** 4 servings.

Nutrition Facts: 1 chicken breast half and 1/2 cup cranberry salsa with 1/2 cup of couscous equals 441 calories, 9 g fat (1 g saturated fat), 66 mg cholesterol, 859 mg sodium, 57 g carbohydrate, 5 g fiber, 31 g protein. **Diabetic Exchanges:** 3 lean meat, 2 vegetable, 1-1/2 starch, 1-1/2 fruit.

🎗🎗🎗
Citrus Grilled Salmon

Margaret Pache, Mesa, Arizona

I grow my own oranges, and I wanted a main dish that really lets that citrus flavor come through. This tasty salmon is definitely one of our favorite recipes.

   1/2 cup orange juice
   1/2 cup honey
     2 teaspoons prepared horseradish
     2 teaspoons teriyaki sauce
     1 teaspoon grated orange peel
     1 salmon fillet (about 2-1/2 pounds)

1. In a small bowl, combine the first five ingredients; mix well. Pour 2/3 cup into a large resealable plastic bag; add salmon. Seal bag and turn to coat; refrigerate for at least 2 hours. Cover and refrigerate remaining marinade.

2. Coat grill rack with nonstick cooking spray before starting the grill. Drain and discard marinade from salmon. Place salmon skin side down on grill rack.

3. Grill, covered, over medium heat for 5 minutes. Brush with some of the reserved marinade. Grill 10-15 minutes longer or until fish flakes easily with a fork, basting occasionally with remaining marinade. **Yield:** 6-8 servings.

🎗🎗🎗
Peppery Herbed
Turkey Tenderloin

Virginia Anthony, Blowing Rock, North Carolina

I won our state's Turkey Cook-Off one year with these full-flavored tenderloins in a rich sauce. Marinating the turkey in wine, garlic, rosemary and thyme gives it a fantastic taste.

☑ Uses less fat, sugar or salt. Includes Nutrition Facts and Diabetic Exchanges.

  3 turkey breast tenderloins (12 ounces *each*)
  1 cup dry white wine *or* apple juice
  3 green onions, chopped
  3 tablespoons minced fresh parsley
  6 teaspoons olive oil, *divided*
  1 tablespoon finely chopped garlic
3/4 teaspoon dried rosemary, crushed
3/4 teaspoon dried thyme
  1 teaspoon coarsely ground pepper
3/4 teaspoon salt, *divided*
  4 teaspoons cornstarch
  1 cup reduced-sodium chicken broth

1. Pat tenderloins dry; flatten to 3/4-in. thickness. In a bowl, combine the wine or juice, onions, parsley, 4 teaspoons oil, garlic, rosemary and thyme; mix well. Pour 3/4 cup marinade into a large resealable plastic bag; add turkey. Seal bag and turn to coat; refrigerate for at least 4 hours, turning occasionally. Cover and refrigerate remaining marinade.

2. Drain and discard marinade from turkey. Sprinkle turkey with pepper and 1/2 teaspoon salt. In a large nonstick skillet, cook turkey in remaining oil for 5-6 minutes on each side or until no longer pink. Remove and keep warm.

3. In a small bowl, combine the cornstarch, broth, reserved marinade and remaining salt until smooth; pour into skillet. Bring to a boil; cook and stir for 1-2 minutes or until thickened. Slice turkey; serve with sauce. **Yield:** 6 servings.

Editor's Note: If using the broth instead of wine, add 1 tablespoon white wine vinegar or cider vinegar to the marinade.

Nutrition Facts: One serving (5 ounces cooked turkey) equals 258 calories, 5 g fat (1 g saturated fat), 116 mg cholesterol, 476 mg sodium, 4 g carbohydrate, trace fiber, 41 g protein. **Diabetic Exchanges:** 6 very lean meat, 1 fat.

Fruited Chicken Curry

Bernadine Dirmeyer, Harpster, Ohio

Any curry lovers you know will be thrilled with this juicy chicken that's served over a bed of hot rice. Dried fruits and toasted almonds make it a wonderful change-of-pace entree for weeknights and even special occasions.

- **4 bone-in chicken breast halves (8 ounces *each*)**
- **1 tablespoon butter**
- **1/4 cup chopped onion**
- **2 teaspoons curry powder**
- **1/2 teaspoon salt**
- **1/8 teaspoon pepper**
- **1 cup dried mixed fruit (such as apples, apricots and prunes)**
- **3/4 cup hot water**
- **1 tablespoon sugar**
- **1 teaspoon lemon juice**

Hot cooked rice
- **1/4 cup slivered almonds, toasted**

1. In a large skillet, brown the chicken in butter on each side; remove and keep warm. In the drippings, cook the onion, curry, salt and pepper until onion is tender. Stir in the fruit, water, sugar and lemon juice.

2. Return chicken to pan. Bring to a boil. Reduce heat; cover and simmer for 25-30 minutes or until meat juices run clear. Serve over rice; sprinkle with almonds. **Yield:** 4 servings.

Ginger Pork Stir-Fry

Jackie Hannahs, Fountain, Michigan

My recipe box is packed with delicious pork recipes, but this fast stir-fry really stands out from the crowd. Everyone likes the citrus glaze that coats the tender pork and vegetables.

✓ Uses less fat, sugar or salt. Includes Nutrition Facts and Diabetic Exchanges.

- **1 tablespoon cornstarch**
- **1 cup orange juice**
- **2 tablespoons soy sauce**
- **2 garlic cloves, minced**
- **1/4 teaspoon ground ginger**
- **1 pork tenderloin (1 pound), cut into thin strips**
- **1 tablespoon canola oil**
- **1 small onion, chopped**
- **1/4 pound fresh snow peas**
- **1/4 cup chopped sweet red pepper**

Hot cooked rice

1. In a small bowl, combine the cornstarch, orange juice, soy sauce, garlic and ginger until smooth; set aside.

2. In a large skillet or wok, stir-fry pork in oil for 5 minutes or until lightly browned; drain. Add the onion, peas and red pepper; cook and stir for 3-5 minutes or until crisp-tender.

3. Stir orange juice mixture; add to the skillet. Bring to a boil; cook and stir for 2 minutes or until thickened. Serve over rice. **Yield:** 4 servings.

Nutrition Facts: 3/4 cup (prepared with reduced-sodium soy sauce; calculated without rice) equals 230 calories, 7 g fat (2 g saturated fat), 74 mg cholesterol, 361 mg sodium, 14 g carbohydrate, 1 g fiber, 26 g protein. **Diabetic Exchanges:** 3 lean meat, 1 vegetable, 1/2 fruit.

✿✿✿
Shrimp Fried Rice

Sandra Thompson, White Hall, Arkansas

My family can't get enough of this delicious dish, and it always vanishes at dinnertime. The bacon adds crispness and a hint of heartiness. Consider this recipe for a brunch buffet, too.

- **4 tablespoons butter, *divided***
- **4 eggs, lightly beaten**
- **3 cups cold cooked rice**
- **1 package (16 ounces) frozen mixed vegetables**
- **1 pound uncooked medium shrimp, peeled and deveined**
- **1/2 teaspoon salt**
- **1/4 teaspoon pepper**
- **8 bacon strips, cooked and crumbled, optional**

1. In a large skillet, melt 1 tablespoon butter over medium-high heat. Pour eggs into skillet. As eggs set, lift edges, letting uncooked portion flow underneath. Remove eggs and keep warm.

2. Melt remaining butter in the skillet. Add rice, vegetables and shrimp; cook and stir for 5 minutes or until shrimp turn pink. Return eggs to the pan; sprinkle with salt and pepper. Cook until heated through. Sprinkle with bacon if desired. **Yield:** 8 servings.

✿✿✿
Tex-Mex Turkey Tacos

Jodi Fleury, West Gardiner, Maine

I normally don't care for ground turkey, but I love the Southwestern flair of this well-seasoned taco meat mixed with red and green peppers, onions and black beans. It's sure to be a hit at your house, too.

> ✓ Uses less fat, sugar or salt. Includes Nutrition Facts and Diabetic Exchanges.

- **1 pound lean ground turkey**
- **2 medium green peppers, chopped**
- **1 medium sweet red pepper, chopped**
- **1 medium onion, chopped**
- **2 medium carrots, halved lengthwise and sliced**
- **2 garlic cloves, minced**
- **1 tablespoon olive oil**
- **2 cans (15 ounces *each*) black beans, rinsed and drained**
- **1 jar (16 ounces) salsa**
- **2 tablespoons chili powder**
- **1 tablespoon ground cumin**
- **24 taco shells, warmed**
- **3 cups shredded lettuce**
- **1-1/2 cups diced fresh tomato**
- **1/2 cup minced fresh parsley**

1. In a large nonstick skillet coated with nonstick cooking spray, cook turkey over medium heat until no longer pink; drain and set aside. In the same skillet, saute the peppers, onion, carrots and garlic in oil for 8-10 minutes or until vegetables are tender.

2. Add the turkey, beans, salsa, chili powder and cumin; bring to a boil. Reduce heat; simmer, uncovered, for 10-15 minutes or until thickened. Fill each taco shell with 1/3 cup turkey mixture. Serve with lettuce, tomato and cilantro. **Yield:** 12 servings.

Nutrition Facts: 2 tacos equals 297 calories, 11 g fat (2 g saturated fat), 30 mg cholesterol, 634 mg sodium, 36 g carbohydrate, 9 g fiber, 14 g protein. **Diabetic Exchanges:** 2 starch, 1-1/2 fat, 1 lean meat, 1 vegetable.

✿✿✿ Southwestern Rice Bake

Sheila Johnson, Red Feather Lakes, Colorado

When I don't know what to make for dinner, my husband requests this popular bake. Often, I use it as an entree and serve it with warm tortillas. Other times, I eliminate the meat and present it as a spicy side dish.

- 3 cups cooked brown *or* white rice
- 1/2 pound ground beef, cooked and drained
- 1-1/4 cups sour cream
- 1 cup (4 ounces) shredded Monterey Jack cheese, *divided*
- 1 cup (4 ounces) shredded cheddar cheese, *divided*
- 1 can (4 ounces) chopped green chilies
- 1/2 teaspoon salt
- 1/4 teaspoon pepper
- Sliced ripe olives, chopped tomatoes and chopped green onions, optional

1. In a large bowl, combine the rice, beef, sour cream, 3/4 cup of Monterey Jack cheese, 3/4 cup of cheddar cheese, chilies, salt and pepper.

2. Spoon into a greased 1-1/2-qt. baking dish. Sprinkle with remaining cheeses. Bake, uncovered, at 350° for 20-25 minutes or until heated through. Serve with olives, tomatoes and onions if desired. **Yield:** 4 servings.

✿✿✿ Beef 'n' Bean Enchiladas

Linda Lundmark, Martinton, Illinois

After cooking ground beef in the microwave, I combine it with ready-made bean dip and green chilies to fill flour tortillas. Cheddar cheese and black olives jazz up the prepared enchilada sauce that tops this swift Mexican specialty.

- 3 tablespoons all-purpose flour
- 1 teaspoon salt, *divided*
- 1/4 teaspoon paprika
- 1-1/2 cups milk
- 1 can (10 ounces) enchilada sauce
- 1 cup (4 ounces) shredded cheddar cheese
- 1 can (2-1/4 ounces) sliced ripe olives, drained
- 3/4 pound ground beef
- 1 medium onion, chopped
- 1 can (9 ounces) bean dip
- 1 can (4 ounces) chopped green chilies
- 1/8 teaspoon pepper
- 1 large tomato, seeded and diced
- 9 white *or* yellow corn tortillas (6 inches), warmed

1. In a 1-qt. microwave-safe bowl, combine the flour, 1/2 teaspoon salt, paprika, milk and enchilada sauce until smooth. Microwave, uncovered, on high for 2 minutes; stir. Cook 4-5 minutes longer or until thickened, stirring every minute. Stir in cheese and olives; set aside.

2. Place beef and onion in a microwave-safe dish. Cover and microwave on high for 5 minutes or until meat is no longer pink; drain. Stir in the bean dip, chilies, pepper and remaining salt.

3. Spoon about 1/3 cup meat mixture and 1 tablespoon of diced tomato down the center of each tortilla; roll up tightly.

4. Place enchiladas seam side down in an ungreased 11-in. x 7-in. x 2-in. microwave-safe dish. Top with sauce. Microwave, uncovered, on high for 10 minutes or until bubbly around the edges, rotating dish twice. **Yield:** 4 servings.

Editor's Note: This recipe was tested with an 850-watt microwave.

🎀🎀🎀
Chicken with Cranberry Stuffing

JoAnne Cloughly, East Worcester, New York

I came up with this dish by combining various elements of other recipes that my family enjoyed. It's a pretty, festive way to dress up plain chicken breasts.

  1/4 **cup chopped onion**
    2 **garlic cloves, minced**
    2 **tablespoons butter**
3-1/2 **cups chicken broth**
  1/2 **cup uncooked brown rice**
  1/2 **cup uncooked wild rice**
  1/2 **cup dried cranberries**
    1 **tablespoon minced fresh parsley**
  1/4 **teaspoon dried thyme**
  1/4 **teaspoon pepper**
    8 **bacon strips**
    4 **boneless skinless chicken breast halves**
      (4 ounces *each*)
  1/4 **cup honey**
CREAMY MUSTARD SAUCE:
    1 **cup heavy whipping cream**
    3 **tablespoons spicy brown mustard**

1. In a large saucepan, saute the onion and garlic in butter until tender. Add the broth, brown rice and wild rice; bring to a boil. Reduce heat; cover and cook for 55-65 minutes or until the rice is tender. Drain excess liquid if necessary. Stir in the cranberries, parsley, thyme and pepper.

2. In a large skillet, cook bacon over medium heat until cooked but not crisp; drain on paper towels.

3. Flatten chicken to 1/4-in. thickness. Top each with 1/4 cup rice mixture; roll up from one end. Wrap two strips of bacon around each roll-up and secure with toothpicks. Place remaining rice mixture in a greased 11-in. x 7-in. x 2-in. baking dish; place roll-ups over rice.

4. In a microwave-safe bowl, heat honey, uncovered, on high for 30 seconds; spoon over chicken. Bake, uncovered, at 325° for 28-30 minutes or until chicken juices run clear. Discard toothpicks.

5. In a small saucepan, combine cream and mustard. Cook over medium-low heat until mixture is reduced and begins to thicken, stirring constantly. Serve warm with chicken. **Yield:** 4 servings.

Poached Perch with Broccoli

Alyce Reed, Elyria, Ohio

We love to fish, and this is our favorite recipe for perch. It's easy to prepare and so delicious. Everyone likes the tender fillets served with broccoli in a creamy garlic sauce.

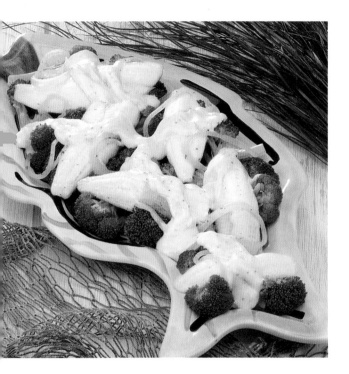

   1 pound fresh broccoli, cut into spears
3/4 cup water
   1 small onion, sliced
   1 bay leaf
   1 teaspoon salt
1/2 teaspoon dried tarragon
   2 pounds perch fillets
GARLIC SAUCE:
   1 cup mayonnaise
   1 tablespoon lemon juice
   1 garlic clove, minced
1/2 teaspoon ground mustard
1/4 teaspoon salt
1/4 teaspoon pepper

1. Place the broccoli spears in a steamer basket. Place basket in a saucepan over 1 in. of water; bring to a boil. Cover and steam the broccoli until crisp-tender; set aside and keep warm.

2. In a large skillet, combine the water, onion, bay leaf, salt and tarragon; bring to a boil. Reduce heat; add the perch fillets in batches. Cover and cook until the fish is firm and flakes easily with a fork. Remove the fish and onions with a slotted spoon; keep warm. Discard the bay leaf.

3. In a large bowl, combine the sauce ingredients; stir in 2-4 tablespoons cooking liquid until sauce reaches desired consistency.

4. Arrange broccoli on a serving platter; top with fish, onions and garlic sauce. **Yield:** 4-6 servings.

Mexican Beef and Mushrooms

Sharon De Motts, Waupun, Wisconsin

This nicely spiced main dish made an impression on our children. Now grown, every one of them has requested the recipe! Sometimes I stir my home-canned salsa into the mix.

2-1/2 pounds boneless beef top round steak, cut into 1-inch cubes
   1 large onion, chopped
   1 garlic clove, minced
   2 tablespoons butter
   2 jars (6 ounces *each*) sliced mushrooms, drained
   1 jar (16 ounces) salsa
   1 cup water
1/2 teaspoon salt
1/4 teaspoon chili powder
   3 cups hot cooked rice
   1 cup (8 ounces) sour cream
   1 cup (4 ounces) shredded cheddar cheese

1. In a Dutch oven over medium-high heat, cook beef, onion and garlic in butter for 4-6 minutes or until meat is no longer pink; drain. Stir in the mushrooms, salsa, water, salt and chili powder. Reduce heat; cover and simmer for 1-1/2 to 2 hours or until the meat is tender.

2. Serve over rice and top with sour cream and cheese. **Yield:** 6-8 servings.

Pork with Apples and Sweet Potatoes

Linda Lacek, Winter Park, Florida

Here's a meal-in-one that's quick, delicious and nutritious. The tenderloin is rubbed with a few simple seasonings, and the baked apples and sweet potatoes round out the dinner perfectly.

☑ Uses less fat, sugar or salt. Includes Nutrition Facts and Diabetic Exchanges.

- 1 teaspoon salt
- 1/2 teaspoon ground cinnamon
- 1/2 teaspoon ground cardamom
- 1/4 teaspoon pepper
- 4-1/2 cups cubed peeled sweet potatoes (about 1-1/2 pounds)
- 4 teaspoons olive oil, *divided*
- 2 pork tenderloins (3/4 pound *each*)
- 4 large Granny Smith *or* other tart apples, peeled and cored

1. In a small bowl, combine the salt, cinnamon, cardamom and pepper. Place sweet potatoes in a large bowl. Sprinkle with 1 teaspoon spice mixture and 3 teaspoons oil; toss to coat.

2. Spread in a single layer in a 15-in. x 10-in. x 1-in. baking pan coated with nonstick cooking spray. Bake, uncovered, at 425° for 10 minutes.

3. Rub the remaining oil over pork; rub with remaining spice mixture. Place over the sweet potatoes. Bake for 15 minutes.

4. Cut each apple into eight wedges. Turn pork; arrange apples around meat. Bake 15 minutes longer or until a meat thermometer reads 160°. **Yield:** 6 servings.

Nutrition Facts: 1 serving equals 321 calories, 8 g fat (2 g saturated fat), 67 mg cholesterol, 452 mg sodium, 37 g carbohydrate, 5 g fiber, 26 g protein. **Diabetic Exchanges:** 3 lean meat, 1-1/2 starch, 1 fruit.

Chicken with Cheese Sauce

(Pictured on page 87)

Joyce Breeding, Falkville, Alabama

Guests are always impressed when I bring this mouth-watering main dish to the table. The recipe makes it easy to dress up plain chicken breasts.

- 4 boneless skinless chicken breast halves (4 ounces *each*)
- 1/2 cup Italian salad dressing, *divided*
- 1/4 cup chopped onion
- 1 cup crushed saltines (about 30 crackers), *divided*
- 1 package (10 ounces) frozen chopped spinach, thawed and drained
- 2 tablespoons minced fresh parsley
- 2 tablespoons butter
- 1 envelope white sauce mix
- 2 cups milk
- 2/3 cup shredded Swiss cheese

Ground nutmeg, optional

1. Flatten chicken to 1/8-in. thickness. Place in a resealable plastic bag; add 1/4 cup salad dressing. Seal bag and turn to coat; refrigerate for 2 hours.

2. In a large skillet, saute onion in remaining salad dressing. Add 1/2 cup cracker crumbs, spinach and parsley. Cook for 5 minutes or until heated through. Remove from the heat.

3. Drain and discard marinade from chicken. Spoon about 1/2 cup spinach mixture on each chicken breast; roll up and overlap ends. Secure with a toothpick. Roll in remaining crumbs.

4. Place in a greased 9-in. square baking dish. Bake, uncovered, at 375° for 35 minutes or until chicken juices run clear.

5. Meanwhile, melt butter in a saucepan. Stir in the white sauce mix until smooth; gradually stir in milk. Bring to boil; cook and stir for 2 minutes or until thickened. Reduce heat; stir in cheese until melted. Serve with chicken. Sprinkle with nutmeg if desired. **Yield:** 4 servings.

1/3 cup grated Parmesan cheese
2 tablespoons all-purpose flour
1/2 teaspoon paprika
1/4 teaspoon salt
1/8 teaspoon pepper
1 egg
2 tablespoons milk
4 orange roughy *or* catfish fillets (4 ounces *each*)

1. In a shallow bowl, combine the Parmesan cheese, flour, paprika, salt and pepper. In another shallow bowl, beat egg and milk. Dip fish fillets into egg mixture, then coat with the Parmesan mixture.

2. Arrange in a greased 13-in. x 9-in. x 2-in. baking dish. Bake, uncovered, at 350° for 25-30 minutes or until fish flakes easily with a fork. **Yield:** 4 servings.

Nutrition Facts: 1 serving (prepared with 2% milk) equals 154 calories, 5 g fat (2 g saturated fat), 83 mg cholesterol, 382 mg sodium, 4 g carbohydrate, trace fiber, 22 g protein. **Diabetic Exchange:** 3 lean meat.

Baked Parmesan Fish

Carolyn Brinkmeyer, Centennial, Colorado

Here's a no-fuss way to work an elegant fish entree into your menu. I sometimes sprinkle the golden fillets with slivered or sliced almonds before baking.

Green Bean Mushroom Pie

Tara Walworth, Maple Park, Illinois

Fresh green-bean flavor stands out in this attractive lattice-topped pie. A flaky, golden crust holds the savory bean, mushroom and cheese filling. It tastes delightfully different every time I make it, depending on the variety of mushroom I use.

3 cups sliced fresh mushrooms
4 tablespoons butter, *divided*
2-1/2 cups chopped onions
6 cups cut fresh green beans (1-inch pieces)
2 teaspoons minced fresh thyme *or* 3/4 teaspoon dried thyme
1/2 teaspoon salt

1/4 teaspoon pepper
1 package (8 ounces) cream cheese, cubed
1/2 cup milk
CRUST:
2-1/2 cups all-purpose flour
2 teaspoons baking powder
1 teaspoon dill weed
1/4 teaspoon salt
1 cup cold butter
1 cup (8 ounces) sour cream
1 egg
1 tablespoon heavy whipping cream

1. In a large skillet, saute mushrooms in 1 tablespoon butter until tender; drain and set aside. In the same skillet, saute onions and beans in remaining butter for 18-20 minutes or until beans are crisp-tender. Add the thyme, salt, pepper, cream cheese, milk and mushrooms. Cook and stir until the cheese is melted. Remove from the heat; set aside.

2. In a large bowl, combine the flour, baking powder, dill and salt. Cut in butter until mixture resembles coarse crumbs. Stir in sour cream to form a soft dough.

3. Divide dough in half. On a well-floured surface, roll out one portion to fit a deep-dish 9-in. pie plate; trim pastry even with edge.

4. Pour the green bean mixture into the crust. Roll out the remaining pastry; make a lattice crust. Trim, seal and flute the edge.

5. In a small bowl, beat the egg and cream; brush over lattice top. Bake at 400° for 25-35 minutes or until golden brown. **Yield:** 8-10 servings.

Spicy Island Shrimp

Teresa Methe, Minden, Nebraska

My husband got this recipe while he was living on St. Croix Island, and we've served the zippy shrimp for several holiday meals. People who say they don't care for shrimp devour them when they're prepared this way!

      1 large green pepper, chopped
      1 large onion, chopped
  1/2 cup butter cubed
2-1/4 pounds uncooked large shrimp, peeled and
            deveined
      2 cans (8 ounces *each*) tomato sauce
      3 tablespoons chopped green onions
      1 tablespoon minced fresh parsley
      1 teaspoon salt
      1 teaspoon pepper
      1 teaspoon paprika
  1/2 teaspoon garlic powder
  1/2 teaspoon dried oregano
  1/2 teaspoon dried thyme
  1/4 to 1/2 teaspoon white pepper
  1/4 to 1/2 teaspoon cayenne pepper
Hot cooked rice

In a large skillet, saute the green pepper and onion in butter until tender. Reduce heat; add shrimp. Cook for 5 minutes. Stir in the tomato sauce, green onions, parsley and seasonings. Bring to a boil. Reduce heat; simmer, uncovered, for 20 minutes or until slightly thickened. Serve with rice. **Yield:** 6 servings.

Santa Fe Supper

Valerie Collier, Charleston, South Carolina

This zesty skillet meal brings a little Southwestern flair to dinnertime without a lot of fuss. Green chilies spice up the rice while chunky salsa, zucchini, onion and cheddar cheese dress up the ground beef mixture.

      1 cup uncooked long grain rice
      1 pound ground beef
      2 small zucchini, cut into 1/4-inch slices
      1 large onion, halved and sliced
1-1/2 cups chunky salsa, *divided*
  1/4 teaspoon salt
  1/4 teaspoon pepper
      1 cup (4 ounces) shredded pepper Jack cheese
      1 can (4 ounces) chopped green chilies, drained
      1 cup (4 ounces) shredded cheddar cheese

1. Cook rice according to package directions. Meanwhile, in a large skillet, cook the beef over medium heat until no longer pink; drain. Stir in the zucchini, onion, 1 cup salsa, salt and pepper; cook until vegetables are crisp-tender.

2. Add pepper Jack cheese and chilies to the rice. Sprinkle cheddar cheese over beef mixture; serve with rice and remaining salsa. **Yield:** 4 servings.

🎀 🎀 🎀
Pizza on a Stick

Charlene Woods, Norfolk, Virginia

My daughter and her friends had fun using sausage, pepperoni, vegetables and pizza dough to create these cute kabobs. Give this version a try…or make your own using the pizza toppings of your choice.

✓ Uses less fat, sugar or salt. Includes Nutrition Facts and Diabetic Exchanges.

    8 ounces turkey Italian sausage links
    2 cups whole fresh mushrooms
    2 cups cherry tomatoes
    1 medium onion, cut into 1-inch pieces
    1 large green pepper, cut into 1-inch pieces
   30 slices turkey pepperoni (2 ounces)
    1 tube (10 ounces) refrigerated pizza crust
1-1/2 cups (6 ounces) shredded part-skim
        mozzarella cheese
1-1/4 cups pizza sauce, warmed

1. In a large nonstick skillet, cook the sausage over medium heat until no longer pink; drain. When cool enough to handle, cut sausage into 20 pieces. On 10 metal or soaked wooden skewers, alternately thread the sausage, vegetables and pepperoni.

2. Unroll the pizza dough onto a lightly floured surface; cut widthwise into 1-in.-wide strips. Starting at the pointed end of a prepared skewer, pierce skewer through one end of dough strip and press dough against last ingredients on the skewer. Spiral-wrap dough strip around skewer, allowing vegetables and meats to peek through. Wrap the remaining end of dough strip around skewer above the first ingredient. Repeat with remaining dough strips and prepared skewers.

3. Arrange kabobs on a baking sheet coated with nonstick cooking spray. Bake at 400° for 10-12 minutes or until vegetables are tender and pizza crust is golden. Immediately sprinkle with cheese. Serve with pizza sauce. **Yield:** 5 servings.

Nutrition Facts: 2 kabobs with 1/4 cup sauce equals 400 calories, 13 g fat (5 g saturated fat), 58 mg cholesterol, 1,208 mg sodium, 42 g carbohydrate, 4 g fiber, 28 g protein. **Diabetic Exchanges:** 3 lean meat, 2 starch, 2 vegetable, 1 fat.

🎗🎗🎗 Apple Halibut Kabobs

Marilyn Rodriguez, Fairbanks, Alaska

I was hesitant to try this recipe at first, but I'm very glad I did! The apple and halibut complement one another so well.

✓ Uses less fat, sugar or salt. Includes Nutrition Facts and Diabetic Exchanges.

- **1/2 cup dry white wine *or* unsweetened apple juice**
- **2 tablespoons lime juice**
- **2 tablespoons olive oil**
- **2 tablespoons diced onion**
- **1 teaspoon salt**
- **1/2 teaspoon dried thyme**
- **1/4 teaspoon pepper**
- **1-1/2 pound halibut, cut into 1-inch cubes**
- **1 small red onion, cut into 1-inch pieces**
- **1 medium Golden Delicious apple, cut into 1-inch pieces**
- **1 medium sweet red pepper, cut into 1-inch pieces**

1. In a large bowl, combine the first seven ingredients; mix well. Pour half into a large resealable plastic bag; add halibut. Seal bag and turn to coat.

2. Pour remaining marinade into another large resealable plastic bag; add the onion, apple and red pepper. Seal bag and turn to coat. Refrigerate fish and apple mixture for 4-6 hours, turning occasionally.

3. If grilling the kabobs, coat grill rack with nonstick cooking spray before starting the grill. Drain fish, discarding marinade. Drain fruit and vegetables, reserving marinade for basting.

4. On eight metal or soaked wooden skewers, alternately thread fish, onion, apple and red pepper. Grill, covered, over medium heat or broil 4-6 in. from the heat for 2-3 minutes on each side or until fish flakes easily with a fork, and fruit and vegetables are tender, turning once. Baste frequently with reserved marinade. **Yield:** 4 servings.

Nutrition Facts: 2 kabobs equals 241 calories, 6 g fat (1 g saturated fat), 54 mg cholesterol, 240 mg sodium, 9 g carbohydrate, 1 g fiber, 36 g protein. **Diabetic Exchanges:** 5 very lean meat, 1 vegetable.

🎗🎗🎗 Italian Swiss Steak

Janice Lyhane, Marysville, Kansas

This family-pleasing dish combines tender beef and vegetables in a tangy sauce and tops it all off with mozzarella. Add a salad and warm bread, and you have a can't-miss meal.

- **3 tablespoons all-purpose flour**
- **2 pounds boneless beef top round steak, cut into serving-size pieces**
- **1/4 cup butter, cubed**
- **1 can (14-1/2 ounces) diced tomatoes, undrained**
- **1-1/2 teaspoons salt**
- **1/4 teaspoon dried basil**
- **1/8 teaspoon pepper**
- **1/2 cup chopped green pepper**
- **1/2 cup chopped onion**
- **1 cup (4 ounces) shredded part-skim mozzarella cheese**

1. Place flour in a large resealable plastic bag. Add beef, a few pieces at a time, and shake to coat. Remove meat from bag; pound to flatten.

2. In a large skillet over medium-high heat, brown steak on both sides in butter. Add the tomatoes, salt, basil and pepper; bring to a boil. Reduce heat; cover and simmer for 1 hour or until meat is tender.

3. Add green pepper and onion. Cover and simmer for 25-30 minutes or until vegetables are tender. Sprinkle with cheese; cook 2 minutes longer or until cheese is melted. **Yield:** 6-8 servings.

Barbecued Turkey Pizza

Krista Frank, Rhododendron, Oregon

My bread machine makes the crust for this mouth-watering pizza. Barbecue sauce, turkey, vegetables and cheese deliver so much flavor that even the biggest pizza fans will be satisfied.

✓ Uses less fat, sugar or salt. Includes Nutrition Facts and Diabetic Exchanges.

    1 cup water (70° to 80°)
    2 tablespoons olive oil
    1 tablespoon sugar
    1 teaspoon salt
    3 cups all-purpose flour
    2 teaspoons active dry yeast
  3/4 cup barbecue sauce
1-1/2 cups cubed cooked turkey breast
  1/2 cup fresh or frozen corn, thawed
    1 small red onion, julienned
    1 small green pepper, julienned
    1 garlic clove, minced
    1 cup (4 ounces) shredded part-skim
        mozzarella cheese
  1/2 cup shredded reduced-fat cheddar cheese
  1/4 cup grated Parmesan cheese

1. In bread machine pan, place the first six ingredients in order suggested by manufacturer. Select dough setting (check dough after 5 minutes of mixing; add 1 to 2 tablespoons of water or flour if needed).

2. When cycle is complete, turn dough onto a lightly floured surface. Punch down; cover and let stand for 10 minutes.

3. Roll dough into a 14-in. circle. Transfer to a 14-in. pizza pan coated with nonstick cooking spray; build up edges slightly.

4. Spread barbecue sauce over crust. Layer with half of the turkey, corn, onion, green pepper, garlic and cheese. Repeat layers. Bake at 400° for 25-30 minutes or until the crust is golden brown. **Yield:** 8 servings.

Nutrition Facts: 1 serving equals 366 calories, 9 g fat (4 g saturated fat), 38 mg cholesterol, 663 mg sodium, 52 g carbohydrate, 2 g fiber, 20 g protein. **Diabetic Exchanges:** 3 starch, 2 lean meat, 1/2 fat.

Grilled Salmon Steaks

Deb Essen, Victor, Montana

I once served this entree to 12 people from the Pacific Northwest, and they said it was the best salmon they'd ever eaten! The marinade mellows the fish taste, and the dill sauce is a wonderful accent.

    2 tablespoons white wine vinegar
    2 tablespoons sugar
    1 tablespoon dill weed
  3/4 teaspoon salt
1/8 to 1/4 teaspoon pepper, optional
    4 salmon steaks (1 inch thick and
        6 ounces each)
MUSTARD DILL SAUCE:
    3 tablespoons mayonnaise
    3 tablespoons Dijon mustard
    3 tablespoons dill weed
    1 tablespoon sugar
    4 teaspoons white wine vinegar
  1/4 teaspoon pepper, optional

1. In a large resealable plastic bag, combine the first five ingredients. Add salmon; seal bag and turn to coat. Refrigerate for 1 hour, turning occasionally.

2. In a small bowl, combine the sauce ingredients; cover and refrigerate.

3. Drain salmon, discarding marinade. Grill salmon, covered, over medium-hot heat for 5 minutes. Turn; grill 7-9 minutes longer or until fish flakes easily with a fork. Serve with the mustard dill sauce. **Yield:** 4 servings.

♜ ♜ ♜
Stir-Fried Beef 'n' Beans

Kristine Lowry, Bowling Green, Kentucky

My mother-in-law took cooking lessons while living in Japan and brought back this exceptional recipe. Garlic, ginger and soy sauce lend a robust flavor to the meaty, marinated dish. It's become popular with our family and friends...even those who don't otherwise care for green beans.

1/4 cup cornstarch
1/2 cup soy sauce
2 tablespoons water
1 teaspoon ground ginger *or* 4 teaspoons minced fresh gingerroot
4 garlic cloves, minced
4 tablespoons vegetable oil, *divided*
1 pound boneless beef sirloin steak, cut into 1/4-inch strips
1/2 pound fresh green beans, cut in half lengthwise
1 teaspoon sugar
1/2 teaspoon salt
Hot cooked rice

1. In a bowl, combine the cornstarch, soy sauce, water, ginger, garlic and 2 tablespoons oil until smooth. Set aside 1/2 cup. Pour the remaining marinade into a large resealable plastic bag; add the beef. Seal bag and turn to coat; refrigerate for 25-30 minutes.

2. Drain and discard marinade from beef. In a wok or skillet, stir-fry beef in remaining oil for 4-6 minutes or until crisp-tender. Remove and keep warm. In the same skillet, stir-fry the beans, sugar and salt for 15 minutes or until crisp-tender. Stir in the beef and reserved marinade. Bring to a boil; cook and stir for 1-2 minutes or until thickened. Serve over rice. **Yield:** 4 servings.

♜ ♜ ♜
Grilled Pineapple Pork Chops

(Also pictured on page 87)

Debby Cole, Wolf Creek, Oregon

This is my all-time favorite way to grill pork chops. The meat turns out wonderfully moist, tender and delicious. Usually, I serve these chops with fresh corn on the cob or green beans and a basket of dinner rolls.

1/2 cup packed brown sugar
1/2 cup Italian salad dressing
1/4 cup pineapple juice
3 tablespoons soy sauce
6 bone-in pork loin chops (1 inch thick and 7 ounces *each*)
1 can (20 ounces) sliced pineapple, drained

1. In a 2-cup measuring cup, combine the brown sugar, salad dressing, pineapple juice and soy sauce. Pour 2/3 cup into a large resealable plastic bag; add the pork chops. Seal bag and turn to coat; refrigerate for at least 3 hours or overnight. Cover and refrigerate remaining marinade for basting.

2. Drain and discard marinade from pork. Grill, uncovered, over medium heat for 8 minutes on each side. Place pineapple slices on grill. Baste pork and pineap-

ple with reserved marinade. Grill 5-8 minutes longer or until meat juices run clear. Place a pineapple slice on each chop. **Yield:** 6 servings.

✦✦✦
Garden Squash Ravioli

Teri Christensen, West Jordan, Utah

I created this pleasing pasta to use up an overabundance of yellow squash and zucchini from our garden. The meatless, cheesy ravioli was an instant hit with the whole family.

1 package (24 ounces) frozen miniature cheese ravioli
1 medium yellow summer squash, cut into 1/2-inch pieces
1 medium zucchini, cut into 1/2-inch pieces
2 cans (one 15 ounces, one 8 ounces) tomato sauce
1 teaspoon garlic salt
1 teaspoon dried minced onion
1 teaspoon dried oregano
1 teaspoon dried basil
1/2 teaspoon sugar
1/2 teaspoon chili powder
1/4 teaspoon pepper

1. In a large saucepan, cook ravioli according to package directions.

2. Meanwhile, in a 1-1/2-qt. microwave-safe dish, combine the squash, zucchini, tomato sauce and seasonings. Cover and cook on high for 6-7 minutes or until vegetables are tender. Drain ravioli; top with sauce. **Yield:** 6 servings.

Editor's Note: This recipe was tested with an 850-watt microwave.

✦✦✦
Saucy Orange Roughy

Bette Hunn, Orosi, California

Both the seafood and citrus lovers in your house will appreciate this entree. Not only do the flaky fillets and sauce taste great, but the dish is ready in moments.

☑ Uses less fat, sugar or salt. Includes Nutrition Facts and Diabetic Exchanges.

1 tablespoon sugar
2 teaspoons cornstarch
1/2 teaspoon chicken bouillon granules
Dash pepper
1/2 cup orange juice
1 teaspoon lemon juice
1/4 teaspoon grated orange peel
1/8 teaspoon dried tarragon
1 pound orange roughy fillets
1/2 teaspoon salt
Orange slices and fresh tarragon, optional

1. In a small microwave-safe dish, combine the first six ingredients until smooth. Microwave, uncovered, on high for 1 minute; stir. Cook 1 minute longer or until thickened. Stir in orange peel and tarragon; set aside.

2. Place fish in an ungreased 11-in. x 7-in. x 2-in. microwave-safe dish, with the thickest side toward the outside of the dish. Sprinkle with salt. Cover and microwave on high for 4 minutes.

3. Top with orange sauce. Microwave, uncovered, on high for 45-60 seconds or until fish flakes easily with a fork. Serve with orange slices and fresh tarragon if desired. **Yield:** 4 servings.

Editor's Note: This recipe was tested with an 850-watt microwave.

Nutrition Facts: 1 serving equals 111 calories, 1 g fat (trace saturated fat), 23 mg cholesterol, 475 mg sodium, 8 g carbohydrate, trace fiber, 17 g protein. **Diabetic Exchanges:** 2-1/2 very lean meat, 1/2 fruit.

🎗 🎗 🎗

Cranberry-Mushroom Beef Brisket

Margaret Welder, Madrid, Iowa

I sampled this fantastic sweet-and-sour brisket at a wedding reception and really enjoyed it. Because the meat needs to be refrigerated overnight, this is a great make-ahead entree.

> 2 cups beef broth
> 1/2 cup cranberry juice concentrate
> 1/4 cup red wine vinegar
> 4-1/2 teaspoons chopped fresh rosemary or 1-1/2
>   teaspoons dried rosemary, crushed
> 4 garlic cloves, minced
> 1 large onion, thinly sliced
> 1 fresh beef brisket (4 pounds)
> 1/2 teaspoon salt
> 1/4 teaspoon pepper
> 1/4 cup all-purpose flour
> 1/4 cup cold water
> 1/4 to 1/2 teaspoon browning sauce, optional

> 1 pound fresh mushrooms, sliced
> 1-1/2 cups dried cranberries

1. In a large bowl, combine the broth, cranberry juice concentrate, vinegar, rosemary and garlic; pour into a large roasting pan. Top with onion slices.

2. Season beef with salt and pepper; place fat side up in the pan. Cover and bake at 325° for 3 to 3-1/2 hours or until meat is tender. Remove meat and thinly slice across the grain. Cover and refrigerate overnight.

3. For gravy, skim fat from cooking juices; pour into a saucepan. Combine flour, water and browning sauce if desired until smooth; stir into cooking juices. Bring to a boil; cook and stir for 2 minutes or until thickened. Cover and refrigerate.

4. Place beef slices in a shallow baking dish; top with mushrooms, cranberries and gravy. Cover and bake at 325° for 60-65 minutes or until heated through and mushrooms are tender. **Yield:** 10-12 servings.

Editor's Note: This is a fresh beef brisket, not corned beef. The meat comes from the first cut of the brisket.

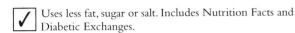

Mustard Chicken Breasts

Tina Footen, Nampa, Idaho

Curry powder, lemon juice, honey and mustard make a lip-smacking sauce for this easy microwaved chicken. The made-in-minutes main dish is a favorite with my family.

✓ Uses less fat, sugar or salt. Includes Nutrition Facts and Diabetic Exchanges.

    4 bone-in chicken breast halves (6 ounces *each*),
      skin removed
    1 teaspoon paprika
    1 medium lemon, thinly sliced
  1/3 cup spicy brown mustard
  1/3 cup honey
    1 teaspoon dried minced onion
  1/2 teaspoon curry powder
  1/2 teaspoon lemon juice

1. Arrange chicken in a 9- or 10-in. microwave-safe pie plate, with a thickest side toward the outside of the plate. Sprinkle with paprika; top with lemon slices. Cover and microwave on high for 8-10 minutes, rotating dish a half turn once.

2. In a small microwave-safe bowl, combine the remaining ingredients. Microwave, uncovered, on high for 1-1/2 to 2 minutes or until heated through; stir.

3. Drain chicken; top with sauce. Cover and cook on high for 2 minutes or until meat juices run clear. **Yield:** 4 servings.

Editor's Note: This recipe was tested with an 850-watt microwave.

Nutrition Facts: 1 serving equals 232 calories, 3 g fat (1 g saturated fat), 63 mg cholesterol, 332 mg sodium, 28 g carbohydrate, 2 g fiber, 27 g protein. **Diabetic Exchanges:** 2-1/2 lean meat, 1-1/2 fruit.

Taco Skillet

Tina Schaubroeck, Greencastle, Pennsylvania

I appreciate the convenience of one-dish dinners, and this Southwestern supper is among the best I've found. Because it looks so good on the stove, I put the skillet right on the table. Just add taco shells or chips for a fun meal.

    1 pound ground beef
    1 medium onion, chopped
    1 can (16 ounces) refried beans
    1 can (4 ounces) chopped green chilies
  1/4 to 1/2 teaspoon garlic powder
  3/4 cup sour cream
  1/2 to 1 teaspoon ground cumin
  1/2 to 1 teaspoon chili powder
    1 medium tomato, seeded and chopped
    1 can (2-1/4 ounces) sliced ripe olives, drained
    1 small green pepper
    1 cup (4 ounces) shredded Mexican cheese blend
Tortilla chips *or* taco shells, shredded lettuce and
  salsa

1. In a large skillet, cook beef and onion over medium heat until meat is no longer pink; drain. Stir in the beans, chilies and garlic powder; heat through.

2. Combine the sour cream, cumin and chili powder; spread over beef mixture. Top with tomato, olives and green pepper. Sprinkle with cheese. Serve with tortilla chips or taco shells, lettuce and salsa. **Yield:** 4-6 servings.

Grilled Vegetable Skewers, p. 136

Sweet-and-Sour Mustard, p. 135

Strawberry-Tomato Salsa, p. 147

Side Dishes & Condiments

Round out your meals with memorable mashed potatoes, standout
sauces, pleasing pasta, tempting toppings and special vegetables.
You'll find all of those and more in this chock-full chapter.

Stuffed Baked Potatoes, p. 147

✓ Uses less fat, sugar or salt. Includes Nutrition Facts and Diabetic Exchanges.

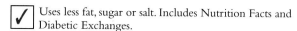

1-1/2 cups ketchup
   1 medium onion, chopped
   1 medium green pepper, chopped
   1 medium sweet red pepper, chopped
1/2 cup water
1/2 cup packed brown sugar
   2 bay leaves
   2 to 3 teaspoons cider vinegar
   1 teaspoon ground mustard
1/8 teaspoon pepper
   1 can (16 ounces) kidney beans, rinsed and drained
   1 can (15-1/2 ounces) great northern beans, rinsed and drained
   1 can (15-1/4 ounces) lima beans
   1 can (15 ounces) black beans, rinsed and drained
   1 can (15-1/2 ounces) black-eyed peas, rinsed and drained

In a 5-qt. slow cooker, combine the first 10 ingredients. Add the beans and peas; mix well. Cover and cook on low for 5-7 hours or until onion and peppers are tender. Remove bay leaves. **Yield:** 16 servings.

Nutrition Facts: 1/2 cup (prepared with no-salt-added ketchup) equals 162 calories, trace fat (trace saturated fat), 0 cholesterol, 305 mg sodium, 34 g carbohydrate, 6 g fiber, 7 g protein. **Diabetic Exchanges:** 2 starch, 1 meat.

🎗️ 🎗️ 🎗️

Partytime Beans

Jean Cantner, Boston, Virginia

A friend brought this colorful bean dish to my house for a potluck dinner years ago. As soon as I tasted the slightly sweet baked beans, I just had to have the recipe. I've served this slow-cooked specialty many times since.

🎗️ 🎗️ 🎗️

German-Style Green Beans

Vivian Steers, Central Islip, New York

My mother-in-law introduced me to this quick, down-home dish when I was a new bride. The tender green beans are topped with diced bacon and a classic glaze.

   1 pound fresh green beans, cut into 2-inch pieces
   3 bacon strips, diced
   1 medium onion, quartered and sliced
   2 teaspoons cornstarch
1/4 teaspoon salt
1/4 teaspoon ground mustard
1/2 cup water
   1 tablespoon brown sugar
   1 tablespoon cider vinegar

1. Place beans in a saucepan and cover with water; bring to a boil. Cook, uncovered, for 8-10 minutes or until crisp-tender; drain and set aside.

2. In a large skillet, cook bacon over medium heat until crisp. Remove to paper towels. Drain, reserving 1 tablespoon drippings. In the same skillet, saute onion in drippings until tender.

3. In a small bowl, combine the cornstarch, salt, mustard and water until smooth. Stir into onion. Bring to a boil; cook and stir for 1-2 minutes or until thickened. Stir in brown sugar and vinegar. Add the beans; heat through. Sprinkle with bacon. **Yield:** 3-4 servings.

★★★
Rhubarb Chutney
Jan Paterson, Anchorage, Alaska

It's always fun to surprise guests with a meat or poultry dish that has a twist. With fine chunks of rhubarb and raisins, this tangy-sweet chutney is a wonderfully different accent.

✓ Uses less fat, sugar or salt. Includes Nutrition Facts and Diabetic Exchanges.

 3/4 cup sugar
 1/3 cup cider vinegar
   1 tablespoon minced garlic
   1 teaspoon ground cumin
 3/4 teaspoon ground ginger
 1/2 teaspoon ground cinnamon
 1/4 to 1/2 teaspoon ground cloves
 1/4 teaspoon crushed red pepper flakes
   4 cups coarsely chopped fresh *or* frozen
     rhubarb, thawed
 1/2 cup chopped red onion
 1/3 cup golden raisins
   1 teaspoon red food coloring, optional

1. In a large saucepan, combine the sugar, vinegar, garlic, cumin, ginger, cinnamon, cloves and red pepper flakes. Bring to a boil. Reduce heat; simmer, uncovered, for 2 minutes or until sugar is dissolved.

2. Add the rhubarb, onion and raisins. Cook and stir over medium heat for 5-10 minutes or until rhubarb is tender and mixture is slightly thickened. Stir in food coloring if desired. Cool completely. Store in the refrigerator. **Yield:** about 3 cups.

Editor's Note: If using frozen rhubarb, measure rhubarb while still frozen, then thaw completely. Drain in a colander, but do not press liquid out.

Nutrition Facts: 1/4 cup equals 75 calories, trace fat (trace saturated fat), 0 cholesterol, 3 mg sodium, 19 g carbohydrate, 1 g fiber, 1 g protein.

★★★
Rice Croquettes
Lucia Edwards, Cotati, California

As a newlywed, I used to agonize over meal preparation. Now I love trying new recipes, and some—like this tasty side dish—turn out to be big hits with my family. The crisp, golden croquettes jazz up a simple dinner such as roast chicken.

 1/2 cup chopped onion
   2 tablespoons butter
   1 cup uncooked long grain rice
2-1/4 cups chicken broth
   2 tablespoons chopped fresh parsley
   1 egg, lightly beaten
 1/2 cup grated Parmesan cheese
   1 teaspoon dried basil
 1/4 teaspoon pepper
 1/2 cup dry bread crumbs
Vegetable oil
Additional fresh parsley, optional

1. In a large saucepan, saute onion in butter until tender. Add rice; saute 3 minutes. Stir in broth and parsley; bring to a boil. Reduce heat; cover and simmer for 20 minutes. Cool for 30 minutes.

2. Stir in egg, cheese, basil and pepper. Moisten hands with water and shape 1/4 cupfuls into logs. Roll in crumbs.

3. In an electric skillet, heat 1/4 in. of oil to 365°. Fry croquettes, a few at a time, for 3-4 minutes or until crisp and golden, turning often. Drain on paper towels. Sprinkle with parsley if desired. **Yield:** 16 croquettes.

Nutty Onion Green Beans

Donna Buckley, Western Springs, Illinois

I never cared for green beans until I tried this recipe. The beans, red onion and chopped pecans are coated in a delicious orange-mustard sauce. I make them for my family on a regular basis.

1/2 **pound fresh green beans, trimmed and cut in half**
1 **small red onion, sliced and separated into rings**
1/3 **cup chopped pecans**
3 **tablespoons butter**
2 **tablespoons brown sugar**
2 **tablespoons orange juice**
1 **tablespoon Dijon mustard**
1/2 **teaspoon salt**

1. Place beans in a saucepan and cover with water; bring to a boil. Cook, uncovered, for 8-10 minutes or until crisp-tender; drain and set aside.

2. In a skillet, cook onion and pecans in butter until onion is tender. In a small bowl, combine the brown sugar, orange juice, mustard and salt; stir into the onion mixture. Cook 2-3 minutes longer or until sauce begins to thicken. Stir in beans; heat through. **Yield:** 3-4 servings.

Great Green Beans

When choosing green beans, pick brightly colored, smooth pods that are unblemished. They should be crisp and have a firm, velvety feel.

Store unwashed beans in a sealed plastic bag or covered container in the crisper drawer of your refrigerator. Beans may be stored this way for up to 3 days.

To trim beans, snap off the stem end and the other end if desired. One-half pound of beans equals about 2 cups cut.

1 whole garlic bulb
1 tablespoon olive oil
8 medium red potatoes, peeled and cut into chunks
1/2 cup butter, cubed
1 cup (8 ounces) sour cream
2 tablespoons milk
1 tablespoon minced fresh parsley
3 green onions, sliced
1 can (11 ounces) whole kernel corn, drained
Salt and pepper to taste
1 cup (4 ounces) shredded cheddar cheese

1. Remove papery outer skin from garlic (do not peel or separate cloves). Brush with oil. Wrap in heavy-duty foil.

2. Bake at 425° for 30-35 minutes or until softened. Cool for 10-15 minutes. Cut top off garlic head, leaving the root end intact. Squeeze softened garlic into a large bowl; set aside.

3. Place potatoes in a large saucepan and cover with water. Bring to a boil. Reduce heat; cover and cook for 15-20 minutes or until tender. Drain and add to garlic. Add the butter, sour cream, milk and parsley; mash. Add the onions, corn, salt and pepper; mix well.

4. Spoon into a greased 11-in. x 7-in. x 2-in. baking dish. Sprinkle with the cheese. Bake, uncovered, at 350° for 25 minutes or until heated through. **Yield:** 8 servings.

Corny Garlic Mashed Potatoes

Patti Lacey, Lincoln, Nebraska

I dreamed up this dish after dining on something similar at a restaurant. These are my family's potatoes of choice for special occasions, but I'll make them any time we want a change from ordinary mashed potatoes.

Cranberry Rice with Caramelized Onions

Tommi Roylance, Charlo, Montana

Rice gives creative cooks so many options—the possibilities for stir-ins are endless. In this recipe, dried cranberries lend a sweet-tart flavor and a festive touch for the holidays.

2-1/2 cups chicken broth
1/2 cup uncooked wild rice
1/2 cup uncooked brown rice
3 medium onions, cut into wedges
2 teaspoons brown sugar
3 tablespoons butter
1 cup dried cranberries
1/2 teaspoon grated orange peel

1. In a large saucepan, bring broth to a boil. Add the wild rice. Reduce heat; cover and simmer for 10 minutes. Add the brown rice; cover and simmer for 45-50 minutes or until rice is tender and liquid is absorbed.

2. In a large skillet over medium heat, cook the onions and brown sugar in butter until golden brown, stirring frequently. Add the cranberries, orange peel and rice; heat through. **Yield:** 4 servings.

🎗🎗🎗
Winter Fruit Chutney

Helen Littrell, Klamath Falls, Oregon

The pairing of sweet and tart fruits makes this chutney a wonderful accompaniment for pork. Not only is the recipe a consistent blue-ribbon winner at fairs, but it's a natural way to capture the best of autumn's harvest in a jar.

- 2 cups cider vinegar
- 1 medium onion, finely chopped
- 1/2 cup water
- 1 tablespoon ground ginger
- 1 tablespoon grated orange peel
- 1-1/2 teaspoons salt
- 2 garlic cloves, minced
- 1/2 teaspoon ground cinnamon
- 1/4 teaspoon crushed red pepper flakes
- 3 cups packed brown sugar
- 2 medium ripe unpeeled pears, finely chopped
- 2 cups fresh *or* frozen cranberries
- 1 large tart unpeeled apple, finely chopped
- 1/2 cup dried currants

1. In a Dutch oven, combine the first nine ingredients. Bring to a boil over medium heat, stirring occasionally. Reduce heat; cover and simmer for 15 minutes.

2. Stir in the brown sugar, pears, cranberries, apple and currants. Return to a boil. Reduce heat; simmer, uncovered, for 1 hour or until fruit is tender and mixture has thickened.

3. Pour hot mixture into hot jars, leaving 1/4-in. headspace. Adjust caps. Process for 15 minutes in a boiling-water bath. **Yield:** 4 half-pints.

🎗🎗🎗
Ranch Mac 'n' Cheese

Michelle Rotunno, Independence, Missouri

I gave this creamy, satisfying macaroni and cheese a flavorful twist with ranch salad dressing mix. My husband requests this stovetop specialty often.

- 1 cup milk
- 1/4 cup butter, cubed
- 2 envelopes ranch salad dressing mix
- 1 teaspoon lemon-pepper seasoning
- 1 teaspoon garlic pepper blend
- 1 teaspoon garlic salt
- 1 cup cubed Colby cheese
- 1 cup cubed Monterey Jack cheese
- 1 cup (8 ounces) sour cream
- 1 pound elbow macaroni, cooked and drained
- 1/2 cup crushed saltines

Grated Parmesan cheese

1. In a Dutch oven, combine the first eight ingredients. Cook and stir over medium heat until cheese has melted and mixture begins to thicken.

2. Fold in the sour cream. Add macaroni and crackers. Cook until heated through, stirring frequently. Spoon into a serving dish; sprinkle with Parmesan cheese. **Yield:** 6-8 servings.

🎀🎀🎀
Sweet-and-Sour Mustard
(Also pictured on page 128)

Cheri White, Richland, Michigan

I like using this mustard in everything from honey-mustard chicken to sandwiches. It doesn't have a "bite"…just a little "zip." Put some in festive jars to make quick Christmas gifts.

- 1 cup packed brown sugar
- 1 cup cider vinegar
- 1/3 cup ground mustard
- 2 tablespoons water
- 2 eggs, lightly beaten

In a large saucepan, whisk together all ingredients. Cook over low heat, stirring constantly, until thickened. Pour into small jars. Cover and refrigerate. **Yield:** 1-1/2 cups.

🎀🎀🎀
Italian Green Beans

Andrea Ibzag, Gordon, Wisconsin

When I was first married, I wasn't a great cook. Now, I have many dishes I'm proud of, including this family favorite. Basil, oregano and Romano cheese give these beans an Italian accent.

- 1 small onion, chopped
- 2 tablespoons olive oil
- 2 to 3 garlic cloves, minced
- 1 can (14-1/2 ounces) stewed tomatoes, coarsely mashed
- 1/2 cup water
- 3 tablespoons minced fresh oregano *or* 1 tablespoon dried oregano
- 4-1/2 teaspoons minced fresh basil *or* 1-1/2 teaspoons dried basil
- 1 teaspoon sugar
- 1 teaspoon salt
- 1/4 to 1/2 teaspoon coarsely ground pepper
- 2 pounds fresh green beans, cut into 1-inch pieces
- 2 tablespoons grated Romano *or* Parmesan cheese

1. In a small saucepan, saute onion in oil until tender. Add garlic; saute 1 minute longer. Add the tomatoes, water, oregano, basil, sugar, salt and pepper. Bring to a boil. Reduce heat; simmer, uncovered, for 40 minutes.

2. Meanwhile, place beans in a large saucepan and cover with water; bring to a boil. Cook, uncovered, for 8-10 minutes or until crisp-tender; drain. Add tomato mixture and cheese; cook for 5 minutes or until heated through. **Yield:** 10 servings.

🏅🏅🏅
Grilled Vegetable Skewers

(Also pictured on page 128)

Susan Bourque, Danielson, Connecticut

To my mother and me, the best way to prepare vegetables is on the grill. Seasoned with fresh herbs, these colorful kabobs showcase summer's bounty.

✓ Uses less fat, sugar or salt. Includes Nutrition Facts and Diabetic Exchanges.

- 1 medium ear fresh *or* frozen sweet corn, thawed and quartered
- 1 small zucchini, quartered
- 1/4 small red onion, halved
- 4 cherry tomatoes
- 1/4 teaspoon dried basil
- 1/4 teaspoon dried rosemary, crushed
- 1/4 teaspoon dried thyme
- 1/8 teaspoon garlic powder
- 1/8 teaspoon salt
- 1/8 teaspoon pepper

1. Place the corn on a microwave-safe plate. Cover with waxed paper. Microwave on high for 2 minutes.

2. Coat grill rack with nonstick cooking spray before starting the grill. On two metal or soaked wooden skewers, alternately thread the corn, zucchini, onion and tomatoes. Lightly coat vegetables with nonstick cooking spray. In a small bowl, combine the seasonings; sprinkle over vegetables.

3. Grill, covered, over medium heat for 3 minutes on each side or until vegetables are tender, turning three times. **Yield:** 2 servings.

Nutrition Facts: 1 kabob equals 69 calories, 1 g fat (trace saturated fat), 0 cholesterol, 131 mg sodium, 16 g carbohydrate, 3 g fiber, 3 g protein. **Diabetic Exchanges:** 1 vegetable, 1/2 starch.

🏅🏅🏅
Rich and Creamy Potato Bake

L. Joy Simpkins, Cambridge City, Indiana

Here's a delicious side dish that goes well with just about any meat entree. The recipe is especially nice for potluck dinners—anyone who likes potatoes will dig right in.

- 3 cups half-and-half cream
- 1/2 cup butter, cubed
- 1-1/2 teaspoons salt
- 1 package (32 ounces) frozen Southern-style hash brown potatoes, thawed
- 1/2 cup grated Parmesan cheese

Minced fresh parsley, optional

1. In a large saucepan, combine cream, butter and salt. Cook and stir over medium heat until butter is melted. Place potatoes in a greased 13-in. x 9-in. x 2-in. baking dish; pour cream mixture over potatoes. Sprinkle with Parmesan cheese.

2. Bake, uncovered, at 350° for 45–55 minutes or until potatoes are tender and top is golden brown. Sprinkle with parsley if desired. **Yield:** 12 servings.

🎗️🎗️🎗️
Homemade Pizza Sauce

Cheryl Kravik, Spanaway, Washington

When I prepare this family-favorite sauce, I usually fix enough for three to four pizzas and freeze it. Feel free to add extra spices if it suits your taste.

- **2 cans (15 ounces *each*) tomato sauce**
- **1 can (12 ounces) tomato paste**
- **1 tablespoon Italian seasoning**
- **1 tablespoon dried oregano**
- **1 to 2 teaspoons fennel seed, crushed**
- **1 teaspoon onion powder**
- **1 teaspoon garlic powder**
- **1/2 teaspoon salt**

1. In a large saucepan over medium heat, combine tomato sauce and paste. Add remaining ingredients; mix well. Bring to a boil, stirring constantly. Reduce heat; cover and simmer for 1 hour, stirring occasionally. Cool.

2. Pour into freezer containers, leaving 1/2-in. headspace. Freeze for up to 12 months. **Yield:** about 4 cups.

Editor's Note: Use the sauce with crust and toppings of your choice to make a pizza; 1-1/3 cups of sauce will cover a crust in a 15-in. x 10-in. x 1-in. pan.

★★★ Creamed New Potatoes

Lillian Julow, Gainesville, Florida

My mother always made this side dish with sour cream, but I substituted buttermilk and added more herbs. Thyme and tarragon give these saucy potatoes a fresh taste I love.

2-1/2 pounds unpeeled small red potatoes, cut into 1-inch slices
   1 teaspoon salt
   1 package (8 ounces) cream cheese, cubed
   1 cup buttermilk
   1 bunch green onions, chopped
   1 teaspoon dried thyme
   1 teaspoon dried tarragon
 1/4 teaspoon pepper
   3 tablespoons minced fresh parsley

1. Place potatoes in a large saucepan and cover with water; add salt. Bring to a boil. Reduce heat; cover and cook for 15-20 minutes or until tender.

2. Meanwhile, in another saucepan, combine the cream cheese and buttermilk; cook and stir over medium heat until cheese is melted and mixture is smooth. Remove from the heat; add the onions, thyme, tarragon and pepper. Drain potatoes and place in a serving bowl; add cream sauce and toss to coat. Sprinkle with parsley. **Yield:** 6 servings.

★★★ Two-Bread Dressing

Vanessa Leeson, Bishop, Texas

I'm originally from Oregon and was raised on herb stuffing, but my Southern husband would eat only his mother's corn bread stuffing. So I created this recipe as a compromise!

   9 bacon strips, diced
   1 cup chopped celery
 1/4 cup chopped onion
   6 slices bread, toasted and cubed
   3 cups coarse corn bread crumbs
 1/3 cup minced fresh parsley
1-1/2 teaspoons rubbed sage
   1 teaspoon dried thyme
   1 teaspoon dried rosemary, crushed
1-1/2 cups chicken broth

1. In a large skillet, cook bacon until crisp. Drain, reserving 2 tablespoons drippings; set bacon aside. Saute celery and onion in drippings until tender.

2. In a large bowl, toss bread, parsley, sage, thyme and rosemary. Add celery, onion, broth and bacon; mix gently.

3. Spoon into a greased 2-qt. baking dish. Bake, uncovered, at 350° for 30-35 minutes or until heated through. **Yield:** 6-8 servings.

🎗🎗🎗 Teapot Cranberry Relish

Carolyn Huston, Jamesport, Missouri

A Christmas party at the tearoom we operate inspired my friend and me to make this relish. It was an instant hit and has turned many people into cranberry lovers.

- 1 package (12 ounces) fresh *or* frozen cranberries
- 2 cups sugar
- 1/2 cup orange juice
- 1/2 cup cranberry juice
- 2 cups dried cherries *or* golden raisins
- 1 teaspoon grated orange peel

In a large saucepan, cook cranberries, sugar and juices over medium heat until berries pop, about 15 minutes. Add cherries and orange peel. Simmer, uncovered, for 10 minutes. Cool slightly. Transfer to a large bowl; cover and refrigerate until serving. **Yield:** 4 cups.

🎗🎗🎗 Asparagus Cheese Bundles

Pat Habiger, Spearville, Kansas

Here's a rich, interesting side dish that'll have folks asking for seconds. I think it's the perfect vegetable for Easter dinner.

- 1 cup water
- 1/2 pound fresh asparagus, trimmed and cut into 2-inch pieces
- 2 medium carrots, julienned
- 1 package (8 ounces) cream cheese, softened
- 1 egg
- 2 tablespoons minced fresh basil *or* 2 teaspoons dried basil
- 1/2 cup crumbled feta cheese
- 8 flour tortillas (8 inches), warrmed
- 2 tablespoons milk
- 2 teaspoons sesame seeds

1. In a large saucepan, bring water to a boil. Add asparagus and carrots. Cook, uncovered, for 5 minutes; drain.

2. In a small mixing bowl, beat cream cheese, egg and basil; stir in feta cheese.

3. Place a mound of vegetables in the center of each tortilla. Top with 2 rounded tablespoonfuls of cheese mixture. Fold ends and sides over filling and roll up.

4. Place seam side down on an ungreased baking sheet. Brush with milk; sprinkle with sesame seeds. Bake at 425° for 10-14 minutes or until heated through and golden brown. **Yield:** 8 servings.

🎖️🎖️🎖️
Herbed Veggie Platter

Patricia Vandiver, Tucson, Arizona

Topped with herb butter and Parmesan, this eye-catching combination is a great addition to buffets. Divide the ingredients between two plates if your microwave can't accommodate one large platter.

- 1 small head cauliflower, broken into florets
- 1 medium bunch broccoli, cut into florets
- 2 medium zucchini, cut into 1/4-inch slices
- 1/2 cup butter, cubed
- 3/4 teaspoon dried thyme
- 3/4 teaspoon dried parsley flakes
- 1/2 teaspoon onion salt
- 2 medium tomatoes, cut into wedges
- 1/3 cup grated Parmesan cheese

1. On a large round microwave-safe platter, arrange the cauliflower, broccoli and zucchini. Cover and microwave on high for 7 minutes or until crisp-tender, stirring occasionally; drain.

2. In a small microwave-safe bowl, combine the butter, thyme, parsley and onion salt. Cover and microwave on high for 1 minute or until the butter is melted. Arrange tomatoes on platter. Drizzle butter mixture over vegetables; sprinkle with Parmesan cheese. Cook, uncovered, on high for 1-2 minutes or until heated through. **Yield:** 8-10 servings.

Editor's Note: This recipe was tested with an 850-watt microwave.

🎖🎖🎖
Shepherd's Bean Pie

Karen Cleveland, Spring Valley, Minnesota

This comforting casserole is a variation on traditional English pie. The fresh beans, carrots, cubed ham, almonds and creamy Swiss cheese sauce are topped with mashed potatoes for a hearty side dish...or even a main course.

1-1/4 **pounds fresh green beans, cut into 2-inch pieces**
1-1/4 **pounds fresh wax beans, cut into 2-inch pieces**
   3 **medium carrots, cut into 2-inch julienned strips**
1/2 **small onion, chopped**
   1 **teaspoon butter**
   1 **can (10-3/4 ounces) condensed cream of chicken soup, undiluted**
1/2 **cup heavy whipping cream**
1/2 **cup chicken broth**
3-1/4 **teaspoons dill weed, *divided***
   6 **ounces cubed fully cooked ham**
1-1/2 **cups (6 ounces) shredded Swiss cheese, *divided***
1/4 **cup slivered almonds**
   7 **cups hot mashed potatoes (with added milk and butter)**

1. Place beans and carrots in a saucepan and cover with water; bring to a boil. Cook, uncovered, for 8-10 minutes or until crisp-tender; drain and set aside. In a small skillet, saute onion in butter for 3-4 minutes or until tender.

2. In a large bowl, whisk soup, cream, broth and 3 teaspoons of dill. Add the beans, carrots and onion; gently stir to coat. Transfer to a greased shallow 3-qt. baking dish. Top with the ham, 1 cup cheese and almonds. Spread mashed potatoes over the top.

3. Cover and bake at 350° for 30 minutes. Uncover; sprinkle with remaining cheese and dill. Bake 5-10 minutes longer or until heated through and the cheese is melted. **Yield:** 12-15 servings.

🎖🎖🎖
Fresh Tomato Relish

Lela Baskins, Windsor, Missouri

I usually make a batch of this garden-fresh relish as soon as the first tomatoes of the season are ready. It can be stored for up to a year in the freezer.

   2 **cups white vinegar**
1/2 **cup sugar**
   8 **cups chopped tomatoes (about 11 large)**
1/2 **cup chopped onion**
   1 **medium green pepper, diced**
   1 **celery rib, diced**
1/4 **cup prepared horseradish**
   2 **tablespoons salt**
   1 **tablespoon mustard seed**
1-1/2 **teaspoons pepper**
1/2 **teaspoon ground cinnamon**
1/2 **teaspoon ground cloves**

1. In a large saucepan, bring vinegar and sugar to a boil. Remove from the heat; cool completely.

2. In a large bowl, combine remaining ingredients; add vinegar mixture and mix well. Spoon into storage containers, allowing 1/2-in. headspace. Refrigerate up to 2 weeks or freeze up to 12 months. Serve with a slotted spoon. **Yield:** about 6 pints.

Three-Berry Sauce

Suzanne Ganatta, Mammoth Lakes, California

I combined cranberries with strawberries and raspberries for a tasty twist on traditional holiday sauce. Cinnamon and cloves spice up this fruity topping that's great over poultry or pork.

✓ Uses less fat, sugar or salt. Includes Nutrition Facts and Diabetic Exchanges.

2 cups fresh *or* frozen cranberries
1/2 cup honey
1/4 cup orange juice
1 tablespoon grated orange peel
1/4 teaspoon salt
1/4 teaspoon ground cinnamon
1/8 teaspoon ground cloves
1/8 teaspoon ground allspice
2/3 cup frozen sweetened sliced strawberries, thawed
2/3 cup frozen sweetened raspberries, thawed
Thinly sliced cooked turkey

In a large saucepan, combine the first eight ingredients. Cook, uncovered, over medium heat for 10 minutes or until the cranberries pop, stirring occasionally. Reduce the heat; add the strawberries and raspberries. Cook until heated through. Remove from the heat;

cool. Serve with turkey. Store in the refrigerator. **Yield:** 2-1/4 cups.

Nutrition Facts: 1/4 cup equals 108 calories, trace fat (trace saturated fat), 0 cholesterol, 67 mg sodium, 29 g carbohydrate, 2 g fiber, trace protein. **Diabetic Exchange:** 2 fruit.

Hungarian Noodle Side Dish

Betty Sugg, Akron, New York

I first served this creamy noodle casserole at a ladies' meeting at church. Everyone liked it, and many people wanted the recipe. It can even make a meatless main dish.

3 chicken bouillon cubes
1/4 cup boiling water
1 can (10-3/4 ounces) condensed cream of mushroom soup, undiluted
1/2 cup chopped onion
2 tablespoons Worcestershire sauce
2 tablespoons poppy seeds
1/8 to 1/4 teaspoon garlic powder
1/8 to 1/4 teaspoon hot pepper sauce
2 cups (16 ounces) cottage cheese
2 cups (16 ounces) sour cream
1 package (16 ounces) medium noodles, cooked and drained
1/4 cup shredded Parmesan cheese
Paprika

1. In a large bowl, dissolve bouillon in water. Add the next six ingredients; mix well. Stir in cottage cheese, sour cream and noodles and mix well.

2. Pour into a greased 2-1/2-qt. baking dish. Sprinkle with the Parmesan cheese and paprika. Cover and bake at 350° for 45 minutes or until heated through. **Yield:** 8-10 servings.

Creamy Chive Mashed Potatoes

Bonnie Thompson, Rathdrum, Idaho

Buttermilk and cream cheese give rich, sour cream-like flavor to these wonderful whipped potatoes. The chives make them attractive for special-occasion dinners.

        5 medium potatoes, peeled
1-1/2 teaspoons salt, *divided*
        4 ounces cream cheese, softened
        2 tablespoons butter, softened
        2 tablespoons snipped chives
    1/4 teaspoon pepper
    1/4 to 1/2 cup buttermilk

1. Place potatoes in a large saucepan and cover with water; add 1 teaspoon salt. Bring to a boil. Reduce heat; cover and cook for 25-30 minutes or until tender. Drain.

2. In a large mixing bowl, mash the potatoes until smooth. Add cream cheese, butter, chives, pepper and remaining salt; gradually beat in the buttermilk. **Yield:** 4-5 servings.

Two-Bean Tomato Bake

Dorothy Rieke, Julian, Nebraska

I add Parmesan cheese, basil and garlic to accent this mouth-watering medley of beans, mushrooms, onion and tomato. With a crunchy crumb topping, the veggie bake is even better when you use your garden harvest.

1-1/2 pounds fresh green beans, cut into 2-inch
        pieces
1-1/2 pounds fresh wax beans, cut into 2-inch pieces
        5 medium tomatoes, peeled and cubed
    1/2 pound fresh mushrooms, sliced
        1 medium sweet onion, chopped
      10 tablespoons butter, *divided*
1-1/2 teaspoons minced garlic, *divided*
1-1/2 teaspoons dried basil, *divided*
1-1/2 teaspoons dried oregano, *divided*
        1 teaspoon salt
1-1/2 cups soft bread crumbs
    1/3 cup grated Parmesan cheese

1. Place the beans in a large saucepan and cover with water; bring to a boil. Cook, uncovered, for 8-10 minutes or until crisp-tender. Drain; add the tomatoes and set aside.

2. In a large skillet, saute mushrooms and onion in 4 tablespoons butter. Add 1 teaspoon garlic, 1 teaspoon basil,

1 teaspoon oregano and salt. Add to the bean mixture; toss to coat. Spoon into a greased 3-qt. baking dish.

3. Melt the remaining butter; toss with bread crumbs, Parmesan cheese and remaining garlic, basil and oregano. Sprinkle over bean mixture.

4. Cover and bake at 400° for 20 minutes. Uncover; bake 15 minutes longer or until golden brown. **Yield:** 14-16 servings.

🎀 🎀 🎀
Tomato Dumplings

Lucille Tucker, Clinton, Illinois

The fresh tomato taste of the sauce wonderfully complements these light, savory dumplings. They make a perfect side dish for a main course of beef.

- 1/2 cup finely chopped onion
- 1/4 cup finely chopped green pepper
- 1/4 cup finely chopped celery
- 1/4 cup butter
- 1 bay leaf
- 1 can (28 ounces) diced tomatoes, undrained
- 1 tablespoon brown sugar
- 1/2 teaspoon dried basil
- 1/2 teaspoon salt
- 1/4 teaspoon pepper

DUMPLINGS:
- 1 cup all-purpose flour
- 1-1/2 teaspoons baking powder
- 1/2 teaspoon salt
- 1 tablespoon cold butter
- 1 tablespoon snipped fresh parsley
- 2/3 cup milk

1. In large skillet, saute onion, green pepper and celery in butter until tender. Add bay leaf, tomatoes, brown sugar, basil, salt and pepper; cover and simmer for 5-10 minutes.

2. Meanwhile, for dumplings, combine flour, baking powder and salt in a bowl. Cut in butter. Add parsley and milk; stir just until mixed.

3. Drop by tablespoonfuls into six mounds onto bubbling tomato mixture; cover tightly and simmer for 12-15 minutes or until a toothpick inserted into dumplings comes out clean. Discard bay leaf. Serve immediately. **Yield:** 6 servings.

Ultimate Scalloped Potatoes

Glenda Malan, Lake Forest, California

My husband found this recipe when I called and informed him we were having guests for dinner. This delicious variation on traditional scalloped potatoes is dressed up with garlic, Swiss cheese and Parmesan cheese.

- 1 teaspoon butter, softened
- 1 cup heavy whipping cream
- 1/3 cup milk
- 1 teaspoon salt
- 1/2 teaspoon pepper
- 2 garlic cloves, crushed
- 6 medium potatoes
- 1 cup (4 ounces) shredded Swiss cheese
- 1/4 cup shredded Parmesan cheese

1. Grease a shallow 1-1/2-qt. baking dish with the butter; set aside. In a large saucepan, combine cream, milk, salt, pepper and garlic. Cook just until bubbles begin to form around sides of pan. Remove from the heat; cool for 10 minutes.

2. Peel and thinly slice the potatoes; pat dry with paper towels. Layer half of the potatoes in prepared baking dish; top with half of the cream mixture and half of the cheeses. Repeat layers.

3. Bake, uncovered, at 350° for 55-65 minutes or until potatoes are tender. Let stand for 5-10 minutes before serving. **Yield:** 6 servings.

Two-Season Squash Medley

Mary Beth LaFlamme, Eagle Bridge, New York

Both winter and summer squash star in this fun, colorful veggie stir-fry. I've cooked in several restaurants and for many guests in my home, and this dish has been well-received for years.

- 2 tablespoons butter
- 2 tablespoons olive oil
- 1 medium yellow summer squash, sliced
- 1 medium zucchini, sliced
- 3/4 pound butternut squash, peeled, seeded and julienned
- 1 medium onion, sliced
- 1 medium green pepper, julienned
- 1 medium sweet red pepper, julienned
- 3 to 4 garlic cloves, minced
- 1 tablespoon minced fresh thyme *or* 1 teaspoon dried thyme
- 1/4 teaspoon garlic salt
- 1/4 teaspoon pepper

In a large skillet, heat the butter and oil over medium heat. Add vegetables, garlic and thyme. Cook and stir until tender, about 15 minutes. Add garlic salt and pepper. **Yield:** 6-8 servings.

🎗🎗🎗 Pepperoni Angel Hair

Julie Mosher, Coldwater, Michigan

This noodle side dish is so versatile that it can accompany everything from steak and pork chops to chicken and hamburgers. You can even chill the leftovers to serve as a cool main-dish salad. For variety, I sometimes replace the pepperoni with sliced cooked chicken.

  8 ounces uncooked angel hair pasta, broken into thirds
  1 small cucumber, peeled and chopped
  1 medium green pepper, chopped
  1 package (8 ounces) sliced pepperoni, quartered
  2 cans (2-1/4 ounces *each*) sliced ripe olives, drained
  1/2 cup Italian salad dressing
  1-1/4 cups shredded Parmesan cheese

Cook the pasta according to package directions. Meanwhile, combine the cucumber, green pepper, pepperoni and olives in a large bowl. Drain pasta and add to pepperoni mixture. Top with salad dressing and Parmesan cheese; toss to coat. **Yield:** 4-6 servings.

🎗🎗🎗 Seasoned Potato Wedges

Karen Trewin, Decorah, Iowa

Seasoned with Parmesan cheese and served with a sour cream dip, these baked wedges make a nice alternative to french fries or baked potatoes. My family enjoys the wedges both as a side dish and as a snack.

  1/3 cup all-purpose flour
  1/3 cup grated Parmesan cheese
    1 teaspoon paprika
    3 large baking potatoes (about 2-3/4 pounds)
  1/3 cup milk
  1/4 cup butter, *divided*
SOUR CREAM DIP:
    2 cups (16 ounces) sour cream
    8 bacon strips, cooked and crumbled
    2 tablespoons snipped chives
  1/2 teaspoon garlic powder

1. In a large resealable plastic bag, combine the flour, Parmesan cheese and paprika. Cut each potato into eight wedges; dip in milk. Place in the bag, a few at a time, and shake to coat.

2. Place in a greased 15-in. x 10-in. x 1-in. baking pan. Drizzle with 2 tablespoons butter. Bake, uncovered, at 400° for 20 minutes. Turn wedges; drizzle with remaining butter. Bake 20-25 minutes longer or until potatoes are tender and golden brown.

3. In a large bowl, combine dip ingredients. Serve with warm potato wedges. **Yield:** 6-8 servings.

🎗️🎗️🎗️
Strawberry-Tomato Salsa

(Also pictured on page 128)

Jean Giroux, Belchertown, Massachusetts

This delightfully different salsa is versatile, fresh-tasting and colorful. People are surprised to find strawberries in it, but it's excellent served over grilled chicken or pork...or even as a dip with your favorite chips.

> 1 pint fresh strawberries, chopped
> 4 plum tomatoes, seeded and chopped
> 1 small red onion, finely chopped
> 1 to 2 medium jalapeno peppers, minced
> Juice of 1 lime
> 2 garlic cloves, minced
> 1 tablespoon olive oil

1. In a large bowl, combine strawberries, tomatoes, onion and peppers. Stir in lime juice, garlic and oil. Cover and chill for 2 hours.

2. Serve with cooked poultry or pork or as a dip for tortilla chips. **Yield:** 4 cups.

Editor's Note: When cutting or seeding hot peppers, use rubber or plastic gloves to protect your hands. Avoid touching your face.

🎗️🎗️🎗️
Stuffed Baked Potatoes

(Also pictured on page 129)

Kristyn Drews, Omaha, Nebraska

My mom gave me the recipe for these twice-baked potatoes, which I altered a bit by adding garlic, bacon and green onions. They're perfect for just about any occasion, from a potluck to an elegant meal. My two boys love them!

> 5 medium baking potatoes
> 1/4 cup butter, softened
> 2 cups (8 ounces) shredded cheddar cheese, divided
> 3/4 cup sour cream
> 1 envelope ranch salad dressing mix
> 1 tablespoon snipped chives
> 1 garlic clove, minced
> Crumbled cooked bacon and chopped green onion

1. Bake potatoes at 400° for 1 hour or until tender. Reduce heat to 375°. Cut each potato in half lengthwise; scoop out the pulp, leaving a thin shell.

2. In a large mixing bowl, beat the pulp with butter. Stir in 1 cup of cheese, sour cream, salad dressing mix, chives and garlic. Spoon into potato shells. Sprinkle with remaining cheese.

3. Place on a baking sheet. Bake for 15-20 minutes or until heated through. Top with bacon and green onions. **Yield:** 10 servings.

Dill Seed Braid, p. 159

Cheddar-Squash Cloverleaf Rolls, p. 153

Apple Streusel Muffins, p. 162

Breads & Rolls

Delight your family and friends anytime with fruit-filled muffins, beautiful braids, classic biscuits and other home-baked goodies. It's easy when you choose these fresh-from-the-oven recipes.

Whole Wheat Bread, p. 163

🎖🎖🎖
Italian Snack Bread

Joan Nowacki, Pewaukee, Wisconsin

This snack bread is so versatile—I've served it with spaghetti, as an appetizer and even as a light main dish. Because it stays so moist, I often bake it the day before.

2-1/2 cups all-purpose flour
    1 package (1/4 ounce) active dry yeast
2-1/2 teaspoons dried oregano
    1/2 teaspoon salt
    1 cup warm water (120° to 130°)
    2 tablespoons olive oil
    1 egg, lightly beaten
TOPPING:
1-1/2 cups thinly sliced onion
    1/4 cup olive oil
    1 teaspoon dried rosemary, crushed
    1 teaspoon coarse salt, optional

1. In a large bowl, combine 1-1/2 cups flour, yeast, oregano and salt. Stir in water, oil and egg; mix well. Stir in enough remaining flour to form a soft dough. Cover and let rest 10 minutes. Pat into a greased 13-in. x 9-in. x 2-in. baking pan; set aside.

2. In a large skillet, saute onion in oil until tender. Spoon evenly over dough. Sprinkle with rosemary and salt if desired. Cover and let rise in a warm place until doubled, about 30 minutes.

3. Bake at 400° for 25-30 minutes or until lightly browned. Cut into small squares. Serve warm or at room temperature. **Yield:** about 8 servings.

🎖🎖🎖
Banana Bran Muffins

Alyce Wyman, Pembina, North Dakota

Several years ago, I experimented with a banana muffin recipe by adding bran cereal. I loved the results and have been making this heartier version ever since. For a twist, try replacing the chocolate chips and nuts with chopped dates.

    1/2 cup butter, softened
    1 cup sugar
    2 eggs
    3 medium ripe bananas, mashed
    1/2 cup buttermilk
1-1/2 cups all-purpose flour
1-1/2 teaspoons baking soda
    1/2 teaspoon salt
    4 cups raisin bran
    1 cup miniature semisweet chocolate chips
    1/2 cup chopped pecans

1. In a large mixing bowl, cream butter and sugar. Add the eggs, bananas and buttermilk. Combine the flour, baking soda and salt; stir into creamed mixture just until moistened. Fold in the cereal, chocolate chips and pecans.

2. Fill greased or paper-lined muffin cups two-thirds full. Bake at 350° for 23-25 minutes or until a toothpick comes out clean. Cool for 5 minutes before removing from pans to wire racks. **Yield:** 2 dozen.

Potato Pan Rolls

LeAnne Hofferichter, Floresville, Texas

Beautiful color and light-as-a-feather texture make these rolls our family's favorite for holiday meals. I won the Reserve Champion award at a 4-H yeast bread competition with this recipe.

2 medium potatoes, peeled and quartered
1-1/2 cups water
2 packages (1/4 ounce *each*) active dry yeast
1 teaspoon sugar

1/2 cup butter, melted
1/2 cup honey
1/4 cup vegetable oil
2 eggs
2 teaspoons salt
6 to 7 cups all-purpose flour

1. In a large saucepan, bring potatoes and water to a boil. Reduce heat; cover and simmer for 15-20 minutes or until tender. Drain, reserving 1 cup cooking liquid; cool liquid to 110°-115°. Mash potatoes; set aside 1 cup to cool to 110°-115° (save remaining potatoes for another use).

2. In a large mixing bowl, dissolve yeast and sugar in reserved potato liquid; let stand for 5 minutes. Add reserved mashed potatoes, butter, honey, oil, eggs, salt and 1-1/2 cups flour; beat until smooth. Stir in enough remaining flour to form a soft dough.

3. Turn onto a floured surface; knead until smooth and elastic, about 6-8 minutes. Place in a greased bowl, turning once to grease top. Cover and let rise in a warm place until doubled, about 1 hour.

4. Punch dough down and turn onto a floured surface; divide into 30 pieces. Shape each piece into a ball. Place 10 balls each in three greased 9-in. round baking pans. Cover and let rise until doubled, about 30 minutes.

5. Bake at 400° for 20-25 minutes or until golden brown. Remove from pans to wire racks to cool. **Yield:** 2-1/2 dozen.

Jumbo Onion Cheese Muffins

Valerie Collier, Charleston, South Carolina

Chopped green onions and three types of cheese perk up these suppertime specialties. The large, golden muffins have a savory flavor that's great with nearly any entree.

2 cups all-purpose flour
3 teaspoons baking powder
1/4 teaspoon pepper
Dash ground nutmeg
1-1/4 cups milk
1/4 cup butter, melted
1 egg
1/4 cup chopped green onions
1/4 cup shredded part-skim mozzarella cheese
1/4 cup grated Romano cheese
1/4 cup shredded Parmesan cheese

1. In a large bowl, combine the flour, baking powder, pepper and nutmeg. In another bowl, combine the milk, butter and egg; stir into dry ingredients just until moistened. Fold in the onions and cheeses.

2. Fill greased jumbo muffin cups two-thirds full. Bake at 400° for 20-25 minutes or until a toothpick comes out clean. Cool for 5 minutes before removing from pan to a wire rack. **Yield:** 6 muffins.

Editor's Note: Muffins may be baked in regular-size muffin cups for 16-18 minutes; recipe makes 1 dozen.

⚜ ⚜ ⚜
Cardamom Wreath

Judy Wilson, Vermont, Illinois

I've been cooking since I was very young, and yeast breads are my favorite things to bake. This sweet-and-spicy ring is perfect for Christmas and scrumptious with the accompanying Cardamom Butter.

      2 **packages (1/4 ounce** *each***) active dry yeast**
   1/3 **cup warm water (110° to 115°)**
   1/2 **cup butter, softened**
   3/4 **cup sugar**
      4 **eggs**
      1 **can (12 ounces) evaporated milk**
   1/4 **cup sour cream**
      1 **tablespoon grated orange peel**
2-1/4 **teaspoons ground cardamom**
      2 **teaspoons salt**
      7 **to 7-1/2 cups all-purpose flour**
      1 **tablespoon milk**
Toasted sliced almonds
Coarse *or* granulated sugar
CARDAMOM BUTTER:
      2 **cups butter, softened**
   1/4 **cup confectioners' sugar**
1-1/2 **teaspoons grated orange peel**
      1 **to 1-1/2 teaspoons ground cardamom**
   1/2 **teaspoon ground nutmeg**

1. In a small bowl, dissolve yeast in warm water. In a large mixing bowl, cream butter and sugar. Beat in 3 eggs, evaporated milk, yeast mixture, sour cream, orange peel, cardamom and salt; mix well. Beat in 6 cups flour until smooth. Stir in enough remaining flour to form a soft dough.

2. Turn onto a floured surface; knead until smooth and elastic, about 6–8 minutes. Place in a greased bowl, turning once to grease top. Cover and let rise in a warm place until doubled, about 1 hour.

3. Punch dough down; turn onto a floured surface. Divide into six portions. Cover and let rest for 10 minutes. Shape each portion into a 24-in. rope. Place three ropes on a greased baking sheet and braid. Form into a ring; pinch ends tightly together. Repeat with remaining dough. Cover and let rise until almost doubled, about 45 minutes.

4. Beat milk and remaining egg; brush over wreaths. Sprinkle with almonds and sugar. Bake at 375° for 25–30 minutes or until golden brown. Remove from pans to wire racks to cool.

5. Meanwhile, in a large mixing bowl, beat cardamom butter ingredients until blended. Serve with bread. **Yield:** 2 loaves (2 cups butter).

🎀🎀🎀
Cheeseburger Mini Muffins

Teresa Kraus, Cortez, Colorado

I created these cute little muffins so I could enjoy the flavor of cheeseburgers without resorting to fast food. I often freeze a batch and reheat however many I need. They're great as snacks and even for lunch.

    1/2 pound ground beef
    1 small onion, finely chopped
    2-1/2 cups all-purpose flour
    1 tablespoon sugar
    2 teaspoons baking powder
    1 teaspoon salt
    3/4 cup ketchup
    3/4 cup milk
    1/2 cup butter, melted
    2 eggs
    1 teaspoon prepared mustard
    2 cups (8 ounces) shredded cheddar cheese

1. In a large skillet, cook beef and onion over medium heat until meat is no longer pink; drain.

2. In a small bowl, combine the flour, sugar, baking powder and salt. In another bowl, combine the ketchup, milk, butter, eggs and mustard; stir into the dry ingredients just until moistened. Fold in the beef mixture and cheese.

3. Fill greased miniature muffin cups three-fourths full. Bake at 425° for 15-18 minutes or until a toothpick comes out clean. Cool for 5 minutes before removing from the pans to wire racks. Refrigerate leftovers. **Yield:** 5 dozen.

Editor's Note: Muffins may be baked in regular-size muffin cups for 20-25 minutes; recipe makes 2 dozen.

🎀🎀🎀
Cheddar-Squash Cloverleaf Rolls

(Also pictured on page 148)

DeDe Waldmann, Monona, Wisconsin

These from-scratch yeast rolls started out as a basic bread recipe, which I adapted to suit my family. Our son-in-law normally can't stand squash, but he loves these treats! They're especially good in fall and winter.

    2 tablespoons sugar
    1/4 cup warm water (110° to 115°)
    1 package (1/4 ounce) active dry yeast
    1 cup warm milk (110° to 115°)
    4 tablespoons butter, melted, *divided*
    1 teaspoon salt
    1 cup mashed cooked winter squash
    3/4 cup shredded cheddar cheese
    4 to 4-1/2 cups all-purpose flour
Sesame seeds, optional

1. In a large mixing bowl, dissolve sugar in water. Sprinkle the yeast over the water and stir gently. Let stand until light and foamy. Stir in milk, 3 tablespoons butter, salt, squash and cheese. Add enough flour to form a soft dough.

2. Turn out onto a lightly floured surface; knead until the dough is no longer sticky, about 5 minutes. Form in-

to a ball and place in a greased bowl, turning once to grease top. Cover and let rise in a warm place until doubled, about 1 hour.

3. Meanwhile, lightly grease 24 muffin cups. Punch down dough. Break off small portions and roll into 1-in. balls. Put three balls into each cup. Cover and let rise in a warm place until doubled, about 30 minutes.

4. Brush tops of rolls with remaining butter; sprinkle with sesame seeds if desired. Bake at 375° for 16-18 minutes or until golden. Serve warm. **Yield:** 2 dozen.

🎀🎀🎀
Almond Bear Claws

Aneta Kish, La Crosse, Wisconsin

These bear claws are absolutely melt-in-your-mouth delicious! It's impossible to resist the delicate pastry, rich almond filling and pretty fanned tops sprinkled with sugar and nuts. I made yummy treats like this years ago when I worked in a bakery.

```
1-1/2  cups cold butter, cut into 1/2-inch pieces
    5  cups all-purpose flour, divided
    1  package (1/4 ounce) active dry yeast
1-1/4  cups half-and-half cream
  1/4  cup sugar
  1/4  teaspoon salt
    2  eggs
    1  egg white
  3/4  cup confectioners' sugar
```

```
  1/2  cup almond paste, cubed
    1  tablespoon water
Coarse or granulated sugar
Sliced almonds
```

1. In a large bowl, toss butter with 3 cups flour until well coated; refrigerate. In a large mixing bowl, combine yeast and remaining flour. In a large saucepan, heat cream, sugar and salt to 120°-130°. Add to yeast mixture with 1 egg; mix well. Stir in butter mixture just until moistened.

2. Turn onto a lightly floured surface; knead 10 times. Roll into a 21-in. x 12-in. rectangle. Starting at a short side, fold dough in thirds, forming a 12-in. x 7-in. rectangle. Cover and chill for 1 hour.

3. For filling, in a large mixing bowl, beat egg white until foamy. Gradually add confectioners' sugar and almond paste; beat until smooth. Cut dough in half widthwise.

4. Roll each portion into a 12-in. square; cut each square into three 12-in. x 4-in. strips. Spread about 2 tablespoons filling down center of each strip. Fold long edges together; seal edges and ends. Cut into three pieces.

5. Place on greased baking sheets with folded edge facing away from you. With scissors, cut strips four times to within 1/2 in. of folded edge; separate slightly. Repeat with remaining dough and filling. Cover and let rise in a warm place until doubled, about 1 hour.

6. Lightly beat water and remaining egg; brush over dough. Sprinkle with sugar and almonds. Bake at 375° for 15 minutes or until golden brown. Remove from pans to wire racks to cool. **Yield:** 1-1/2 dozen.

🎀🎀🎀
Cranberry Cream Cheese Muffins

Sharon Hartman, Twin Falls, Idaho

The sweet, creamy filling in these sugar-sprinkled muffins makes them popular at my house. The recipe calls for just six ingredients, including a convenient quick bread mix.

```
    1  package (3 ounces) cream cheese, softened
    4  tablespoons sugar, divided
    1  package (15.6 ounces) cranberry-orange quick
       bread mix
    1  cup milk
  1/3  cup vegetable oil
    1  egg
```

1. In a small mixing bowl, beat the cream cheese and 2 tablespoons sugar until smooth; set aside. Place the bread mix in another bowl. Combine the milk, oil and egg; stir into bread mix just until moistened.

2. Fill paper-lined muffin cups one-fourth full with batter. Place 2 teaspoons cream cheese mixture in the center of each; top with remaining batter. Sprinkle with remaining sugar. Bake at 400° for 18-20 minutes or until a toothpick comes out clean. Cool for 5 minutes before removing from pan to a wire rack. **Yield:** 1 dozen.

1/2 cup chopped onion
3 tablespoons butter
1 cup plus 2 tablespoons warm milk
(120° to 130°)
1 tablespoon sugar
1-1/2 teaspoons salt
1/2 teaspoon dill weed
1/2 teaspoon dried basil
1/2 teaspoon dried rosemary, crushed
1 package (1/4 ounce) active dry yeast
3 to 3-1/2 cups all-purpose flour
Melted butter

1. In a large skillet, cook onion in butter over low heat until tender, about 8 minutes. Cool for 10 minutes. Place in a large mixing bowl. Add milk, sugar, salt, herbs, yeast and 3 cups flour; beat until smooth. Stir in enough remaining flour to form a soft dough.

2. Turn onto a floured surface; knead until smooth and elastic, about 6-8 minutes. Place in a greased bowl, turning once to grease top. Cover and let rise in a warm place until doubled, about 45 minutes.

3. Punch the dough down. Shape into a ball and place on a greased baking sheet. Cover and let rise until doubled, about 45 minutes.

4. Bake at 375° for 25-30 minutes. Remove to a wire rack; brush with melted butter. Cool. **Yield:** 1 loaf.

Herbed Peasant Bread

Ardath Effa, Villa Park, Illinois

I received the recipe for this beautiful, moist loaf from our daughter-in-law. Everyone who samples a slice wants to know how to make it, and I'm always happy to oblige.

Milk-and-Honey White Bread

Kathy McCreary, Goddard, Kansas

My state is the wheat capital of the country, so this bread represents my region well. Thick slices are great for sandwiches.

2 packages (1/4 ounce *each*) active dry yeast
2-1/2 cups warm milk (110° to 115°)
1/3 cup honey
1/4 cup butter, melted
2 teaspoons salt
8 to 8-1/2 cups all-purpose flour

1. In a large mixing bowl, dissolve yeast in warm milk. Add honey, butter, salt and 5 cups of flour; beat until smooth. Add enough remaining flour to form a soft dough.

2. Turn onto a floured surface; knead until smooth and elastic, about 6-8 minutes. Place in a greased bowl, turning once to grease top. Cover and let rise in a warm place until doubled, about 1 hour.

3. Punch dough down and shape into two loaves. Place in greased 9-in. x 5-in. x 3-in. loaf pans. Cover and let rise until doubled, about 30 minutes.

4. Bake at 375° for 30-35 minutes or until golden brown. Cover loosely with foil if top browns too quickly. Remove from pans and cool on wire racks. **Yield:** 2 loaves.

✿✿✿
Berry Pleasing Muffins

Julie Wood, Vancouver, Washington

These goodies are scrumptious with sausage and scrambled eggs for breakfast…or with cottage cheese and a sliced apple for a light lunch. After one taste, you'll want to keep extras for your coffee break or afternoon tea, too!

    1 cup fresh *or* frozen blueberries
  1/2 cup chopped fresh *or* frozen cranberries
    1 cup sugar, *divided*
    1 package (8 ounces) cream cheese, softened
    2 eggs
    1 teaspoon vanilla extract
    1 cup all-purpose flour
    1 teaspoon baking soda
  1/2 teaspoon salt
  1/4 teaspoon ground nutmeg
TOPPING:
  1/4 cup finely chopped walnuts
  1/4 cup flaked coconut
    2 tablespoons brown sugar
  1/4 teaspoon ground cinnamon

1. In a large bowl, combine the blueberries, cranberries and 1/4 cup sugar; set aside. In a large mixing bowl, beat cream cheese and remaining sugar until smooth. Add eggs, one at a time, beating well after each addition. Beat in vanilla. Combine the flour, baking soda, salt and nutmeg; add to the creamed mixture. Fold in the berry mixture.

2. Fill greased or paper-lined muffin cups two-thirds full. Combine topping ingredients; sprinkle over batter. Bake at 400° for 18-20 minutes or until a toothpick comes out clean. Cool for 5 minutes before removing to a wire rack. **Yield:** 1 dozen.

Editor's Note: Muffins may be baked in miniature muffin cups for 10-12 minutes; recipe makes 4 dozen. If using frozen berries, do not thaw.

✿✿✿
Cinnamon Swirl Quick Bread

Helen Richardson, Shelbyville, Michigan

When I was first married, I bought two popular cookbooks to learn the "basics." Now, I have over 2,000 cookbooks, booklets and recipe magazines that I read like others read novels! This bread is one of my longtime favorites and great for get-togethers.

      2 cups all-purpose flour
  1-1/2 cups sugar, *divided*
      1 teaspoon baking soda
    1/2 teaspoon salt
      1 cup buttermilk
      1 egg
    1/4 cup vegetable oil
      1 tablespoon ground cinnamon
GLAZE:
    1/4 cup confectioners' sugar
  1-1/2 to 2 teaspoons milk

1. In a large bowl, combine the flour, 1 cup sugar, baking soda and salt. Combine the buttermilk, egg and oil; stir into dry ingredients just until moistened. In a small bowl, combine the cinnamon and remaining sugar.

2. Grease the bottom only of a 9-in. x 5-in. x 3-in. loaf pan. Pour half of the batter into pan; sprinkle with half of the cinnamon-sugar. Carefully spread with remaining batter and sprinkle with remaining cinnamon-sugar; swirl knife through batter. Bake at 350° for 45-50 minutes or until a toothpick inserted near the center comes out clean. Cool in pan 10 minutes before removing to a wire rack to cool completely.

3. For glaze, combine confectioner's sugar and enough milk to achieve drizzling consistency. Drizzle over bread. **Yield:** 1 loaf.

🎀 🎀 🎀

Peanut Butter 'n' Jelly Mini Muffins

Vickie Barrow, Edenton, North Carolina

Kids love these little jelly-filled treats...and so do adults. Packed with peanut butter flavor, the muffins are a fun and easy way to start off the day or tide over children after school.

  1 cup all-purpose flour
1/3 cup packed brown sugar
  1 teaspoon baking powder
1/2 teaspoon baking soda
1/4 teaspoon salt
  2 eggs
1/2 cup vanilla yogurt
  3 tablespoons creamy peanut butter
  2 tablespoons vegetable oil
  3 tablespoons strawberry *or* grape jelly

1. In a large bowl, combine flour, sugar, baking powder, baking soda and salt. In a small mixing bowl, beat eggs, yogurt, peanut butter and oil on low speed until smooth; stir into dry ingredients just until moistened.

2. Fill greased or paper-lined miniature muffin cups half full. Top each with 1/4 teaspoon jelly and remaining batter. Bake at 400° for 10-12 minutes or until golden brown. Cool for 5 minutes before removing from pans to wire racks. **Yield:** 2-1/2 dozen.

Editor's Note: Muffins may be baked in regular-size muffin cups for 16-18 minutes; use 3/4 teaspoon jelly for each instead of 1/4 teaspoon. Recipe makes 10 muffins.

Mess-Free Muffins

Using a spoon to fill muffin cups with batter can get messy. To quickly put batter into muffin cups with little fuss, try using an ice cream scoop that has a quick release. Or pour the batter from a liquid measuring cup.

✿✿✿ Overnight Swedish Rye Bread

Caroline Carr, Lyons, Nebraska

This bread delights family and friends who are of Scandinavian origin—and everyone else who tastes it! The overnight recipe allows me to do the baking early in the morning, leaving time to take care of other things.

    2 packages (1/4 ounce *each*) active dry yeast
  1/2 cup warm water (110° to 115°)
    1 teaspoon sugar
    4 cups warm milk (110° to 115°)
    1 cup molasses
    1 cup packed brown sugar
    1 cup vegetable oil
    1 cup quick-cooking oats
    2 tablespoons grated orange peel
    1 tablespoon salt
    1 teaspoon fennel seed
    1 teaspoon aniseed
    1 teaspoon caraway seed
    2 cups rye flour
  11 to 12 cups all-purpose flour

1. In a large mixing bowl, dissolve yeast in water; stir in sugar and let stand for 5 minutes. Add milk, molasses, brown sugar, oil, oats, orange peel, salt, fennel, aniseed, caraway, rye flour and 6 cups of all-purpose flour. Add enough remaining all-purpose flour to form a soft but sticky dough. Cover and let rise in a warm place overnight.

2. Punch dough down. Turn onto a floured surface; knead until smooth and elastic, about 6-8 minutes. Shape into four loaves. Place in greased 9-in. x 5-in. x 3-in. loaf pans. Cover and let rise until doubled, about 1 hour.

3. Bake at 350° for 35-45 minutes. Remove from the pans to cool on wire racks. **Yield:** 4 loaves.

✿✿✿ Triple Berry Muffins

Michelle Turnis, Hopkinton, Iowa

Fresh blueberries, raspberries and strawberries add eye-catching color and summertime flavor to these moist muffins spiced with cinnamon. The sweet treats come together in no time and bake up in a snap.

    3 cups all-purpose flour
1-1/2 cups sugar
4-1/2 teaspoons ground cinnamon
    3 teaspoons baking powder
  1/2 teaspoon salt
  1/2 teaspoon baking soda
    2 eggs
1-1/4 cups milk
    1 cup butter, melted
    1 cup fresh blueberries
  1/2 cup fresh raspberries
  1/2 cup chopped fresh strawberries

1. In a large bowl, combine the first six ingredients. In another bowl, beat the eggs, milk and butter; stir into dry ingredients just until moistened. Fold in berries.

2. Fill greased or paper-lined muffin cups three-fourths full. Bake at 375° for 18-20 minutes or until a toothpick comes out clean. Cool for 5 minutes before removing from pans to wire racks. **Yield:** about 1-1/2 dozen.

Pineapple Carrot Bread

Paula Spink, Elkins Park, Pennsylvania

This yummy bread not only tastes like carrot cake, it's nutritious and economical—two important qualities in my home! The recipe yields two loaves, so there's plenty to share.

       3 cups all-purpose flour
       2 cups sugar
       1 teaspoon baking soda
       1 teaspoon ground cinnamon
     3/4 teaspoon salt
       3 eggs
       2 cups shredded carrots
       1 cup vegetable oil
       1 can (8 ounces) unsweetened crushed
          pineapple, drained
       2 teaspoons vanilla extract
       1 cup chopped pecans or walnuts
     3/4 cup confectioners' sugar, optional
       1 to 1-1/2 teaspoons milk, optional

1. In a large bowl, combine the flour, sugar, baking soda, cinnamon and salt. In another bowl, beat eggs; add carrots, oil, pineapple and vanilla. Stir into the dry ingredients just until moistened. Fold in nuts.

2. Spoon into two greased and floured 8-in. x 4-in. x 2-in. loaf pans. Bake at 350° for 65-75 minutes or until a toothpick inserted near the center comes out clean. Cool for 10 minutes before removing to wire racks to cool completely.

3. If glaze is desired, combine confectioners' sugar and milk; drizzle over loaves. **Yield:** 2 loaves.

Dill Seed Braid

(Also pictured on page 148)

Lori Jameson, Walla Walla, Washington

With an attractive braided shape and pleasant dill flavor, this golden-brown bread stands out from other yeast breads. My family loves it alongside soup, roast beef or pot roast. I almost always make a second loaf—one just isn't enough!

       1 package (1/4 ounce) active dry yeast
     1/4 cup warm water (110° to 115°)
       1 cup plain yogurt
       1 small onion, finely chopped
     1/4 cup sugar
       2 tablespoons butter, softened
       1 egg
       1 tablespoon dill seed
       1 teaspoon salt
       3 to 3-1/2 cups all-purpose flour

1. In a large mixing bowl, dissolve yeast in warm water. Add the yogurt, onion, sugar, butter, egg, dill seed, salt and 1 cup flour. Beat until smooth. Stir in enough remaining flour to form a soft dough.

2. Turn onto a floured surface; knead until smooth and elastic, about 6-8 minutes. Place in a greased bowl, turning once to grease top. Cover and let rise in a warm place until doubled, about 1 hour.

3. Punch dough down. Turn onto a lightly floured surface; divide into thirds. Shape each portion into a 20-in. rope. Place ropes on a large greased baking sheet and braid; pinch ends to seal and tuck under. Cover and let rise until doubled, about 30 minutes.

4. Bake at 350° for 35-40 minutes or until golden brown. Remove from pan to a wire rack to cool. **Yield:** 1 loaf.

Raspberry Corn Bread Muffins

Sue Santulli, Sea Girt, New Jersey

My son calls these "surprise muffins" because I pipe raspberry preserves into the centers. He likes them so much that sometimes I bake them in jumbo muffin tins, adding more preserves than I do for the standard size.

      3 cups all-purpose flour
      1 cup cornmeal
      1 cup sugar
      6 teaspoons baking powder
  1-1/2 teaspoons salt
      2 eggs
  1-1/2 cups milk
      1 cup butter, melted
    1/2 cup raspberry preserves

1. In a large mixing bowl, combine the flour, cornmeal, sugar, baking powder and salt. In another bowl, combine the eggs, milk and butter; add to dry ingredients and beat on low speed just until blended.

2. Fill paper-lined muffin cups two-thirds full. Bake at 350° for 17-19 minutes or until a toothpick comes out clean. Cool for 5 minutes before removing from pans to wire racks to cool completely.

3. Using the end of a 3/8-in.-wide wooden spoon handle, make a hole in the center of each muffin. Place preserves in a resealable plastic bag; cut a small hole in a corner of bag. Fill the hole in each muffin with preserves. **Yield:** about 2 dozen.

Molasses Oat Bread

Patricia Finch Kelly, Rindge, New Hampshire

This recipe for three hearty loaves has been passed down through my family from my Swedish great-grandmother. One Christmas, my mom made and distributed 25 of them! The slightly sweet bread always receives high praise.

 Uses less fat, sugar or salt. Includes Nutrition Facts and Diabetic Exchanges.

      4 cups boiling water
      2 cups old-fashioned oats
      1 cup molasses
      3 tablespoons canola oil
    1/4 cup sugar
      3 teaspoons salt
      1 package (1/4 ounce) active dry yeast
      9 to 10 cups all-purpose flour

1. In a large mixing bowl, combine the first six ingredients. Cool to 110°-115°. Add yeast; mix well. Add enough flour to form a soft dough. Turn onto a floured surface; knead until smooth and elastic, about 6-8 minutes. Place in a greased bowl, turning once to grease top. Cover and let rise in a warm place until doubled, about 1-1/2 hours.

2. Punch dough down and divide into thirds; shape into loaves. Place in three greased 9-in. x 5-in. x 3-in. loaf pans. Cover and let rise until doubled, about 1 hour.

3. Bake at 350° for 45-50 minutes or until golden brown. Remove from pans to wire racks to cool. **Yield:** 3 loaves (12 slices each).

Nutrition Facts: 1 slice equals 183 calories, 2 g fat (trace saturated fat), 0 cholesterol, 200 mg sodium, 37 g carbohydrate, 1 g fiber, 4 g protein. **Diabetic Exchange:** 2-1/2 starch.

🎗 🎗 🎗
Nutty Sweet Potato Biscuits

Mrs. India Thacker, Clifford, Virginia

Back in the 1920s and '30s, Mom always had something yummy for us to eat when we got home from school. She often surprised us with a plate of these wonderful biscuits warm from the oven. What a treat!

2-3/4 **cups all-purpose flour**
4 **teaspoons baking powder**
1-1/4 **teaspoons salt**
1/2 **teaspoon ground cinnamon**
1/2 **teaspoon ground nutmeg**
3/4 **cup chopped nuts**
2 **cups mashed sweet potatoes**
3/4 **cup sugar**
1/2 **cup butter, melted**
1 **teaspoon vanilla extract**

1. In a large mixing bowl, combine flour, baking powder, salt, cinnamon, nutmeg and nuts. In another bowl, combine sweet potatoes, sugar, butter and vanilla; add to flour mixture and mix well.

2. Turn onto a lightly floured surface; knead slightly. Roll dough to 1/2-in. thickness. Cut with a 2-1/2-in. biscuit cutter and place on lightly greased baking sheets. Bake at 450° for 12 minutes or until golden brown. **Yield:** 18 servings.

✿ ✿ ✿
Sausage Cheese Braid

Christena Weed, Levant, Kansas

This braided bread looks so beautiful on a buffet table. And when people take a bite, they discover the delicious sausage-and-cheese filling tucked into each slice.

> **2 packages (1/4 ounce *each*) active dry yeast**
> **1-1/4 cups warm water (110° to 115°)**
> **2 tablespoons sugar**
> **1-1/2 teaspoons salt**
> **1 teaspoon Italian seasoning**
> **1 egg**
> **1/4 cup butter, softened**
> **4 to 4-1/2 cups all-purpose flour**
> **1 pound bulk hot pork sausage**
> **1 cup (4 ounces) shredded part-skim mozzarella or cheddar cheese**
> **GLAZE:**
> **1 egg**

1. In a large mixing bowl, dissolve yeast in water. Add sugar, salt, Italian seasoning, 1 egg, butter and 2 cups flour; beat until smooth. Add enough remaining flour to form a soft dough.

2. Turn onto a floured surface; knead until smooth and elastic, about 6-8 minutes. Place in a greased bowl, turning once to grease top. Cover and let rise in a warm place until doubled, about 1 hour.

3. Meanwhile, in a large skillet, cook sausage until no longer pink; drain and set aside to cool.

4. Punch the dough down; divide in half. On a floured surface, roll each half into a 14-in. x 12-in. rectangle. Cut each one into three 14-in. x 4-in. strips. Combine cheese and sausage; spoon 1/2 cup down the center of each strip. Bring long edges together over filling; pinch to seal.

5. Place three strips with seam side down on greased baking sheets. Braid strips together; secure ends. Cover and let rise until doubled, about 45 minutes.

6. Beat the egg for glaze and brush over loaves. Bake at 400° for 20-25 minutes or until golden. Immediately remove from baking sheets to wire racks. Serve warm. **Yield:** 2 loaves.

✿ ✿ ✿
Apple Streusel Muffins

(Also pictured on page 148)

Elizabeth Calabrese, Yucaipa, California

I wanted to make something warm and special for my daughter before school on a rainy morning. So I jazzed up a boxed muffin mix with a chopped apple, walnuts, brown sugar and a fast-to-fix vanilla glaze. The yummy results really hit the spot.

> **1 package (6-1/2 ounces) apple cinnamon muffin mix**
> **1 large tart apple, peeled and diced**
> **1/3 cup chopped walnuts**
> **3 tablespoons brown sugar**
> **4-1/2 teaspoons all-purpose flour**
> **1 tablespoon butter, melted**
> **GLAZE:**
> **3/4 cup confectioners' sugar**
> **1/2 teaspoon vanilla extract**
> **1 to 2 tablespoons milk**

1. Prepare muffin mix according to package directions; fold in apple. Fill greased muffin cups three-fourths full.

In a small bowl, combine the walnuts, brown sugar, flour and butter; sprinkle over batter.

2. Bake at 400° for 15-20 minutes or until a toothpick comes out clean. Cool for 5 minutes before removing from pan to a wire rack. Combine the glaze ingredients; drizzle over warm muffins. **Yield:** 6 muffins.

Editor's Note: This recipe was tested with Betty Crocker apple cinnamon muffin mix.

🏵 🏵 🏵
Rhubarb Streusel Muffins

Sandra Moreside, Regina, Saskatchewan

It's a pleasure to set out a basket of these rhubarb goodies for my children and grandchildren...although the basket doesn't stay full for long! The muffins are based on a recipe for coffee cake.

1/2 cup butter, softened
1 cup packed brown sugar
1/2 cup sugar
1 egg
2 cups all-purpose flour
1 teaspoon baking powder
1/2 teaspoon baking soda
1/8 teaspoon salt
1 cup (8 ounces) sour cream
3 cups chopped fresh *or* frozen rhubarb, thawed
TOPPING:
1/2 cup chopped pecans
1/4 cup packed brown sugar
1 teaspoon ground cinnamon
1 tablespoon cold butter

1. In a large mixing bowl, cream butter and sugars. Add egg; beat well. Combine the flour, baking powder, baking soda and salt; add to creamed mixture alternately with sour cream. Fold in rhubarb. Fill paper-lined or greased muffin cups three-fourths full.

2. For topping, combine the pecans, brown sugar and cinnamon in a small bowl; cut in butter until crumbly. Sprinkle over batter. Bake at 350° for 22-25 minutes or until a toothpick comes out clean. Cool for 5 minutes before removing from pans to wire racks. **Yield:** about 1-1/2 dozen.

Editor's Note: If using frozen rhubarb, measure rhubarb while still frozen, then thaw completely. Drain in a colander, but do not press liquid out.

🏵 🏵 🏵
Whole Wheat Bread

(Also pictured on page 149)

Freida Stutman, Fillmore, New York

I like to make this bread with my mother, who got the recipe from her mother. Slices of the fresh-baked loaves are a real treat.

1 package (1/4 ounce) active dry yeast
3 cups warm water (110° to 115°), *divided*
3/4 cup vegetable oil
1/4 cup molasses
1/4 cup sugar
1 tablespoon salt
3 cups whole wheat flour
5 to 5-1/2 cups all-purpose flour

1. In a large mixing bowl, dissolve yeast in 3/4 cup water. Add the oil, molasses, sugar, salt and remaining water; mix well. Combine flours; add 3 cups to batter. Beat until smooth. Add enough remaining flour to form a firm dough.

2. Turn onto a floured surface; knead until smooth and elastic, about 6-8 minutes. Place in a greased bowl,

turning once to grease top. Cover and let rise in a warm place until doubled, about 1 hour.

3. Punch dough down. Turn onto a lightly floured surface; divide in half. Shape each portion into a loaf. Place in two greased 9-in. x 5-in. x 3-in. loaf pans. Cover and let rise until doubled, about 30 minutes.

4. Bake at 350° for 40-45 minutes or until golden brown. Remove from pans to cool on wire racks. **Yield:** 2 loaves.

🎖🎖🎖
Sesame Onion Braid

Patrice Stribling Donald, Edwardsville, Illinois

Convenient soup mix gives mild onion flavor to this stunning loaf, which is even more delicious spread with the accompanying butter. As a music professor/conductor, I sometimes share this bread with my musicians to give us all an energy boost!

> 1 package (1/4 ounce) active dry yeast
> 1-1/4 cups warm water (110° to 115°), *divided*
> 1 cup warm sour cream (110° to 115°)
> 3 eggs
> 1 envelope onion soup mix
> 2 tablespoons butter, softened
> 2 tablespoons sugar
> 2 teaspoons salt
> 1/4 teaspoon baking soda
> 6-1/2 to 6-3/4 cups all-purpose flour
> 1 tablespoon cold water
> 3 tablespoons sesame seeds

CARAMELIZED ONION BUTTER:

> 1 tablespoon diced onion
> 6 tablespoons butter, softened, *divided*
> 1 garlic clove, minced
> 1 package (3 ounces) cream cheese, cubed
> 1/2 teaspoon minced fresh parsley

1. In a large mixing bowl, dissolve yeast in 1/4 cup warm water; let stand for 5 minutes. Add sour cream, 2 eggs, onion soup mix, butter, sugar, salt, baking soda and remaining warm water; mix well. Stir in enough flour to form a soft dough.

2. Turn onto a floured surface; knead until smooth and elastic, about 6-8 minutes. Place dough in a greased bowl, turning once to grease top. Cover and let rise in a warm place until doubled, about 1 hour.

3. Punch dough down. Turn onto a lightly floured surface; divide into six portions. Shape each into a 15-in. rope. Place three ropes on a greased baking sheet; braid. Pinch ends to seal; tuck under. Repeat. Cover and let rise until doubled, about 1 hour.

4. Beat cold water and remaining egg; brush over dough. Sprinkle with sesame seeds. Bake at 350° for 35-40 minutes or until golden brown.

5. In large skillet, saute onion in 1 tablespoon butter until golden brown. Add garlic; cook 1-2 minutes longer or until golden.

6. In a large mixing bowl, beat the cream cheese, onion mixture, parsley and remaining butter until creamy. Serve with bread. **Yield:** 2 loaves (2/3 cup butter).

🎀🎀🎀
Poteca Nut Roll

Mrs. Anthony Setta, Saegertown, Pennsylvania

This traditional Yugoslavian treat has a wonderful walnut filling. You'll need a large surface for rolling out the dough.

   1 **package (1/4 ounce) active dry yeast**
 1/4 **cup warm water (110° to 115°)**
 3/4 **cup warm milk (110° to 115°)**
 1/4 **cup sugar**
   1 **teaspoon salt**
   1 **egg, lightly beaten**
 1/4 **cup shortening**
   3 **to 3-1/2 cups all-purpose flour**
FILLING:
 1/2 **cup butter, softened**
   1 **cup packed brown sugar**
   2 **eggs, lightly beaten**
   1 **teaspoon vanilla extract**
   1 **teaspoon lemon extract, optional**
   4 **cups ground or finely chopped walnuts**
Milk
 1/2 **cup confectioners' sugar, optional**

1. In a large mixing bowl, dissolve yeast in warm water. Add the milk, sugar, salt, egg, shortening and 1-1/2 cups flour; beat until smooth. Add enough remaining flour to form a soft dough.

2. Turn onto a floured surface; knead until smooth and elastic, about 6-8 minutes. Place in a greased bowl,

turning once to grease top. Cover and let rise in a warm place until doubled, about 1 hour.

3. Punch down. Turn onto a lightly floured surface; roll into a 30-in. x 20-in. rectangle. In a bowl, combine the butter, brown sugar, eggs, vanilla, lemon extract if desired and nuts. Add milk until mixture reaches spreading consistency, about 1/2 cup. Spread over rectangle to within 1 in. of edges.

4. Roll up jelly-roll style, starting with a long side; pinch seams and ends to seal. Place on a greased baking sheet; shape into a tight spiral. Cover and let rise until nearly doubled, about 1 hour.

5. Bake at 350° for 35 minutes or until golden brown. Remove from pan to a wire rack to cool. If desired, combine confectioners' sugar and enough milk to make a thin glaze; brush over roll. **Yield:** 1 coffee cake.

🎀🎀🎀
Brown Sugar Oat Muffins

Regina Stock, Topeka, Kansas

These scrumptious, hearty muffins are great to have for breakfast, as a pick-me-up in the afternoon or as a late-night snack with a cup of hot cocoa. The recipe is so simple that I can bake a fresh-from-the-oven batch in no time.

   1 **cup old-fashioned oats**
   1 **cup whole wheat flour**
 1/2 **cup all-purpose flour**
   2 **teaspoons baking powder**
 1/2 **teaspoon salt**
   2 **eggs**
 3/4 **cup packed brown sugar**
 3/4 **cup milk**
 1/4 **cup vegetable oil**
   1 **teaspoon vanilla extract**

1. In a small bowl, combine the oats, flours, baking powder and salt. In another small bowl, beat the eggs, brown sugar, milk, oil and vanilla. Stir into the dry ingredients just until moistened.

2. Fill greased or paper-lined muffin cups two-thirds full. Bake at 400° for 15-17 minutes or until a toothpick comes out clean. Cool for 5 minutes before removing from pan to a wire rack. **Yield:** 1 dozen.

🎀🎀🎀
Herbed Cheese Ring

Evelyn Bear, Kingston, Idaho

This savory cheese loaf is terrific sliced in thin wedges to go with soup, salads or casseroles. I've served it to large crowds and even given it as a Christmas gift.

> 1 package (1/4 ounce) active dry yeast
> 1/4 cup warm water (110° to 115°)
> 1 cup warm milk (110° to 115°)
> 1/4 cup vegetable oil
> 2 tablespoons honey
> 1 egg
> 1 teaspoon salt
> 1 cup whole wheat flour
> 2-1/2 cups all-purpose flour
> 1 teaspoon *each* dried oregano, basil and rosemary, crushed

FILLING:
> 1-1/2 cups (6 ounces) shredded cheddar cheese
> 1/2 teaspoon dried parsley flakes
> 1/4 teaspoon garlic powder
> 1/4 teaspoon paprika

TOPPING:
> 1 egg, beaten
> 2 teaspoons sesame seeds
> 4 teaspoons grated Parmesan cheese

1. In a large mixing bowl, dissolve yeast in warm water. Add milk, oil, honey, egg, salt, whole wheat flour, 1 cup all-purpose flour and herbs; beat until blended. Stir in enough remaining all-purpose flour to form a soft dough. Cover and refrigerate overnight.

2. Punch dough down and turn onto a floured surface; divide in half. Roll one portion into a 15-in. x 10-in. rectangle. Combine filling ingredients; sprinkle half over dough. Roll up jelly-roll style, starting with a long side; pinch seams to seal.

3. Place seam side down on a greased baking sheet; pinch ends together to form a ring. With a sharp knife, cut 1/2-in. slashes at 2-in. intervals. Repeat with remaining dough and filling. Cover and let rise in a warm place until doubled, about 30 minutes.

4. Brush each ring with egg; sprinkle with sesame seeds and Parmesan. Bake at 350° for 20-25 minutes or until golden brown. Remove from pans to wire racks. **Yield:** 2 loaves.

🎀🎀🎀
Pecan Pear Muffins

Laura Ward, Las Vegas, Nevada

When you have an abundance of fresh pears, pull out this recipe. Chock-full of down-home goodness, the moist treats are wonderful with a glass of cold milk or a steaming cup of coffee.

> 3 cups all-purpose flour
> 2 cups sugar
> 2 teaspoons baking soda
> 1 teaspoon ground cinnamon
> 1/2 teaspoon salt
> 2 eggs
> 1 cup vegetable oil
> 1 teaspoon vanilla extract
> 4 cups chopped peeled ripe pears (about 6 medium)
> 1 cup chopped pecans

1. In a large bowl, combine the flour, sugar, baking soda, cinnamon and salt. In another bowl, combine the eggs, oil and vanilla; stir into dry ingredients just until moistened. Fold in the pears and pecans.

2. Fill paper-lined muffin cups two-thirds full. Bake at 350° for 25-30 minutes or until a toothpick comes out clean. Cool for 5 minutes before removing from pans to wire racks. **Yield:** about 2 dozen.

🎀🎀🎀 Rosemary Garlic Braid

Cori Oakley, Traverse City, Michigan

This attractive, flavorful bread pairs nicely with a variety of soups and main dishes. It also makes a delicious grilled ham and cheese sandwich. I created the recipe when I wanted to use up the fresh rosemary in my garden.

- **5 whole garlic bulbs**
- **2 teaspoons olive oil**
- **1/4 cup minced fresh rosemary *or* 4 teaspoons dried rosemary, crushed**
- **1 tablespoon chicken broth**
- **9 to 9-1/2 cups bread flour**
- **1/2 cup sugar**
- **3 packages (1/4 ounce *each*) quick-rise yeast**
- **3 teaspoons salt**
- **1-1/2 cups milk**
- **1 cup water**
- **3/4 cup butter, *divided***
- **1 egg**
- **1-1/2 teaspoons garlic salt**

1. Remove papery outer skin from garlic (do not peel or separate cloves). Cut top off garlic heads, leaving root end intact. Place cut side up in a small baking dish. Brush with oil; sprinkle with rosemary.

2. Cover and bake at 425° for 30-35 minutes or until softened. Cool for 10 minutes; squeeze softened garlic into a bowl. Add broth; lightly mash.

3. In a large mixing bowl, combine 3 cups flour, sugar, yeast and salt. In a saucepan, heat milk, water and 1/2 cup butter to 120°-130°. Add to dry ingredients; beat just until moistened. Beat in egg and garlic paste until smooth. Stir in enough remaining flour to form a soft dough (dough will be sticky). Turn onto a floured surface; knead until smooth and elastic, about 6-8 minutes. Cover and let rest for 10 minutes.

4. Turn dough onto a lightly floured surface; divide into thirds. Divide each portion into three pieces; shape each into an 18-in. rope. Place three ropes on a greased baking sheet and braid; pinch ends to seal and tuck under. Repeat with remaining dough. Cover and let rise in a warm place until doubled, about 30 minutes.

5. Bake at 350° for 15 minutes. Melt remaining butter; add garlic salt. Brush over bread. Bake 10-15 minutes longer or until golden brown. Remove from pans to wire racks to cool. **Yield:** 3 loaves.

🎀🎀🎀 Sausage Swiss Muffins

Patsy Spires, Cheshire, Ohio

Sage and thyme really perk up these tasty sausage bites made with a baking mix. I like to keep a few muffins in the refrigerator because they're perfect for a quick breakfast.

- **8 ounces pork sausage**
- **1-3/4 cups biscuit/baking mix**
- **3/4 teaspoon rubbed sage**
- **1/4 teaspoon dried thyme**
- **1 egg**
- **1/2 cup milk**
- **1/2 cup shredded Swiss cheese**

1. In a small skillet, cook sausage over medium heat until no longer pink; drain. Meanwhile, in a large bowl, combine the baking mix, sage and thyme. In another bowl, combine the egg and milk; stir into dry ingredients just until moistened. Fold in the cheese and sausage.

2. Fill greased muffin cups two-thirds full. Bake at 375° for 15-18 minutes or until a toothpick comes out clean. Cool for 5 minutes before removing from pan to a wire rack. Serve warm. Refrigerate leftovers. **Yield:** 9 muffins.

Fudgy Mint Squares, p. 180

Chunky Blond Brownies, p. 184

Cherry Crunch Cookies, p. 183

Brownies, Bars & Cookies

You'll have sweet treats well in hand when you prepare the yummy goodies in this chapter, from fruit-filled diamonds and dressed-up shortbread to luscious fudge squares and Christmasy cutouts.

Blueberry Lattice Bars, p. 179

Orange Cheesecake Bars

Connie Faulkner, Moxee, Washington

I still remember the last day of first grade, when our teacher treated the class to little cups of orange sherbet and vanilla ice cream swirled together. I tried to capture that same yummy flavor when I created these layered bars.

      2 cups crushed vanilla wafers (about 40)
  1/4 cup butter, melted
      3 packages (8 ounces *each*) cream cheese, softened
      1 can (14 ounces) sweetened condensed milk
      3 eggs
      2 teaspoons vanilla extract
      2 tablespoons orange juice concentrate
      1 teaspoon grated orange peel
      1 teaspoon orange extract
      5 drops yellow food coloring
      3 drops red food coloring

1. In a large bowl, combine the wafer crumbs and butter. Press into a greased 13-in. x 9-in. x 2-in. baking pan.

2. In a large mixing bowl, beat cream cheese until smooth. Add the milk, eggs and vanilla; beat just until combined. Pour half over crust.

3. Add the orange juice concentrate, orange peel, extract and food coloring to the remaining cream cheese mixture; beat until combined. Pour over first layer.

4. Bake at 325° for 45-50 minutes or until center is almost set. Cool on a wire rack. Refrigerate for at least 2 hours before cutting. **Yield:** 3 dozen.

Mountain Cookies

Jeanne Adams, Richmond, Vermont

I've been making these deliciously different cookies for years, and people always ask for the recipe. My kids especially like the coconut filling. You'll be hard-pressed to eat just one!

      1 cup butter, softened
      1 cup confectioners' sugar
      2 teaspoons vanilla extract
      2 cups all-purpose flour
  1/2 teaspoon salt
FILLING:
      1 package (3 ounces) cream cheese, softened
      1 cup confectioners' sugar
      2 tablespoons all-purpose flour
      1 teaspoon vanilla extract
  1/2 cup finely chopped pecans
  1/2 cup flaked coconut
TOPPING:
  1/2 cup semisweet chocolate chips
      2 tablespoons butter
      2 tablespoons water
  1/2 cup confectioners' sugar

1. In a large mixing bowl, cream butter, sugar and vanilla. Combine flour and salt; gradually add to the creamed mixture and mix well.

2. Shape into 1-in. balls; place 2 in. apart on ungreased baking sheets. Make a deep indentation in the center

of each cookie. Bake at 350° for 10-12 minutes or until the edges just start to brown. Remove to wire racks to cool completely.

3. For the filling, in a large mixing bowl, beat cream cheese, sugar, flour and vanilla. Add pecans and coconut; mix well. Spoon 1/2 teaspoon into each cookie.

4. For topping, heat chocolate chips, butter and water in a small saucepan until melted. Stir in sugar. Drizzle over cookies. **Yield:** 4 dozen.

★★★
Chocolate Chip Brownies

Brenda Kelly, Ashburn, Virginia

People love these extra-rich brownies so much that I never take them anywhere without bringing copies of the recipe to hand out. I often make these goodies for picnics because I don't have to worry about frosting melting.

- 1 cup butter, softened
- 3 cups sugar
- 6 eggs
- 1 tablespoon vanilla extract
- 2-1/4 cups all-purpose flour
- 1/2 cup baking cocoa
- 1 teaspoon baking powder
- 1/2 teaspoon salt
- 1 cup (6 ounces) semisweet chocolate chips
- 1 cup vanilla *or* white chips
- 1 cup chopped walnuts

1. In a large mixing bowl, cream butter and sugar. Add eggs and vanilla; mix well. Combine flour, cocoa, baking powder and salt; stir into creamed mixture just until blended (do not overmix).

2. Pour into two greased 9-in. square baking pans. Sprinkle with chips and nuts. Bake at 350° for 30-35 minutes or until a toothpick inserted near the center comes out clean. Cool. **Yield:** 3-4 dozen.

★★★
Frosted Pumpkin Cranberry Bars

Barbara Nowakowski, Mesa, Arizona

With tangy dried cranberries tucked inside and a creamy brown butter frosting on top, these mildly spiced pumpkin treats are doubly delightful. It's a good thing the recipe makes a big batch, because one bar is never enough!

- 1-1/2 cups all-purpose flour
- 1-1/4 cups sugar
- 2 teaspoons baking powder
- 2 teaspoons ground cinnamon
- 1 teaspoon baking soda
- 1/2 teaspoon ground ginger
- 3 eggs
- 1 can (15 ounces) solid-pack pumpkin
- 3/4 cup butter, melted
- 3/4 cup chopped dried cranberries
- **BROWN BUTTER FROSTING:**
- 1/2 cup butter
- 4 cups confectioners' sugar
- 1 teaspoon vanilla extract
- 4 to 6 tablespoons milk

1. In a large bowl, combine the first six ingredients. In another bowl, whisk the eggs, pumpkin and butter; stir into dry ingredients until well combined. Stir in cranberries.

2. Spread into a greased 15-in. x 10-in. x 1-in. baking pan. Bake at 350° for 20-25 minutes or until a toothpick inserted near the center comes out clean. Cool on a wire rack.

3. For frosting, heat the butter in a saucepan over medium heat until golden brown, about 7 minutes. Remove from the heat; cool for 5 minutes. Stir in confectioners' sugar, vanilla and enough milk to achieve spreading consistency. Spread over bars before cutting. **Yield:** about 4 dozen.

⚜ ⚜ ⚜
Chocolate Cheese Layered Bars

Sharon Schaa, Murray, Iowa

These rich, nutty bars are a hit at church and family gatherings. People love the layers of chocolate and cream cheese.

- 1/2 cup butter, softened
- 1 cup sugar
- 2 eggs
- 1 square (1 ounce) unsweetened chocolate, melted
- 1 teaspoon vanilla extract
- 1 cup all-purpose flour
- 1 teaspoon baking powder
- 1/2 cup chopped pecans

CHEESE LAYER:
- 6 ounces cream cheese, softened
- 1/4 cup butter, softened
- 1/2 cup sugar
- 1 egg
- 2 tablespoons all-purpose flour
- 1/2 teaspoon vanilla extract
- 1/4 cup chopped pecans
- 1 cup (6 ounces) semisweet chocolate chips
- 3 cups miniature marshmallows

TOPPING:
- 1/4 cup butter
- 2 ounces cream cheese, softened
- 1 square (1 ounce) unsweetened chocolate
- 2 tablespoons milk
- 3 cups confectioners' sugar
- 1 teaspoon vanilla extract

1. In a large mixing bowl, cream butter and sugar. Add eggs, chocolate and vanilla; mix well. Combine flour and baking powder; stir into chocolate mixture. Fold in pecans. Pour into a greased 13-in. x 9-in. x 2-in. baking pan.

2. In a large mixing bowl, combine cream cheese and butter. Beat in the sugar, egg, flour and vanilla; mix well. Fold in pecans. Spread over the chocolate layer; sprinkle with chips.

3. Bake at 350° for 20-25 minutes or until edges pull away from sides of pan. Sprinkle with marshmallows; bake 2 minutes longer or until puffed. Spread evenly over cream cheese layer. Cool on a wire rack.

4. In a large saucepan, combine first four topping ingredients. Cook and stir over low heat until smooth. Transfer to a large mixing bowl. Add the confectioners' sugar and vanilla; beat until smooth. Spread over cooled bars. Store in the refrigerator. **Yield:** 2 dozen.

⚜ ⚜ ⚜
Mint Sandwich Cookies

Melissa Thompson, Anderson, Ohio

Canned frosting, peppermint extract and chocolate candy coating quickly turn butter-flavored crackers into these wonderful no-bake cookies. My children and I like to assemble them for parties and holiday get-togethers.

- 1 can (16 ounces) vanilla frosting
- 1/2 teaspoon peppermint extract
- 3 to 5 drops green food coloring, optional
- 72 butter-flavored crackers
- 1 pound dark chocolate candy coating, coarsely chopped

1. In a large bowl, combine the frosting, extract and food coloring if desired. Spread over half of the crackers; top with remaining crackers.

2. Place candy coating in a microwave-safe bowl. Microwave on high for 1-2 minutes or until smooth. Dip the cookies in coating. Place on waxed paper until chocolate is completely set. Store in an airtight container at room temperature. **Yield:** 3 dozen.

🏅🏅🏅
Frosted Raspberry Bars

Esther Horst, Augusta, Wisconsin

While I was visiting a friend, her daughter baked a batch of these tempting treats. After one bite, I knew I had to have the recipe! The cake-like bars have a luscious raspberry layer and sweet drizzled frosting.

    1 **cup butter, softened**
1/4 **cup sugar**
    3 **cups all-purpose flour**
    3 **teaspoons baking powder**
    1 **teaspoon salt**
    2 **eggs**
1/2 **cup milk**
    1 **teaspoon vanilla extract**
    1 **can (21 ounces) raspberry pie filling**
FROSTING:
    1 **tablespoon butter, softened**
    1 **tablespoon shortening**
    1 **ounce cream cheese, softened**
    2 **tablespoons marshmallow creme**
1/2 **cup plus 1 tablespoon confectioners' sugar**
    1 **tablespoon milk**

1. In a large mixing bowl, cream the butter and sugar. Combine the flour, baking powder and salt. Combine the eggs, milk and vanilla. Add the dry ingredients to the creamed mixture alternately with the egg mixture; mix well. Divide the dough in half; chill for 2 hours or until firm.

2. Roll out one portion of dough into a 15-in. x 10-in. rectangle; carefully transfer to a greased 15-in. x 10-in. x 1-in. baking pan. Spread with raspberry filling.

3. Roll out remaining dough to 1/4-in. thickness. Cut into 1/2-in.-wide strips; make a lattice crust over filling. Bake at 350° for 30 minutes or until golden brown. Cool on a wire rack.

4. In a large mixing bowl, beat the butter, shortening, cream cheese and marshmallow creme until smooth. Add the confectioners' sugar and milk; mix well. Drizzle over bars. Refrigerate until set before cutting. **Yield:** about 2 dozen.

Rhubarb-Filled Cookies

Pauline Bondy, Grand Forks, North Dakota

I won a blue ribbon at our local fair for these tender, pretty treats. When not just any cookie will do, try making these and watch the smiles appear.

   1 cup butter, softened
   1 cup sugar
   1 cup packed brown sugar
   4 eggs
4-1/2 cups all-purpose flour
   1 teaspoon baking soda
   1 teaspoon salt

FILLING:
3-1/2 cups chopped fresh *or* frozen rhubarb, thawed
1-1/2 cups sugar
   6 tablespoons water, *divided*
 1/4 cup cornstarch
   1 teaspoon vanilla extract

1. In a mixing bowl, cream butter and sugars. Add eggs, one at a time, beating well after each addition. Combine the flour, baking soda and salt; gradually add to creamed mixture and mix well (dough will be sticky).

2. For filling, combine the rhubarb, sugar and 2 tablespoons water in a large saucepan; bring to a boil. Reduce heat; simmer, uncovered, for 10 minutes or until thickened, stirring frequently. Combine cornstarch and remaining water until smooth; stir into rhubarb mixture. Bring to a boil; cook and stir for 2 minutes or until thickened. Remove from the heat; stir in vanilla.

3. Drop dough by tablespoonfuls 2 in. apart onto ungreased baking sheets. Using the end of a wooden spoon handle, make an indentation in the center of each cookie; fill with a rounded teaspoon of filling. Top with 1/2 teaspoon of dough, allowing some filling to show. Bake at 375° for 8–10 minutes or until lightly browned. **Yield:** about 4-1/2 dozen.

Editor's Note: If using frozen rhubarb, measure rhubarb while still frozen, then thaw completely. Drain in a colander, but do not press liquid out.

Cherry Cocoa Shortbread Squares

Bettie Martin, Oneida, Wisconsin

Whenever there's a potluck at work or a family gathering, I'm asked to bring these delectable bars. I found the recipe years ago and have made it countless times since.

1/2 cup plus 2 tablespoons butter, softened, *divided*
1/4 cup sugar
   1 cup all-purpose flour
   2 tablespoons baking cocoa
   2 cups confectioners' sugar
   2 tablespoons milk
1/2 teaspoon vanilla extract
 18 maraschino cherries, halved
GLAZE:
   1 square (1 ounce) unsweetened chocolate
1-1/2 teaspoons butter

1. In a large mixing bowl, cream 1/2 cup butter and sugar. Beat in flour and cocoa (mixture will be crumbly). Spread into a greased 9-in. square baking pan. Bake at 350° for 15 minutes or until surface is set. Cool on a wire rack for 15 minutes.

2. Meanwhile, in a large mixing bowl, combine confectioners' sugar and remaining butter; beat in milk and vanilla until smooth. Spread over crust. Pat cherries dry with a paper towel; arrange over frosting and press down gently.

3. In a microwave-safe bowl, melt chocolate and butter; stir until smooth. Drizzle over cherries. Refrigerate until glaze has hardened. Cut into squares. **Yield:** 3 dozen.

✿ ✿ ✿
Almond Raspberry Stars

Darlene Weaver, Lebanon, Pennsylvania

Guests will think you bought these impressive-looking goodies at a gourmet bakery. With a star shape and ruby-red jam, the cookies are festive for Christmas.

3/4 cup butter
1/2 cup confectioners' sugar
1 teaspoon vanilla extract
1/2 teaspoon almond extract
1-3/4 cups plus 2 tablespoons all-purpose flour
2 tablespoons finely chopped almonds
1 tablespoon sugar
1/2 teaspoon ground cinnamon
1 egg white, lightly beaten
1/3 cup raspberry jam

1. In a large mixing bowl, cream the butter and confectioners' sugar until light and fluffy. Beat in extracts. Stir in flour. Shape into a ball; cover and chill for 15 minutes.

2. On a lightly floured surface, roll dough to a 1/4-in. thickness. Cut into about 72 stars, half 2-1/2 in. and half 1-1/2 in. Combine almonds, sugar and cinnamon. Brush small stars with egg white and immediately sprinkle with cinnamon-sugar mixture. Leave large stars plain.

3. Place 1 in. apart on ungreased baking sheets. Bake small stars at 350° for 10 minutes and large stars for 12 minutes or until the tips just begin to brown. Cool on wire racks.

4. To assemble, spread enough jam over large stars to cover the center. Top each with a small star; press lightly (jam should show around edge of small stars). Let jam set before storing. **Yield:** about 3 dozen.

✿ ✿ ✿
Chocolate Chip Graham Bars

Sandi Michalski, Macy, Indiana

These chewy, moist bars are a satisfying snack any time of day. Packed with oats, chocolate chips, crunchy peanuts and graham cereal, they have something for everyone.

3/4 cup butter, softened
3/4 cup sugar
3/4 cup packed brown sugar
2 eggs
1 teaspoon vanilla extract
1-1/2 cups all-purpose flour
1-1/2 cups Golden Grahams, crushed
3/4 cup plus 2 tablespoons quick-cooking oats, *divided*
1 teaspoon baking soda
1/2 teaspoon baking powder
1/2 teaspoon salt
1 cup salted peanuts, *divided*
1 cup (6 ounces) semisweet chocolate chips, *divided*

1. In a large mixing bowl, cream butter and sugars. Add eggs, one at a time, beating well after each addition. Beat in vanilla. Combine the flour, cereal, 3/4 cup oats, baking soda, baking powder and salt; gradually add to creamed mixture. Stir in 3/4 cup peanuts and 2/3 cup chocolate chips.

2. Spread into a greased 13-in. x 9-in. x 2-in. baking pan. Coarsely chop remaining peanuts; sprinkle over the top with remaining oats and chips. Bake at 350° for 25-30 minutes or until golden brown. Cool on a wire rack. Cut into bars. **Yield:** 2 dozen.

🎗️ 🎗️ 🎗️

Walnut Horn Cookies

Sharon Allen, Allentown, Pennsylvania

At our house, it just wouldn't be Christmas without a batch of these Pennsylvania Dutch treats. The nutty cookies are known locally as "kiffels."

  1 **pound butter, softened**
  2 **packages (one 8 ounces, one 3 ounces) cream cheese, softened**
  4 **egg yolks**
4-1/4 **cups all-purpose flour**
FILLING:
  4 **cups ground walnuts (about 1 pound)**
5-3/4 **cups confectioners' sugar,** *divided*
  4 **egg whites**
 1/2 **teaspoon vanilla extract**
 1/2 **teaspoon almond extract**

1. In a large mixing bowl, combine butter, cream cheese, egg yolks and flour; beat until smooth. Shape into 1-in. balls; place in a container with waxed paper separating each layer. Cover and refrigerate overnight.

2. For filling, combine walnuts and 3-3/4 cups sugar (the mixture will be dry). In a small mixing bowl, beat egg whites until soft peaks form; fold into nut mixture. Add extracts and a few drops of water if necessary until filling reaches a spreading consistency.

3. Place remaining sugar in a bowl; roll cream cheese balls in sugar until completely covered. Place a few balls at a time between two sheets of waxed paper.

4. Roll balls into 2-1/2-in. circles. Gently spread about 2 teaspoons of filling over each. Roll up; place seam side down on ungreased baking sheets. Curve the ends slightly. Bake at 350° for 20 minutes or until lightly browned. Cool on wire racks. **Yield:** about 8 dozen.

✿✿✿
Peanut Butter Squares

Rachel Keller, Roanoke, Virginia

As a child, I spent a lot of time in the kitchen with my mom and grandmother making all kinds of old-fashioned desserts. This scrumptious recipe, which combines peanut butter and chocolate, is one I adapted.

> 3/4 cup cold butter, cubed
> 2 squares (1 ounce *each*) semisweet chocolate
> 1-1/2 cups graham cracker crumbs (about 24 squares)
> 1 cup flaked coconut
> 1/2 cup chopped salted peanuts
> 1/4 cup toasted wheat germ

FILLING:
> 2 packages (8 ounces *each*) cream cheese, softened
> 3/4 cup sugar
> 2/3 cup chunky peanut butter
> 1 teaspoon vanilla extract

TOPPING:
> 4 squares (1 ounce *each*) semisweet chocolate
> 1/4 cup butter, cubed

1. In a microwave-safe bowl, heat butter and chocolate on high for 1 minute; stir. Microwave 30-60 seconds longer or until melted; stir until smooth. Stir in cracker crumbs, coconut, peanuts and wheat germ. Press into a greased 13-in. x 9-in. x 2-in. pan. Cover and refrigerate for at least 30 minutes.

2. In a small mixing bowl, combine filling ingredients; mix well. Spread over crust. Cover and refrigerate for at least 30 minutes.

3. In a microwave-safe bowl, heat the chocolate and butter on high for 45 seconds; stir. Microwave 30 seconds longer or until melted; stir until smooth. Pour over filling. Cover and refrigerate for at least 30 minutes or until topping is set. Cut into squares. Refrigerate leftovers. **Yield:** 4 dozen.

Editor's Note: This recipe was tested with an 850-watt microwave.

✿✿✿
Double Chip Cheesecake Bars

Beth Allard, Belmont, New Hampshire

I love to cook in my spare time, and sometimes I do a little experimenting to come up with my own recipes. I got creative one afternoon with my baking, and these rich cheesecake squares were the yummy result.

> 2 cups all-purpose flour
> 1/2 cup confectioners' sugar
> 1 cup cold butter

FILLING:
> 2 packages (8 ounces *each*) cream cheese, softened
> 1/2 cup packed brown sugar
> 2 eggs
> 1 teaspoon almond extract
> 1 cup (6 ounces) semisweet chocolate chips, *divided*
> 1/2 cup butterscotch chips
> 1/2 cup chopped walnuts

1. In a large bowl, combine flour and confectioners' sugar. Cut in butter until mixture resembles coarse crumbs. Press into an ungreased 13-in. x 9-in. x 2-in. baking pan. Bake at 350° for 18-22 minutes or until lightly browned.

2. Meanwhile, in a large mixing bowl, beat cream cheese and brown sugar until smooth. Add eggs and extract; beat on low speed just until combined. Stir in 1/2 cup chocolate chips, butterscotch chips and walnuts. Spread over crust. Sprinkle with the remaining chocolate chips.

3. Bake at 350° for 20-25 minutes or until center is almost set. Cool completely on a wire rack before cutting. Refrigerate leftovers. **Yield:** 3 dozen.

🎗️🎗️🎗️ Brownie Kiss Cupcakes

Pamela Lute, Mercersburg, Pennsylvania

It's fun to prepare and share these individual brownie "cup-cakes." Each one has a surprise center—a milk chocolate kiss—that delights young and old alike.

- 1/3 cup butter, softened
- 1 cup sugar
- 2 eggs
- 1 teaspoon vanilla extract
- 3/4 cup all-purpose flour
- 1/2 cup baking cocoa
- 1/4 teaspoon baking powder
- 1/4 teaspoon salt
- 9 milk chocolate kisses

1. In a large mixing bowl, cream butter and sugar. Beat in eggs and vanilla; mix well. Combine flour, cocoa, baking powder and salt; add to the creamed mixture and mix well.

2. Fill paper- or foil-lined muffin cups two-thirds full. Place a chocolate kiss, tip end down, in the center of each. Bake at 350° for 20-25 minutes or until top of brownie springs back when lightly touched. **Yield:** 9 cupcakes.

🎗️🎗️🎗️ Meringue Candy Canes

Anne Lindway, Indianapolis, Indiana

These red-and-white striped treats get lots of compliments for their cute look and mint flavor. The Christmasy confections are easy to make and so light that they melt in your mouth.

✓ Uses less fat, sugar or salt. Includes Nutrition Facts and Diabetic Exchanges.

- 3 egg whites
- 1/2 teaspoon cream of tartar
- 3/4 cup sugar
- 1/4 teaspoon peppermint extract
- Red paste food coloring

1. In a large mixing bowl, beat egg whites until foamy. Add cream of tartar; beat on medium speed until soft peaks form. Gradually add sugar, 1 tablespoon at a time, beating on high until stiff peaks form and sugar is dissolved, about 6 minutes. Beat in peppermint extract.

2. Cut a small hole in the corner of a pastry bag; insert star tip #21. On the inside of the bag, brush three evenly spaced 1/4-in. strips of red food coloring from the tip to three-fourths of the way to the top of the bag. Carefully fill bag with meringue.

3. Pipe 3-in. candy canes onto parchment-lined baking sheets. Bake at 225° for 25 minutes; rotate baking sheets to a different oven rack. Bake 25 minutes longer or until firm to the touch. Turn oven off; leave cookies in oven with door ajar for at least 1 hour or until cool. **Yield:** 4 dozen.

Nutrition Facts: 1 cookie equals 13 calories, 0 fat (0 saturated fat), 0 cholesterol, 3 mg sodium, 3 g carbohydrate, 0 fiber, trace protein. **Diabetic Exchange:** Free food.

Frosted Ginger Cookies

Jeanne Matteson, South Dayton, New York

Baking is one of the things I do in the evening to relax. The wonderful aroma of these soft spiced cookies in our oven is irresistible, and they taste just as good.

1-1/2 cups butter, softened
   1 cup sugar
   1 cup packed brown sugar
   2 eggs
  1/2 cup molasses
   2 teaspoons vanilla extract
4-1/2 cups all-purpose flour
   1 tablespoon ground ginger
   2 teaspoons baking soda
   2 teaspoons ground cinnamon
  1/2 teaspoon salt
  1/2 teaspoon ground cloves
FROSTING:
  1/3 cup packed brown sugar
  1/4 cup milk
   2 tablespoons butter
   2 cups confectioners' sugar
  1/2 teaspoon vanilla extract
Pinch salt

1. In a large mixing bowl, cream butter and sugars. Add the eggs, one at a time, beating well after each addition. Stir in molasses and vanilla; mix well. Combine dry ingredients; gradually add to creamed mixture.

2. Drop by tablespoonfuls 2 in. apart onto ungreased baking sheets. Bake at 325° for 12-15 minutes or until cookies spring back when touched lightly (do not overbake). Remove to wire racks.

3. For frosting, in a medium saucepan, bring brown sugar, milk and butter to a boil; boil for 1 minute, stirring constantly. Remove from the heat (mixture will look curdled at first). Cool for 3 minutes. Add confectioners' sugar, vanilla and salt; mix well. Frost warm cookies. **Yield:** about 6 dozen.

Blueberry Lattice Bars

(Also pictured on page 169)

Debbie Ayers, Baileyville, Maine

Our area has an annual blueberry festival, and my daughters and I are always looking for new berry recipes to enter in the cooking contest. These lovely, yummy bars won a blue ribbon.

   1 cup butter, softened
  1/2 cup sugar
   1 egg
2-3/4 cups all-purpose flour
  1/2 teaspoon vanilla extract
  1/4 teaspoon salt
FILLING:
   3 cups fresh *or* frozen blueberries
   1 cup sugar
   3 tablespoons cornstarch

1. In a large mixing bowl, cream butter and sugar. Add the egg, flour, vanilla and salt; mix well. Cover and refrigerate for 2 hours.

2. Meanwhile, in a saucepan, bring the blueberries, sugar and cornstarch to a boil. Cook and stir for 2 minutes or until thickened.

3. Roll two-thirds of the dough into a 14-in. x 10-in. rectangle. Place in a greased 13-in. x 9-in. x 2-in. baking dish. Top with filling. Roll out remaining dough to 1/4-in. thickness. Cut into 1/2-in.-wide strips; make a lattice crust over filling.

4. Bake at 375° for 30-35 minutes or until top is golden brown. Cool on a wire rack. Cut into bars. **Yield:** 2 dozen.

Coconut Washboards

Tommie Sue Shaw, McAlester, Oklahoma

This traditional coconut cookie is simple to fix yet tastes special. Pressing a fork into the top of the dough creates the look of an old-fashioned washboard.

- 1/2 cup butter, softened
- 1/2 cup shortening
- 2 cups packed brown sugar
- 2 eggs
- 1/4 cup water
- 1 teaspoon vanilla extract
- 4 cups all-purpose flour
- 1-1/2 teaspoons baking powder
- 1/2 teaspoon baking soda
- 1/4 teaspoon salt
- 1 cup flaked coconut

1. In a large mixing bowl, cream butter, shortening and sugar until light and fluffy. Beat in eggs. Gradually add water and vanilla; mix well. Combine the flour, baking powder, baking soda and salt; add to the creamed mixture and mix well. Fold in coconut. Cover and refrigerate for 2-4 hours.

2. Shape into 1-in. balls. Place 2 in. apart on greased baking sheets; flatten with fingers into 2-1/2-in. x 1-in. rectangle shapes. Press lengthwise with a floured fork. Bake at 400° for 8-10 minutes or until lightly browned. Cool 2 minutes before removing to a wire rack to cool completely. **Yield:** 9 dozen.

Fudgy Mint Squares

(Also pictured on page 168)

Heather Campbell, Lawrence, Kansas

I've had this recipe since I was in junior high school. No one can resist the fudgy brownie base, minty cheesecake filling and chocolate glaze in these mouth-watering bars.

- 10 tablespoons butter, *divided*
- 3 squares (1 ounce *each*) unsweetened chocolate, chopped
- 3 eggs

- 1-1/2 cups sugar
- 2 teaspoons vanilla extract
- 1 cup all-purpose flour
- 1 package (8 ounces) cream cheese, softened
- 1 tablespoon cornstarch
- 1 can (14 ounces) sweetened condensed milk
- 1 teaspoon peppermint extract
- 4 drops green food coloring, optional
- 1 cup (6 ounces) semisweet chocolate chips
- 1/2 cup heavy whipping cream

1. In a microwave-safe bowl, melt 8 tablespoons butter and unsweetened chocolate; cool slightly. In a small mixing bowl, beat 2 eggs, sugar and vanilla. Add the chocolate mixture; mix until blended. Gradually beat in flour. Spread into a greased 13-in. x 9-in. x 2-in. baking pan. Bake at 350° for 15-20 minutes or until top is set.

2. In a large mixing bowl, beat cream cheese and remaining butter. Add cornstarch; beat until smooth. Gradually beat in milk and remaining egg. Add extract and food coloring if desired. Pour over crust. Bake for 15-20 minutes or until center is almost set. Cool on a wire rack.

3. In a heavy saucepan, combine chocolate chips and cream. Cook and stir over medium heat until chips are melted. Cool for 30 minutes or until lukewarm, stirring occasionally. Pour over cream cheese layer. Chill for 2 hours or until set before cutting. **Yield:** about 4 dozen.

Cranberry Chip Cookies

Betty Albee, Buhl, Idaho

Chock-full of cranberries, chocolate chips and nuts, these cookies have delectable flavor. They offer a change of pace from traditional Christmas cookies...but you won't want to wait until December to make them. My family requests them year-round.

   1 **cup butter, softened**
   1 **cup sugar**
   2 **egg yolks**
   1 **teaspoon vanilla extract**
2-1/4 **cups all-purpose flour**
  1/2 **teaspoon baking powder**
  1/4 **teaspoon salt**
1-1/2 **cups (9 ounces) semisweet chocolate chips**
1-1/2 **cups dried cranberries**
  3/4 **cup chopped pecans**
  1/2 **cup English toffee bits *or* almond brickle chips, optional**

1. In a large mixing bowl, cream butter and sugar. Add egg yolks and vanilla; mix well. Combine the flour, baking powder and salt; gradually add to the creamed mixture and mix well. Stir in chocolate chips, cranberries, pecans and toffee bits if desired (dough will be stiff).

2. Drop by rounded tablespoonfuls 2 in. apart onto ungreased baking sheets. Flatten slightly. Bake at 350° for 11-14 minutes or until set and edges are lightly browned. Cool for 2 minutes before removing to wire racks. **Yield:** about 6 dozen.

🎗🎗🎗
Sugared Raisin Pear Diamonds

Jeanne Allen, Rye, Colorado

With their tender golden crust and tempting pear-and-raisin filling, these fabulous bars cut into diamond shapes really stand out on buffet tables. Substitute apples for the pears, and the results will be just as yummy.

  2-1/2 cups plus 4-1/2 teaspoons all-purpose flour, *divided*
    1/4 cup plus 6 tablespoons sugar, *divided*
    1/2 teaspoon salt
    3/4 cup cold butter
    1/2 teaspoon grated lemon peel
    1/2 cup half-and-half cream
      6 cups diced peeled ripe pears (about 7)
      6 tablespoons golden raisins
    1/4 cup lemon juice
    1/8 to 1/4 teaspoon ground cinnamon
      1 egg, lightly beaten
Additional sugar

1. In a bowl, combine 2-1/2 cups flour, 1/4 cup sugar and salt. Cut in butter and lemon peel until the mixture resembles coarse crumbs. Gradually add cream, tossing with a fork until dough forms a ball.

2. Divide in half. Roll out one portion of dough onto lightly floured waxed paper or pastry cloth into a 16-in. x 11-1/2-in. rectangle. Transfer to an ungreased 15-in. x 10-in. x 1-in. baking pan.

3. Bake at 350° for 10-15 minutes or until lightly browned. Cool on a wire rack. Increase temperature to 400°.

4. In a bowl, combine the pears, raisins, lemon juice, cinnamon and remaining flour and sugar. Spread over crust. Roll out remaining dough into a 16-in. x 12-in. rectangle; place over filling. Trim and seal edges. Brush top with egg; sprinkle with additional sugar.

5. Bake for 30-34 minutes or until golden brown. Cool on a wire rack. Cut into diamond-shaped bars. **Yield:** about 2 dozen.

🎗🎗🎗
Peanut Mallow Bars

Janice Huelsmann, Trenton, Illinois

Kids of all ages gobble up these sweet snacks, which taste like Payday candy bars. Not only do these treats beat the clock when time is tight, but they're great additions to bake sales.

    1 package (18-1/4 ounces) yellow cake mix
    2 tablespoons water
  1/3 cup butter, softened
    1 egg
    4 cups miniature marshmallows
PEANUT TOPPING:
    1 package (10 ounces) peanut butter chips
  2/3 cup light corn syrup
  1/4 cup butter, cubed
    2 teaspoons vanilla extract
    2 cups crisp rice cereal
    2 cups salted peanuts

1. In a large mixing bowl, beat the cake mix, water, butter and egg until blended (batter will be thick). Spread into a greased 13-in. x 9-in. x 2-in. baking pan.

2. Bake at 350° for 22-25 minutes or until a toothpick inserted near the center comes out clean. Sprinkle with marshmallows. Bake 2 minutes longer. Place on a wire rack while preparing topping.

3. In a large saucepan, combine the peanut butter chips, corn syrup and butter; cook and stir over medium-low heat until melted and smooth. Remove from the heat; stir in vanilla, cereal and peanuts. Spread over marshmallows. Cool completely. **Yield:** 2-1/2 dozen.

Caramel Chip Bars

LaDonna Reed, Ponca City, Oklahoma

This recipe turns a yellow cake mix into something rich and special. We like eating the chocolaty bars when they're cold, right out of the refrigerator. I think they're best with a tall glass of milk.

    1/2 cup butter
     32 caramels
      1 can (14 ounces) sweetened condensed milk
      1 package (18-1/4 ounces) yellow cake mix
    1/2 cup vegetable oil
      2 eggs
      2 cups miniature semisweet chocolate chips
      1 cup vanilla *or* white chips
      1 Heath candy bar (1.4 ounces), chopped

1. In a large saucepan, combine the butter, caramels and sweetened condensed milk; cook and stir over medium-low heat until smooth. Cool.

2. In a large mixing bowl, combine the cake mix, oil and eggs; mix well. Stir in chips and chopped candy bar (dough will be stiff). Press three-fourths into a greased 13-in. x 9-in. x 2-in. baking pan. Bake at 350° for 15 minutes. Place on a wire rack for 10 minutes.

3. Pour caramel mixture over the crust. Drop remaining dough by spoonfuls onto caramel layer. Bake for 25-30 minutes or until edges are golden brown. Cool for 10 minutes; run a knife around edges of pan. Cool 40 minutes longer; cover and refrigerate for at least 1 hour or until serving. **Yield:** 2 dozen.

Cherry Crunch Cookies

(Also pictured on page 168)

Lora Reynolds, Grants Pass, Oregon

These crispy cookies provide a nice change of pace from the traditional chocolate chip, sugar and peanut butter varieties. The crushed cornflakes make a pretty coating.

    3/4 cup butter, softened
      1 cup sugar
      2 eggs
      2 tablespoons milk
      1 teaspoon vanilla extract
  2-1/4 cups all-purpose flour
      1 teaspoon baking powder
    1/2 teaspoon salt
    1/2 teaspoon baking soda
      1 cup chopped pecans
      1 cup chopped dates
    1/3 cup chopped maraschino cherries
  1-3/4 cups finely crushed cornflakes
     30 to 34 maraschino cherries, halved

1. In a mixing bowl, cream butter and sugar. Add eggs, one at a time, beating well after each addition. Add milk and vanilla; mix well. Combine the flour, baking powder, salt and baking soda; add to creamed mixture. Stir in the pecans, dates and chopped cherries. Cover and refrigerate for 30 minutes.

2. Shape dough into 1-in. balls; roll in cornflakes. Place 2 in. apart on ungreased baking sheets; press a cherry half into center of each. Bake at 350° for 14-15 minutes or until golden brown. Remove to wire racks to cool. **Yield:** 5-1/2 dozen.

★★★ Chocolate Pretzel Cookies

Priscilla Anderson, Salt Lake City, Utah

These pretzel-shaped cookies are covered in a mocha glaze and drizzled with white chocolate. Your family will love them!

- 1/2 cup butter, softened
- 2/3 cup sugar
- 1 egg
- 2 squares (1 ounce *each*) unsweetened chocolate, melted and cooled
- 2 teaspoons vanilla extract
- 1-3/4 cups all-purpose flour
- 1/2 teaspoon salt

MOCHA GLAZE:
- 1 cup (6 ounces) semisweet chocolate chips
- 1 teaspoon shortening
- 1 teaspoon light corn syrup
- 1 cup confectioners' sugar
- 4 to 5 tablespoons strong brewed coffee
- 2 squares (1 ounce *each*) white baking chocolate

1. In a large mixing bowl, cream butter and sugar until light and fluffy. Add the egg, chocolate and vanilla; mix well. Combine flour and salt; gradually add to creamed mixture and mix well. Cover and refrigerate for 1 hour or until firm.

2. Divide dough into fourths; form each portion into a 6-in. roll. Cut each roll into 1/2-in. slices; roll each into a 9-in. rope. Place ropes on greased baking sheets; form into pretzel shapes and space 2 in. apart. Bake at 400° for 5-7 minutes or until firm. Cool 1 minute before removing to wire racks to cool completely.

3. For the glaze, melt the chocolate chips and shortening with corn syrup in a heavy saucepan or microwave; stir until smooth. Stir in the confectioners' sugar and enough coffee to make a smooth glaze. Dip the cookies; place on waxed paper until set. Melt the white chocolate; drizzle the cookies with white chocolate. Let stand until the chocolate is completely set. Store in an airtight container. **Yield:** 4 dozen.

★★★ Chunky Blond Brownies

(Also pictured on page 168)

Rosemary Dreiske, Keldron, South Dakota

Every bite of these chewy blond brownies is packed with chunks of white and semisweet chocolate and macadamia nuts. I like to bring a pan of these crowd-pleasing treats to potlucks.

- 1/2 cup butter, softened
- 3/4 cup sugar
- 3/4 cup packed brown sugar
- 2 eggs
- 2 teaspoons vanilla extract
- 1-1/2 cups all-purpose flour
- 1 teaspoon baking powder
- 1/2 teaspoon salt
- 1 cup vanilla *or* white chips
- 1 cup semisweet chocolate chunks
- 1 jar (3-1/4 ounces) macadamia nuts *or* 3/4 cup blanched almonds, chopped, *divided*

1. In a large mixing bowl, cream butter and sugars until light and fluffy. Add eggs and vanilla; mix well. Combine flour, baking powder and salt; add to creamed mixture and mix well. Stir in vanilla chips, chocolate chunks and 1/2 cup nuts.

2. Spoon into a greased 13-in. x 9-in. x 2-in. baking pan; spread to evenly cover bottom of pan. Sprinkle with remaining nuts. Bake at 350° for 25-30 minutes or until top begins to crack and is golden brown. Cool on a wire rack. Cut into bars. **Yield:** 2 dozen.

🎖 🎖 🎖

Apricot Meringue Bars

Krissy Fossmeyer, Huntley, Illinois

I'm expected to bake these wonderful bars for our family picnic each year, and I'm happy to oblige. The apricot filling and delicate meringue topping make them everyone's favorite.

3 cups all-purpose flour
1 cup sugar, *divided*
1 cup cold butter
4 eggs, *separated*
1 teaspoon vanilla extract

2 cans (12 ounces *each*) apricot filling
1/2 cup chopped pecans

1. In a large bowl, combine flour and 1/2 cup sugar; cut in butter until crumbly. Add egg yolks and vanilla; mix well. Press into a greased 15-in. x 10-in. x 1-in. baking pan. Bake at 350° for 12-15 minutes or until lightly browned. Spread apricot filling over crust.

2. In a small mixing bowl, beat the egg whites until soft peaks form. Gradually add the remaining sugar, beating until stiff peaks form. Spread over apricot layer; sprinkle with pecans. Bake for 25-30 minutes or until lightly browned. Cool on a wire rack. Cut into bars. Refrigerate leftovers. **Yield:** 32 bars.

🎀🎀🎀
Chocolate Orange Cookies

Ruth Rumple, Rockford, Ohio

Decorated cutout cookies are a time-honored holiday tradition for many families, including mine. This version combines the fabulous flavors of orange and chocolate.

1 cup butter, softened
3/4 cup sugar, *divided*
1 egg
1 teaspoon vanilla extract
2-1/2 cups all-purpose flour
1/2 teaspoon salt
1/4 cup finely grated orange peel
1 cup (6 ounces) semisweet chocolate chips, melted

1. In a large mixing bowl, cream butter and 1/2 cup sugar until light and fluffy. Add egg and vanilla. Gradually add flour and salt; mix well. Cover and refrigerate for 15 minutes.

2. On a floured surface, roll out dough to 1/4-in. thickness. Cut with a floured 2-in. cookie cutter or shape into 2-in. x 1-in. rectangles. Place 2 in. apart on ungreased baking sheets. Combine orange peel and remaining sugar; sprinkle over cookies.

3. Bake at 350° for 14-16 minutes or until edges just begin to brown. Remove to wire racks to cool. Melt chocolate chips; decorate cookies. **Yield:** about 3 dozen.

🎀🎀🎀
Apple Pie Bars

Janet English, Pittsburgh, Pennsylvania

This is one of the many wonderful recipes my mother handed down to me. The down-home bars, with their flaky pastry crust and scrumptious fruit filling, are the ideal way to serve apple pie to a crowd.

4 cups all-purpose flour
1 teaspoon salt
1 teaspoon baking powder
1 cup shortening
4 egg yolks
2 tablespoons lemon juice
8 to 10 tablespoons cold water
FILLING:
7 cups finely chopped peeled apples
2 cups sugar
1/4 cup all-purpose flour
2 teaspoons ground cinnamon
Dash ground nutmeg
GLAZE:
1 cup confectioners' sugar
1 tablespoon milk
1 tablespoon lemon juice

1. In a large bowl, combine flour, salt and baking powder. Cut in shortening until mixture resembles coarse crumbs. In a small bowl, whisk egg yolks, lemon juice and water; gradually add to flour mixture, tossing with a fork until dough forms a ball. Divide in half. Chill for 30 minutes.

2. Roll out one portion of dough between two large sheets of waxed paper into a 17-in. x 12-in. rectangle. Transfer to an ungreased 15-in. x 10-in. x 1-in. baking pan. Press pastry onto the bottom and up the sides of pan; trim pastry even with top edge.

3. In a large bowl, toss the apples, sugar, flour, cinnamon and nutmeg; spread over crust. Roll out remaining pastry to fit top of pan; place over filling. Trim edges; brush edges between pastry with water or milk; pinch to seal. Cut slits in top.

4. Bake at 375° for 45-50 minutes or until golden brown. Cool on a wire rack. Combine glaze ingredients until smooth; drizzle over bars before cutting. **Yield:** about 2 dozen.

✿✿✿ Honey Pecan Triangles

Debbie Fogel, East Berne, New York

I've been stirring up batches of these tasty bar cookies for many years, and they're a big hit wherever I share them. The triangles have all the goodness of traditional pecan pie and will feed a big group.

    2 teaspoons plus 1/2 cup butter, softened,
        divided
  1/2 cup packed brown sugar
    1 egg yolk
1-1/2 cups all-purpose flour
TOPPING:
    1 cup packed brown sugar
  1/2 cup butter
  1/4 cup honey
  1/2 cup heavy whipping cream
    4 cups chopped pecans

1. Line a 13-in. x 9-in. x 2-in. baking pan with foil; butter the foil with 2 teaspoons butter. In a mixing bowl, cream remaining butter with brown sugar. Add egg yolk; mix well. Gradually add flour. Press into prepared pan. Bake at 350° for 15 minutes or until golden brown.

2. Meanwhile, in a large saucepan, combine the brown sugar, butter and honey. Bring to a boil over medium heat; cook and stir for 3 minutes. Remove from the heat; stir in cream and pecans. Pour over crust. Bake for 30 minutes or until hot and bubbly. Cool completely on a wire rack.

3. Use foil to lift the bars out of the pan and place on a cutting board. Carefully remove foil. Cut into 24 bars; cut each in half diagonally. **Yield:** 4 dozen.

✿✿✿ Very Chocolate Brownies

Arlene Kay Butler, Ogden, Utah

I think this just might be the perfect brownie recipe. The mouthwatering goodies are topped off with a fluffy, chocolate-cream layer that's absolutely heavenly.

    4 squares (1 ounce *each*) unsweetened chocolate
  3/4 cup butter
    2 cups sugar
    3 eggs
    1 teaspoon vanilla extract
    1 cup all-purpose flour
    1 cup coarsely chopped walnuts
TOPPING:
    1 cup (6 ounces) semisweet chocolate chips
  1/4 cup water
    2 tablespoons butter
    1 cup heavy whipping cream, whipped

1. In a microwave or double boiler, melt chocolate and butter; cool for 10 minutes. Add sugar; mix well. Stir in eggs and vanilla. Add flour; mix well. Stir in the walnuts.

2. Line a 13-in. x 9-in. x 2-in. baking pan with foil and grease the foil. Pour batter into pan. Bake at 350° for 25-30 minutes or until a toothpick inserted near the center comes out with moist crumbs (do not overbake). Cool completely.

3. For topping, melt chocolate chips, water and butter in a microwave or double boiler; stir until smooth. Cool to room temperature. Fold in whipped cream. Spread over brownies. Chill before cutting. Store leftovers in the refrigerator. **Yield:** 3 dozen.

Chocolate Strawberry Torte, p. 204

Frozen Chocolate Mint Pie, p. 207

Rhubarb Jelly-Roll Cake, p. 198

Cakes & Pies

Dreaming of a tender, moist cake fresh from the oven? Craving a slice of home-style pie? Whichever delectable dessert you prefer, you'll love all of the tantalizing varieties lined up for you here.

Cranberry Crumb Cake, p. 207

🎗 🎗 🎗
Cranberry-Carrot Layer Cake

Nellie Runne, Rockford, Illinois

Dotted with cranberries and smothered with rich cream cheese frosting, this carrot cake makes any dinner festive.

    4 eggs
1-1/2 cups packed brown sugar
1-1/4 cups vegetable oil
    1 teaspoon grated orange peel
    2 cups all-purpose flour

    1 teaspoon baking soda
    1 teaspoon ground cinnamon
    3/4 teaspoon baking powder
    1/2 teaspoon salt
    1/4 teaspoon ground cloves
    2 cups shredded carrots
    1 cup dried cranberries
CREAM CHEESE FROSTING:
    2 packages (8 ounces *each*) cream cheese, softened
    3/4 cup butter, softened
    4 cups confectioners' sugar
    1 tablespoon milk
    1/2 teaspoon ground ginger
    1/2 teaspoon grated orange peel, optional

1. In a large mixing bowl, combine the eggs, brown sugar, oil and orange peel; mix well. Combine the flour, baking soda, cinnamon, baking powder, salt and cloves; beat into egg mixture. Stir in carrots and cranberries.

2. Pour into two greased and floured 9-in. round baking pans. Bake at 350° for 25-30 minutes or until a toothpick inserted near the center comes out clean. Cool for 10 minutes before removing from pans to wire racks to cool completely.

3. For frosting, in a large mixing bowl, beat cream cheese and butter until fluffy. Gradually beat in sugar, milk, ginger and peel if desired. Split each cake into two horizontal layers. Spread frosting between layers and over top and sides of cake. **Yield:** 12-14 servings.

🎗 🎗 🎗
Chocolate-Caramel Supreme Pie

Diana Stewart, Oelwein, Iowa

At a fund-raiser, I bought a "pie-a-month" package from a local family. Of all the pies they made, this was the best.

    30 caramels
    3 tablespoons butter, melted
    2 tablespoons water
    1 chocolate crumb crust (9 inches)
1/2 cup chopped pecans, toasted
    1 package (3 ounces) cream cheese, softened
1/3 cup confectioners' sugar
3/4 cup milk chocolate chips
    3 tablespoons hot water
    1 carton (8 ounces) frozen whipped topping, thawed
Chocolate hearts *or* curls, optional

1. In a large saucepan, add the caramels, butter and water. Cook and stir over medium heat until caramels are melted. Spread over crust; sprinkle with pecans. Refrigerate for 1 hour.

2. In a large mixing bowl, beat cream cheese and sugar until smooth; spread over caramel layer. Refrigerate.

3. In a large saucepan, melt chocolate chips with hot water over low heat; stir until smooth. Cool slightly.

4. Fold in whipped topping. Spread over cream cheese layer. Garnish with chocolate hearts or curls if desired. Chill until serving. Refrigerate leftovers. **Yield:** 8 servings.

🎖🎖🎖
Apple Bundt Cake

Virginia Horst, Mesa, Washington

This delectable cake has a thin, crunchy crust and is soft inside. The apple-filled slices are wonderful served with the accompanying Butter Cream Sauce.

       2 eggs
       2 cups sugar
  1-1/2 cups vegetable oil
       3 cups all-purpose flour
       1 teaspoon baking soda
       1 teaspoon ground cinnamon
     1/2 teaspoon salt
       3 cups diced peeled apples
       1 cup chopped pecans
BUTTER CREAM SAUCE:
     1/2 cup butter, cubed
       1 cup sugar
     1/2 cup heavy whipping cream
       1 teaspoon vanilla extract

1. In a large mixing bowl, beat the eggs, sugar and oil. Combine the flour, baking soda, cinnamon and salt; gradually add to batter (batter will be very stiff). Fold in apples and pecans.

2. Pour into a greased 10-in. fluted tube pan. Bake at 325° for 1-1/4 to 1-1/2 hours or until a toothpick inserted near the center comes out clean. Cool for 10 minutes before removing from pan to a wire rack.

3. For sauce, melt butter in a small saucepan. Add the sugar, cream and vanilla. Cook and stir over low heat until sugar is dissolved and sauce is heated through. Slice cake; serve with warm sauce. Refrigerate leftover sauce. **Yield:** 12-16 servings.

🎖🎖🎖
Raspberry Ribbon Pie

Anita Ohlson, Cheyenne, Wyoming

We freeze fresh raspberries when they're in season so we can make this tangy, ruby-red pie year-round. I've found that strawberries also work well in this dessert—just follow the variation at the end of the recipe.

       1 cup vanilla wafer crumbs (about 29 wafers)
     1/4 cup butter, melted
       1 package (3 ounces) raspberry gelatin
       1 cup boiling water
     1/4 cup sugar
       1 cup fresh raspberries
       1 tablespoon lemon juice
       1 package (3 ounces) cream cheese, softened
     1/3 cup confectioners' sugar
       1 teaspoon vanilla extract
Pinch salt
       1 cup heavy whipping cream
Additional whipped cream and fresh raspberries

1. In a small bowl, combine the wafer crumbs and butter; press onto the bottom and up the sides of an ungreased 9-in. pie plate. Bake at 350° for 10 minutes or until golden brown.

2. In a bowl, dissolve gelatin in boiling water. Add the sugar, raspberries and lemon juice. Refrigerate until partially set, about 1-1/2 hours.

3. In a mixing bowl, beat cream cheese and confectioners' sugar until smooth. Add vanilla and salt. In another mixing bowl, beat whipping cream until stiff peaks form. Fold into cream cheese mixture. Spread 3/4 cup over bottom of crust.

4. Spread 3/4 cup raspberry mixture over the top; repeat layers. Refrigerate for 8 hours or overnight before serving. Garnish pie with additional whipped cream and berries. Refrigerate leftovers. **Yield:** 8 servings.

Strawberry Ribbon Pie: Use strawberry gelatin for the raspberry gelatin and use 1 cup sliced strawberries for the raspberries.

🎖🎖🎖
Peanut Ice Cream Pie

Lois Sieck, Goodland, Kansas

Everyone is "nuts" about this peanutty pie! It always comes in handy as an easy, no-bake dessert for church dinners, card parties, showers and unexpected guests. Judges at a northwestern Kansas fair declared it a grand-prize winner.

- 1-1/2 cups graham cracker crumbs (about 24 squares)
- 1/4 cup sugar
- 1/3 cup butter, softened
- 1 quart vanilla ice cream, softened
- 1/2 cup light corn syrup
- 1/3 cup chunky peanut butter
- 2/3 cup dry roasted peanuts

1. In a large bowl, combine the cracker crumbs, sugar and butter; press onto the bottom and up the sides of an ungreased 9-in. pie plate. Spoon half of the ice cream into crust.

2. In a small bowl, combine the corn syrup and peanut butter; spoon half over ice cream. Sprinkle with half of the peanuts. Repeat layers. Freeze until firm. **Yield:** 6-8 servings.

🎖🎖🎖
Cranberry Cake With Orange Sauce

Shirley Dehler, Columbus, Wisconsin

I love the tart cranberry flavor of this homemade cake. Served with a warm citrus sauce, it's a wonderful treat to share at get-togethers with family and friends.

 Uses less fat, sugar or salt. Includes Nutrition Facts and Diabetic Exchanges.

- 2 tablespoons butter
- 1 cup sugar
- 1 teaspoon vanilla extract
- 2 cups cake flour
- 3 teaspoons baking powder
- 1/2 teaspoon salt
- 1 cup 2% milk
- 2 cups fresh *or* frozen cranberries

ORANGE SAUCE:
- 3/4 cup sugar
- 2 teaspoons cornstarch
- 1/4 teaspoon salt
- 1-1/2 cups water
- 3 tablespoons orange juice
- 4 teaspoons butter
- 1-1/2 teaspoons grated orange peel
- 1/4 teaspoon orange extract

1. In a large mixing bowl, beat the butter and sugar until crumbly, about 2 minutes. Add the vanilla. Combine the flour, baking powder and salt; add to butter mixture alternately with milk. Fold in cranberries.

2. Transfer to an 11-in. x 7-in. x 2-in. baking dish coated with nonstick cooking spray. Bake at 350° for 30-35 minutes or until the top springs back when lightly touched. Cool on a wire rack.

3. For sauce, combine the sugar, cornstarch and salt in a saucepan. Gradually add water. Bring to a boil; cook and stir for 2 minutes or until thickened. Add the orange juice, butter, orange peel and extract; mix well. Serve warm sauce over cake. **Yield:** 12 servings.

Nutrition Facts: 1 piece with 2 tablespoons sauce equals 233 calories, 4 g fat (2 g saturated fat), 10 mg cholesterol, 250 mg sodium, 49 g carbohydrate, 1 g fiber, 2 g protein. **Diabetic Exchanges:** 1-1/2 starch, 1-1/2 fruit, 1/2 fat.

🎗 🎗 🎗
Maple Sugar Cake

Elin Lee, Lancaster, Massachusetts

Old-fashioned maple sugar frosting makes the perfect topping for this down-home spice cake. I sprinkle on chopped walnuts for a fast finishing touch.

- 1/2 **cup butter, softened**
- 1-1/4 **cups packed brown sugar**
- 3 **eggs**
- 1/2 **cup maple syrup**
- 1/4 **cup milk**
- 1/4 **cup sour cream**
- 1 **teaspoon maple flavoring**
- 2-1/2 **cups cake flour**
- 2 **teaspoons baking powder**
- 1/2 **teaspoon baking soda**
- 1/2 **teaspoon salt**
- 1/2 **teaspoon ground cloves**
- 1/4 **teaspoon** *each* **ground allspice, nutmeg and mace**

MAPLE SUGAR FROSTING:
- 6 **tablespoons butter, softened**
- 1-1/2 **teaspoons maple flavoring**
- 4-1/2 **cups confectioners' sugar**
- 1/2 **to 3/4 cup sour cream**

Chopped walnuts, optional

1. In a large mixing bowl, cream butter and brown sugar. Add eggs, one at a time, beating well after each addition. In a small bowl, combine the syrup, milk, sour cream and maple flavoring. In another bowl, combine the flour, baking powder, baking soda, salt, cloves, allspice, nutmeg and mace; add to creamed mixture alternately with syrup mixture.

2. Pour into two greased and floured 9-in. round baking pans. Bake at 350° for 20-25 minutes or until a toothpick inserted near the center comes out clean. Cool for 10 minutes before removing from pans to a wire rack to cool.

3. For frosting, in a large mixing bowl, cream butter and maple flavoring. Gradually beat in the confectioners' sugar. Add enough sour cream to achieve spreading consistency. Spread frosting between layers and over top and sides of cake. Sprinkle with walnuts if desired. Store in the refrigerator. **Yield:** 12-14 servings.

🎀🎀🎀
Fluffy Caramel Pie

Ginger Hendericksen, Wisconsin Rapids, Wisconsin

I bake a variety of pies, but my husband likes this one best. The gingersnap crust complements the sweet caramel filling.

✓ Uses less fat, sugar or salt. Includes Nutrition Facts.

1-1/2 cups crushed gingersnaps (about 30 cookies)
  1/4 cup butter, melted
FILLING:
  1 envelope unflavored gelatin

1/4 cup cold water
  28 caramels
  1 cup milk
Dash salt
  1/2 cup chopped pecans
  1 teaspoon vanilla extract
  1 cup heavy whipping cream, whipped
Caramel ice cream topping and additional pecans, optional

1. In a small bowl, combine the cookie crumbs and butter; press onto the bottom and up the sides of a greased 9-in. pie plate. Cover and refrigerate.

2. Meanwhile, in a small saucepan, sprinkle gelatin over cold water; let stand for 1 minute. Add caramels, milk and salt. Heat over low heat, stirring until gelatin is completely dissolved and caramels are melted. Refrigerate for 1-2 hours or until mixture mounds when stirred with a spoon.

3. Stir pecans and vanilla into caramel mixture. Fold in whipped cream. Pour into crust. Refrigerate for 6 hours or overnight. Garnish with topping and pecans if desired. Store in the refrigerator. **Yield:** 6-8 servings.

Nutrition Facts: 1 piece equals 471 calories, 28 g fat (14 g saturated fat), 63 mg cholesterol, 362 mg sodium, 51 g carbohydrate, 2 g fiber, 6 g protein.

🎀🎀🎀
White Chocolate Lime Mousse Cake

Margery Richmond, Fort Collins, Colorado

When I took this pretty cake to a party and people lined up at the dessert table for a slice, I knew it was a winner. It bakes up nice and high, and the lime flavor really comes through.

2 cups crushed gingersnaps (about 38 cookies)
  2 tablespoons sugar
  1/3 cup butter, melted
FILLING:
  1 envelope unflavored gelatin
  6 tablespoons lime juice
  9 squares (1 ounce *each*) white baking chocolate, chopped
2-1/2 cups heavy whipping cream
  3 packages (8 ounces *each*) cream cheese, softened
  1 cup sugar
  1 tablespoon grated lime peel

1. In a large bowl, combine the gingersnaps, sugar and butter; press onto the bottom and 1 in. up the sides of a greased 9-in. springform pan. Set aside.

2. In a microwave-safe dish, sprinkle gelatin over juice. Let stand for 1 minute. Microwave on high for 10-20 seconds; stir until gelatin is dissolved. Set aside. In a heavy saucepan or microwave, melt chocolate with 1/2 cup cream; stir until smooth. Cool slightly; stir in gelatin.

3. In a large mixing bowl, beat cream cheese and sugar until smooth. Gradually add chocolate mixture and lime peel; mix well. In another large mixing bowl, beat remaining cream until stiff peaks form. Gently fold into cream cheese mixture. Spoon over the crust. Cover and chill overnight. Refrigerate leftovers. **Yield:** 12-16 servings.

✦✦✦
Spiced Peach Pie

Lois Dunlop, Venice, Florida

If you want a change from the traditional baked fruit pie, give this chilled peach pie a try. With its gelatin filling and fluffy cream, it slices beautifully and gets many compliments.

- 1 can (15 ounces) sliced peaches
- 2 tablespoons brown sugar
- 1/4 teaspoon ground ginger
- 1 cinnamon stick (3 inches)
- 1 package (3 ounces) peach gelatin *or* orange gelatin
- 4 ounces cream cheese, softened
- 2 tablespoons butter, softened
- 1/8 teaspoon ground nutmeg
- 1 pastry shell (9 inches), baked
- 1 carton (8 ounces) frozen whipped topping, thawed

Fresh mint, optional

1. Drain syrup from peaches into a 2-cup measuring cup. Add enough water to measure 1-1/3 cups. Chop peaches and set aside.

2. In a large saucepan, combine syrup, sugar, ginger and cinnamon stick. Bring to a boil. Reduce heat; cook and stir for 5 minutes. Remove from the heat.

3. Discard cinnamon stick. Stir gelatin into syrup mixture until dissolved. Add peaches. Refrigerate until partially set, about 40 minutes.

4. In a large mixing bowl, beat cream cheese, butter and nutmeg until smooth. Spread over the bottom and up the sides of the crust. Pour gelatin mixture over cream cheese layer. Chill until serving. Spread with whipped topping. Serve with mint if desired. **Yield:** 6-8 servings.

✦✦✦
Apple Gingerbread

Pam Blockey, Bozeman, Montana

This nicely spiced cake, with chunks of apple and a hint of ginger, cinnamon and nutmeg, always wins raves. No one guesses that the recipe uses reduced-fat ingredients.

✓ Uses less fat, sugar or salt. Includes Nutrition Facts and Diabetic Exchanges.

- 2/3 cup sugar
- 1/3 cup unsweetened applesauce
- 1 egg
- 3 tablespoons molasses
- 1 cup all-purpose flour
- 1/2 cup whole wheat flour
- 2 teaspoons ground ginger
- 1 teaspoon baking powder
- 1 teaspoon baking soda
- 1 teaspoon ground cinnamon
- 1/4 teaspoon ground nutmeg
- 1/8 teaspoon ground allspice
- 1/2 cup reduced-fat plain yogurt
- 1-1/2 cups chopped peeled Granny Smith or other tart apples (about 1 medium)
- 1 cup plus 2 tablespoons reduced-fat whipped topping

1. In a mixing bowl, combine the sugar, applesauce, egg and molasses; mix well. Combine the flours, ginger, baking powder, baking soda and spices; add to the molasses mixture alternately with yogurt, beating just until combined. Fold in the apples.

2. Pour into an 8-in. square baking dish coated with nonstick cooking spray. Bake at 350° for 30-35 minutes or until a toothpick inserted near the center comes out clean. Cool on a wire rack. Cut into squares; dollop with whipped topping. **Yield:** 9 servings.

Nutrition Facts: 1 piece with 2 tablespoons whipped topping equals 203 calories, 2 g fat (1 g saturated fat), 24 mg cholesterol, 186 mg sodium, 42 g carbohydrate, 2 g fiber, 4 g protein. **Diabetic Exchanges:** 2 starch, 1 fruit.

🎗️ 🎗️ 🎗️
Banana Cream Pie

Anne Schroeder, Yarrow, British Columbia

I whip up this creamy dessert whenever I need a fuss-free treat. People are always surprised to hear that it's made in the microwave because the banana filling and buttery crust taste like I slaved over the stove for hours.

  1/3 **cup butter, cubed**
1-1/4 **cups graham cracker crumbs**
  3 **tablespoons sugar**
FILLING:
  1/2 **cup sugar**
  2 **tablespoons all-purpose flour**
  2 **tablespoons cornstarch**
2-1/4 **cups milk**
  3 **egg yolks, lightly beaten**
  2 **tablespoons butter**
  1 **teaspoon vanilla extract**
  1/4 **teaspoon salt**
  1 **to 2 medium firm bananas, cut into 1/4-inch slices**
Whipped topping and additional banana slices, optional

1. Place butter in a greased 9-in. microwave-safe pie plate. Heat, uncovered, on high for 1 minute or until melted, turning once. Stir in crumbs and sugar; mix well. Press onto the bottom and up the sides of plate. Cook, uncovered, on high for 1-1/2 to 2 minutes or until crust is firm and holds together. Cool completely.

2. For filling, in a 2-qt. microwave-safe bowl, combine sugar, flour and cornstarch. Gradually whisk in the milk until smooth.

3. Microwave, uncovered, on high for 9-10 minutes or until thickened, stirring every 2 minutes. Stir a small amount of hot liquid into egg yolks. Gradually return to the bowl, stirring constantly. Cool 1 to 1-1/2 minutes longer or until bubbly, stirring every 30 seconds. Stir in butter, vanilla and salt until butter is melted. Cool for 20 minutes, stirring several times.

4. Arrange bananas in crust. Top with filling. Cover and chill 8 hours or overnight. Top with whipped topping and additional bananas if desired. **Yield:** 6-8 servings.

Editor's Note: This recipe was tested with an 850-watt microwave.

🎗🎗🎗
Raspberry Pie with Oat Crust

Ginny Arandas, Greensburg, Pennsylvania

As a diabetic, I adapted this recipe to suit my needs. Whenever I serve this pie, no one can believe it's sugarless. The oatmeal crust is so tender...and the filling is "berry" delicious!

 Uses less fat, sugar or salt. Includes Nutrition Facts and Diabetic Exchanges.

- 3/4 cup all-purpose flour
- 1/2 cup quick-cooking oats
- 1/2 teaspoon salt
- 1/4 cup canola oil
- 3 to 4 tablespoons cold water

FILLING:
- 2 cups water
- 1 package (.8 ounces) sugar-free cook-and-serve vanilla pudding mix
- 1 package (.3 ounce) sugar-free raspberry gelatin
- 4 cups fresh raspberries

1. In a food processor, combine the flour, oats and salt. While processing, slowly drizzle in oil. Gradually add water until a ball forms. Roll out dough between two sheets of waxed paper. Remove top sheet of waxed paper; invert dough onto a 9-in. pie plate. Remove remaining waxed paper. Trim, seal and flute edges. Prick bottom of crust with a fork in several places. Bake at 400° for 10-12 minutes or until golden brown. Cool completely on a wire rack.

2. In a saucepan, heat water over medium heat. Whisk in pudding mix. Cook and stir 5 minutes or until thickened and bubbly. Whisk in gelatin until completely dissolved. Remove from the heat; cool slightly. Fold in raspberries. Spoon into crust. Chill for at least 3 hours or overnight. Refrigerate leftovers. **Yield:** 8 servings.

Nutrition Facts: 1 piece equals 167 calories, 8 g fat (1 g saturated fat), 0 cholesterol, 238 mg sodium, 22 g carbohydrate, 5 g fiber, 3 g protein. **Diabetic Exchanges:** 1-1/2 fat, 1 starch, 1/2 fruit.

🎗🎗🎗
Chocolate Cake With Fudge Sauce

Lydia Briscoe, Scott Depot, West Virginia

My family makes sure to leave room for dessert when this decadent cake is on the menu. We all love chocolate and agree that this rich treat is one of the best ways to enjoy it.

- 1 package (3.4 ounces) cook-and-serve chocolate pudding/pie filling mix
- 2 cups milk
- 1 package (18-1/4 ounces) chocolate cake mix

SAUCE:
- 1/2 cup butter, cubed
- 1 cup (6 ounces) semisweet chocolate chips
- 1 can (12 ounces) evaporated milk
- 2 cups confectioners' sugar
- 1 teaspoon vanilla extract

Fresh mint, optional

1. In a heavy saucepan or microwave, prepare pudding with milk according to package directions for pudding. Pour into a mixing bowl; add dry cake mix and beat until well blended.

2. Spread into a greased 13-in. x 9-in. x 2-in. baking pan. Bake at 350° for 30-35 minutes or until cake springs back when lightly touched and edges pull away from sides of pan. Cool on a wire rack.

3. For sauce, in a heavy saucepan, melt butter and chocolate over low heat. Stir in evaporated milk and sugar until smooth. Bring to a boil over medium heat; cook and stir for 8 minutes or until thickened. Remove from the heat; stir in vanilla. Serve warm sauce over cake. Serve with mint if desired. **Yield:** 12-15 servings.

Rhubarb Jelly-Roll Cake

(Pictured on page 188)

Donna Stratton, Carson City, Nevada

This jelly-roll recipe came from my mother's cookbook, circa 1940. The lovely cake has long been a family favorite and is popular at potlucks, too.

> 6 cups chopped fresh *or* frozen rhubarb, thawed
> 2-3/4 cups sugar, *divided*
> 2 teaspoons ground cinnamon
> 1/4 teaspoon ground allspice
> 1/8 teaspoon ground cloves
> 4 eggs
> 1 teaspoon lemon extract
> 3/4 cup all-purpose flour
> 1 teaspoon baking powder
> 1/2 teaspoon salt
> Confectioners' sugar

1. In a large saucepan, combine the rhubarb, 2 cups sugar, cinnamon, allspice and cloves. Bring to a boil. Reduce heat; cook, uncovered, over medium heat until thickened. Cool completely.

2. In a large mixing bowl, beat eggs on high speed until thick and lemon-colored. Gradually add remaining sugar, beating until thick and light-colored. Beat in extract. Combine the flour, baking powder and salt; gradually add to egg mixture.

3. Grease a 15-in. x 10-in. x 1-in. baking pan and line with waxed paper; grease and flour the paper. Spread batter into pan. Bake at 375° for 15 minutes or until cake springs back when lightly touched. Cool for 5 minutes.

4. Turn onto a kitchen towel dusted with confectioners' sugar. Peel off waxed paper. Roll up cake in towel jelly-roll style, starting with a short side. Cool.

5. Carefully unroll cake. Spread filling over cake to within 1 in. of edges. Roll up again. Store in the refrigerator. Dust with confectioners' sugar just before serving. **Yield:** 10-12 servings.

Editor's Note: If using frozen rhubarb, measure rhubarb while still frozen, then thaw completely. Drain in a colander, but do not press liquid out.

Blueberries 'n' Cream Pie

Roger Meyers, Chambersburg, Pennsylvania

After taking one bite of this home-style pie, guests always ask for the recipe. It's especially good served warm. For a change of pace, substitute peaches for the blueberries.

✓ Uses less fat, sugar or salt. Includes Nutrition Facts and Diabetic Exchanges.

> 1/2 cup plus 1 tablespoon fat-free milk, *divided*
> 3 tablespoons butter, melted
> 1 egg
> 3/4 cup all-purpose flour
> 1 package (.8 ounces) sugar-free cook-and-serve vanilla pudding mix
> 1 teaspoon baking powder
> 1/8 teaspoon salt
> 2 cups fresh *or* frozen blueberries, thawed
> 1 package (8 ounces) reduced-fat cream cheese
> 1/2 cup sugar
> **TOPPING:**
> 2 teaspoons sugar
> 1/8 teaspoon ground cinnamon

1. In a large mixing bowl, beat 1/2 cup milk, butter and egg. Combine the flour, pudding mix, baking powder and salt; stir into egg mixture just until moistened. Pour into a 9-in. pie plate coated with nonstick cooking spray. Arrange blueberries over batter to within 1/2 in. of edge of plate.

2. In a large mixing bowl, beat cream cheese, sugar and remaining milk until smooth. Spread over blueberries to within 1 in. of berry edge. For topping, combine sugar and cinnamon; sprinkle over the cream cheese mixture. Bake at 350° for 30-35 minutes or until set. Serve warm. Refrigerate leftovers. **Yield:** 8 servings.

Nutrition Facts: 1 piece equals 249 calories, 12 g fat (7 g saturated fat), 60 mg cholesterol, 302 mg sodium, 31 g carbohydrate, 1 g fiber, 6 g protein. **Diabetic Exchanges:** 2 fat, 1-1/2 starch, 1/2 fruit.

🎀🎀🎀
Favorite Chocolate Sheet Cake

Mary Lewis, Escondido, California

My mother adapted this crowd-pleaser from a vanilla cake recipe in a church cookbook. The cake itself is so luscious, it wouldn't need frosting—but I always feel you can never have too much chocolate!

>   1 cup butter, softened
>   2 cups sugar
>   4 eggs
>   2 teaspoons vanilla extract
> 2-1/4 cups cake flour
>   1 teaspoon baking soda
>   1 teaspoon salt
>   1 cup buttermilk
>   3 squares (1 ounce *each*) bittersweet chocolate, melted
> FROSTING:
>   1/4 cup baking cocoa
>   1/3 cup milk
>   1/2 cup butter, cubed
>   1 teaspoon vanilla extract
> 3-1/2 cups confectioners' sugar

1. In a large mixing bowl, cream butter and sugar. Add eggs, one at a time, beating well after each addition. Beat in vanilla. Combine the flour, baking soda and salt; add to creamed mixture alternately with buttermilk. Beat in chocolate until combined.

2. Pour into a greased 15-in. x 10-in. x 1-in. baking pan. Bake at 350° for 23-27 minutes or until a toothpick inserted near the center comes out clean. Cool on a wire rack.

3. For frosting, in a small saucepan, bring cocoa and milk to a boil over medium heat, stirring constantly. Remove from the heat; stir in butter and vanilla until butter is melted. Whisk in confectioners' sugar until smooth. Drizzle over cake and spread quickly. Let stand until set. **Yield:** 24 servings.

🎀🎀🎀
Mocha Pie

Barbara Keller, Highlands Ranch, Colorado

When a friend of mine served this divine pie, I couldn't believe that she had managed to make such an elegant dessert after a long day at work. Then she gave me the recipe, which is a breeze to assemble with refrigerated cookie dough, marshmallow creme and instant coffee.

>   1 tube (18 ounces) refrigerated chocolate chip cookie dough
>   1 package (3 ounces) cream cheese, softened
>   2 tablespoons milk
>   1 jar (7 ounces) marshmallow creme
>   1 tablespoon instant coffee granules
>   1 tablespoon hot water
>   1 carton (8 ounces) frozen whipped topping, thawed
>   2 tablespoons chocolate syrup, *divided*
>   3 tablespoons chopped walnuts

1. Cut cookie dough in half widthwise; let one half stand at room temperature for 5-10 minutes to soften (save the other half for another use).

2. Press dough onto bottom and up the sides of an ungreased 9-in. pie plate. Bake, uncovered, at 375° for 11-12 minutes or until lightly browned. Cool on a wire rack.

3. In a large mixing bowl, beat cream cheese and milk until smooth. Add the marshmallow creme; beat until blended. Dissolve coffee granules in water. Fold the coffee, whipped topping and 1 tablespoon chocolate syrup into the cream cheese mixture. Pour into cooled crust. Chill for 1 hour.

4. Just before serving, sprinkle with nuts and drizzle with remaining chocolate syrup. **Yield:** 6-8 servings.

Cakes & Pies **199**

Strawberry Poke Cake

Mary Jo Griggs, West Bend, Wisconsin

That classic summertime treat—strawberry shortcake—gets a whole new look and taste with this recipe.

   1 package (18-1/4 ounces) white cake mix
1-1/4 cups water
   1/4 cup vegetable oil
   2 eggs
   1 package (16 ounces) frozen sweetened sliced strawberries, thawed

   2 packages (3 ounces *each*) strawberry gelatin
   1 carton (12 ounces) frozen whipped topping, thawed, *divided*
Fresh strawberries, optional

1. In a large mixing bowl, beat cake mix, water, oil and eggs on low speed until moistened. Beat on medium for 2 minutes. Pour into two greased and floured 9-in. round baking pans. Bake at 350° for 25-35 minutes or until a toothpick inserted near the center comes out clean. Cool for 10 minutes; remove from pans to wire racks to cool completely.

2. Using a serrated knife, level top of each cake if necessary. Return layers, top side up, to two clean 9-in. round baking pans. Pierce cakes with a meat fork at 1/2-in. intervals.

3. Drain juice from strawberries into a 2-cup measuring cup; refrigerate berries. Add water to juice to measure 2 cups; pour into a saucepan. Bring to a boil; stir in gelatin until dissolved. Chill for 30 minutes. Gently spoon over each cake layer. Chill for 2-3 hours.

4. Dip bottom of one pan in warm water for 10 seconds. Invert cake onto a serving platter. Top with reserved strawberries and 1 cup whipped topping. Place second cake layer over topping. Frost cake with remaining whipped topping. Chill for at least 1 hour. Serve with fresh berries if desired. Refrigerate leftovers. **Yield:** 10-12 servings.

Editor's Note: This cake was tested with Pillsbury white cake mix.

🏅🏅🏅

Frosty Pumpkin Pie

Janet Jackson, Homedale, Illinois

This frozen dessert is so yummy that no one will guess it's made with reduced-fat ingredients. My family actually prefers this layered pie to traditional pumpkin pie at Christmastime.

✓ Uses less fat, sugar or salt. Includes Nutrition Facts and Diabetic Exchanges.

   2 cups frozen reduced-fat vanilla yogurt, softened
   1 reduced-fat graham cracker crust (9 inches)
   1 cup canned pumpkin
   1/2 cup sugar
   1 teaspoon pumpkin pie spice
   1/2 teaspoon salt
   1/2 teaspoon ground ginger
   1 carton (8 ounces) frozen reduced-fat whipped topping, thawed

1. Spread yogurt into crust. Freeze for 30 minutes.

2. Meanwhile, in a bowl, combine the pumpkin, sugar, pumpkin pie spice, salt and ginger. Fold in whipped topping. Spoon over frozen yogurt. Freeze for 6 hours or overnight. Remove from the freezer 20 minutes before cutting. **Yield:** 8 servings.

Nutrition Facts: 1 piece equals 282 calories, 7 g fat (5 g saturated fat), 3 mg cholesterol, 273 mg sodium, 47 g carbohydrate, 1 g fiber, 4 g protein. **Diabetic Exchanges:** 2 starch, 1 fruit, 1 fat.

200 *Contest Winning Annual Recipes 2007*

🎗🎗🎗
Lemon Meringue Cake

Debra Blair, Glenwood, Minnesota

When you can't decide whether to make a cake or pie, reach for this unique recipe and make both! It's like getting two delectable desserts in one.

 1/4 cup butter, softened
 1/2 cup sugar
   1 egg
   2 egg yolks
 1/2 teaspoon vanilla extract
   1 cup all-purpose flour
   1 teaspoon baking powder
 1/3 cup milk
FILLING:
 3/4 cup sugar
 1/3 cup all-purpose flour
   1 cup water
   2 egg yolks, lightly beaten
 1/4 cup fresh lemon juice
   1 tablespoon butter
 1/2 teaspoon grated lemon peel
MERINGUE:
   4 egg whites
 1/2 teaspoon cream of tartar
 1/2 cup sugar

1. In a large mixing bowl, cream butter and sugar until light and fluffy. Add egg and yolks; mix well. Beat in vanilla. Combine the flour and baking powder; add to creamed mixture alternately with milk, beating well after each addition.

2. Pour into greased and floured 9-in. round baking pan. Bake at 350° for 25-30 minutes or until a toothpick inserted near the center comes out clean. Cool for 10 minutes before removing to a wire rack to cool completely.

3. For filling, combine sugar and flour in a heavy saucepan. Stir in water until smooth. Cook and stir over medium-high heat until thickened and bubbly. Reduce heat; cook and stir 2 minutes longer. Remove from the heat. Stir a small amount of hot filling into egg yolks; return all to the pan, stirring constantly. Bring to a gentle boil; cook and stir 2 minutes longer. Remove from the heat. Gently stir in lemon juice, butter and lemon peel. Cool to room temperature without stirring. Place cake on a baking sheet; spoon filling on top of cake to within 1/2 in. of edge.

4. For meringue, let egg whites stand at room temperature for 30 minutes. In a small mixing bowl and with clean beaters, beat egg whites and cream of tartar on medium speed until soft peaks form. Gradually add sugar, 1 tablespoon at a time, beating on high until stiff peaks form. Carefully spread over filling, sealing to edges of cake. Bake at 350° for 12-15 minutes or until lightly browned. **Yield:** 6-8 servings.

1-1/2 cups cold water
   1 package (3 ounces) peach, apricot *or* orange gelatin
   2 cups frozen unsweetened sliced peaches
   1 package (3 ounces) cream cheese, softened
   3 tablespoons confectioners' sugar
   1 tablespoon milk
1-1/2 cups whipped topping
   1 extra-servings-size graham cracker crust (9 ounces)

1. In a large saucepan, combine the sugar and cornstarch. Stir in water until smooth. Bring to a boil; cook and stir for 1-2 minutes or until thickened. Remove from the heat; whisk in gelatin until dissolved. Add the peaches. Refrigerate until slightly thickened, about 20 minutes.

2. In a large mixing bowl, beat the cream cheese, confectioners' sugar and milk until smooth. Fold in whipped topping. Spoon into pie crust. Spoon gelatin mixture over cream cheese layer. Refrigerate until set, about 3 hours. **Yield:** 8 servings.

Editor's Note: This recipe was tested with a Keebler extra-servings-size graham cracker crust. This pie crust size is needed for the large amount of filling.

🎗🎗🎗
Peachy Cream Pie

Gina Glassford, Provo, Utah

It's easy to turn a store-bought graham cracker crust, frozen peaches and whipped topping into this pretty pie.

  3/4 cup sugar
   5 teaspoons cornstarch

2-1/2 cups self-rising flour
   1 teaspoon ground cinnamon
   1 cup sliced almonds
FROSTING:
  1/2 cup butter, cubed
   1 cup packed brown sugar
   1 cup evaporated milk
   3 egg yolks, beaten
1-1/2 cups flaked coconut
   1 cup sliced almonds
   1 teaspoon vanilla extract

1. In a large mixing bowl, beat oil and sugar. Add eggs, one at a time, beating well after each addition. Add sweet potato, water and vanilla; mix well. Combine flour and cinnamon; add to potato mixture. Stir in almonds.

2. Pour into a greased 13-in. x 9-in. x 2-in. baking pan. Bake at 350° for 40-45 minutes or until a toothpick inserted near the center comes out clean.

3. For frosting, melt butter in a saucepan; whisk in sugar, milk and egg yolks until smooth. Bring to a boil over medium heat; boil gently for 2 minutes. Remove from the heat; stir in coconut, almonds and vanilla. Spread over warm cake. Cool on a wire rack. **Yield:** 12-15 servings.

Editor's Note: As a substitute for each cup of self-rising flour, place 1-1/2 teaspoons baking powder and 1/2 teaspoon salt in a measuring cup. Add all-purpose flour to measure 1 cup.

🎗🎗🎗
Sweet Potato Cake

Wanda Rolen, Sevierville, Tennessee

I often bake for church dinners, and many people have told me how much they like this sweet, Southern-style dessert.

   1 cup vegetable oil
   2 cups sugar
   4 eggs
1-1/2 cups finely shredded uncooked sweet potato (about 1 medium)
  1/4 cup hot water
   1 teaspoon vanilla extract

🎗🎗🎗
Rich Chocolate Cake

Connie Scheffer, Salina, Kansas

For Valentine's Day and other special occasions, I treat all of my sweeties to this fudgy cake. A small slice satisfies even the most passionate chocolate fan.

2-2/3 cups (16 ounces) semisweet chocolate chips
    1 cup butter, softened
    1 cup half-and-half cream
    1 cup sugar
    8 eggs
    2 tablespoons vanilla extract
GLAZE:
    1 cup (6 ounces) semisweet chocolate chips
    3 tablespoons half-and-half cream
    2 tablespoons butter, softened
    2 tablespoons corn syrup
Fresh raspberries and fresh mint, optional

1. Grease a 10-in. springform pan and wrap bottom of pan with heavy-duty foil; set aside.

2. In a large saucepan, combine the chips, butter, cream and sugar; cook over low heat until chocolate is melted, stirring occasionally. Remove from the heat; stir until smooth. Pour into a large mixing bowl; cool.

3. In another large mixing bowl, beat the eggs on high for 3 minutes or until light and fluffy. Beat into the chocolate mixture, a third at a time, until well blended. Stir in the vanilla.

4. Pour into prepared pan; place on a baking sheet. Bake at 350° for 45-50 minutes or until a toothpick inserted near the center comes out with moist crumbs (top will crack). Cool on a wire rack (cake will settle). Cover and chill for 1 hour. Run a knife around edge of pan before removing sides.

5. For glaze, in a large saucepan, combine the chips, cream, butter and corn syrup; cook over low heat until chocolate is melted, stirring occasionally. Remove from the heat; stir until smooth.

6. Spread enough of the glaze over top and sides of cake to cover. Chill for 10 minutes. Repeat with remaining glaze. Chill overnight. Serve with raspberries and mint if desired. Refrigerate leftovers. **Yield:** 12-16 servings.

🎗🎗🎗
Soda Fountain Pie

Marsha Hanson, Ponsford, Minnesota

The first time I made this frosty pie was during winter, using frozen berries, and it was a hit. It's an even bigger hit on hot summer days when you're craving something cool.

1-1/2 cups crushed sugar cones (about 12)
    1/2 cup butter, melted
    1/4 cup sugar
3-1/2 cups fresh strawberries, *divided*
    1 quart vanilla ice cream, softened
    1/3 cup malted milk powder
1-1/2 cups fudge ice cream topping, softened
Additional strawberries, optional

1. Combine crushed sugar cones, butter and sugar. Press onto the bottom and up the sides of an ungreased 10-in. pie plate. Freeze.

2. Place 3 cups of strawberries in a blender or food processor; cover and puree. Chop remaining berries. Place pureed and chopped berries in a large bowl. Add ice cream and malted milk powder; stir to blend. Pour into prepared crust. Cover and freeze overnight.

3. Spread fudge topping over the pie to within 1 in. of edge; freeze for at least 2 hours. Remove from the freezer 20 minutes before serving. Serve with additional berries if desired. **Yield:** 8-10 servings.

🎀🎀🎀
Chocolate Strawberry Torte

(Also pictured on page 188)

Paula Magnus, Republic, Washington

This impressive torte boasts a tantalizing combination—chocolate and fresh strawberries. When you're looking for an extra-special dessert, this is the one!

        5 squares (1 ounce *each*) semisweet chocolate
    3/4 cup butter, cubed
1-1/2 cups sugar
        3 eggs
        2 teaspoons vanilla extract
2-1/2 cups all-purpose flour
        1 teaspoon baking soda
        1/4 teaspoon salt
1-1/2 cups water
STRAWBERRY FILLING:
        4 cups sliced fresh strawberries
        2 tablespoons sugar
        1 teaspoon vanilla extract
GLAZE:
        3 squares (1 ounce *each*) semisweet chocolate
        1 tablespoon butter

        1 cup confectioners' sugar
        3 tablespoons water
    1/2 teaspoon vanilla extract
        1 carton (8 ounces) frozen whipped topping, thawed

1. In a heavy saucepan or microwave, melt chocolate and butter; stir until smooth. Transfer to a large mixing bowl; add sugar. Add the eggs, one at a time, beating well after each addition. Add vanilla. Combine the flour, baking soda and salt; add to chocolate mixture alternately with water and beat until smooth.

2. Pour into two greased and floured 9-in. round baking pans. Bake at 350° for 28-33 minutes or until a toothpick inserted near the center comes out clean. Cool for 10 minutes before removing from the pans to wire racks.

3. In a large bowl, combine filling ingredients; set aside. For glaze, melt chocolate and butter in a heavy saucepan or microwave; stir until smooth. Stir in confectioners' sugar, water and vanilla until smooth. Cool slightly.

4. To assemble, place one cake layer on a serving plate. Spread with half of the whipped topping; drizzle with half of the glaze. Top with half of the filling. Repeat layers. Store in the refrigerator. **Yield:** 10-12 servings.

★ ★ ★
Frosted Orange Pie

Delores Edgecomb, Atlanta, New York

With its tangy citrus filling and fluffy frosting, this coconut-topped pie is truly an elegant ending for a meal.

- 3/4 cup sugar
- 1/2 cup all-purpose flour
- 1/4 teaspoon salt
- 1-1/4 cups water
- 2 egg yolks, lightly beaten
- 2 to 3 tablespoons grated orange peel
- 1/2 teaspoon grated lemon peel
- 1/2 cup orange juice
- 2 tablespoons lemon juice
- 1 pastry shell (9 inches), baked

FROSTING:
- 1/2 cup sugar
- 2 egg whites
- 2 tablespoons water
- 1/8 teaspoon cream of tartar
- 1/8 teaspoon salt
- 1/2 cup flaked coconut, toasted

1. In a saucepan, combine sugar, flour and salt; gradually add water. Cook and stir over medium-high heat for 2-3 minutes or until thickened and bubbly. Remove from heat. Gradually stir 1/2 cup into egg yolks; return all to pan. Bring to a gentle boil; cook and stir for 2 minutes. Remove from the heat; stir in orange and lemon peel. Gently stir in juices. Pour into pastry shell. Cool on a wire rack for 1 hour. Chill at least 3 hours.

2. In a heavy saucepan or double boiler, combine sugar, egg whites, water, cream of tartar and salt. With a portable mixer, beat on low speed for 1 minute. Continue beating on low over low heat until frosting forms stiff peaks, about 7 minutes. Spread over chilled pie. Just before serving, sprinkle with coconut. Store in the refrigerator. **Yield:** 6-8 servings.

★ ★ ★
Pecan Chip Tube Cake

Janet Keppinger, Salem, Oregon

This quick, crowd-size recipe is a fun one to make with children. They love sprinkling the pecans, chocolate chips and miniature marshmallows over the batter, and they're so proud of the final result.

- 1 package (18-1/4 ounces) yellow cake mix
- 1 package (3.4 ounces) instant vanilla pudding mix
- 4 eggs
- 1 cup vegetable oil
- 1 cup (8 ounces) sour cream
- 1 cup chopped pecans
- 1 cup (6 ounces) semisweet chocolate chips
- 1 cup miniature marshmallows

1. In a large mixing bowl, combine the first five ingredients. Beat on low speed for 2 minutes or until the ingredients are combined.

2. Pour half of the batter into a greased and floured 10-in. tube pan. Combine pecans and chocolate chips; sprinkle half over batter. Top with marshmallows and remaining batter; sprinkle with remaining pecan mixture.

3. Bake at 350° for 55-60 minutes or until a toothpick inserted near the center comes out clean. Cool for 10 minutes; invert cake to remove from pan and immediately invert again onto a serving plate. **Yield:** 12-16 servings.

✿✿✿
Hawaiian Sunset Cake

Kara De la Vega, Suisun City, California

This three-layer orange cake is special enough for guests, but it's so simple to fix that you'll find yourself making it all the time. Store-bought mixes keep this dessert convenient while the pineapple-coconut filling makes it a crowd-pleaser.

1 package (18-1/4 ounces) **white** *or* **orange cake mix**
1 package (3.4 ounces) **instant vanilla pudding mix**
1 package (3 ounces) **orange gelatin**
4 **eggs**
1-1/2 cups **milk**
1/2 cup **vegetable oil**
FILLING:
1 can (20 ounces) **crushed pineapple, drained**
2 cups **sugar**
1 package (10 ounces) **flaked coconut**
1 cup (8 ounces) **sour cream**
1 carton (8 ounces) **frozen whipped topping, thawed**
Toasted coconut, optional

1. In a large mixing bowl, combine the first six ingredients. Pour into three greased and floured 9-in. round baking pans. Bake at 350° for 25-30 minutes or until a toothpick inserted near the center comes out clean. Cool for 10 minutes before removing from pans to wire racks to cool completely.

2. In a large bowl, combine the pineapple, sugar, coconut and sour cream. Remove 1 cup to another bowl; set aside. Place one cake on a serving plate; top with a third of the remaining pineapple mixture. Repeat layers twice.

3. Fold whipped topping into the reserved pineapple mixture. Spread over top and sides of cake. Sprinkle with toasted coconut if desired. Refrigerate. **Yield:** 12-16 servings.

✿✿✿
Cheddar Pear Pie

Cynthia LaBree, Elmer, New Jersey

With the sprinkling of cheddar cheese on top of this pie, some people may think you're serving an apple pie. They'll be delightfully surprised when they take a bite and discover the subtle sweetness of the pears.

4 large ripe **pears, peeled and thinly sliced**
1/3 cup **sugar**
1 tablespoon **cornstarch**
1/8 teaspoon **salt**
1 unbaked **pastry shell (9 inches)**
TOPPING:
1/2 cup **shredded cheddar cheese**
1/2 cup **all-purpose flour**
1/4 cup **sugar**
1/4 teaspoon **salt**
1/4 cup **butter, melted**

1. In a large bowl, combine pears, sugar, cornstarch and salt; toss gently to coat. Pour into pastry shell.

2. For topping, combine the cheese, flour, sugar and salt; stir in butter until crumbly. Sprinkle over filling. Bake at 425° for 25-35 minutes or until crust is golden and cheese is melted. Cool on wire rack for 15-20 minutes. Serve warm. Store in refrigerator. **Yield:** 6-8 servings.

✿✿✿ Frozen Chocolate Mint Pie

(Pictured on page 188)

Jenny Falk, Sauk Rapids, Minnesota

This refreshing treat was served at a small resort my family visited regularly when I was growing up. Every time I make the pie now, I relish fond memories of sunny days at the beach and home-style cooking.

        3 egg whites
    1/4 teaspoon cream of tartar
        1 cup sugar
CHOCOLATE SAUCE:
    1/4 cup butter
        1 square (1 ounce) unsweetened chocolate
        1 cup sugar
    3/4 cup evaporated milk
    1/2 teaspoon vanilla extract
    1/8 teaspoon peppermint extract
Dash salt

        2 cups vanilla ice cream, softened
    1-1/3 cups heavy whipping cream, whipped

1. In a large mixing bowl, beat egg whites until foamy. Add cream of tartar; beat until soft peaks form. Gradually add sugar, 1 tablespoon at a time, beating until stiff glossy peaks form.

2. Spread onto the bottom and up the sides of a greased and floured 9-in. deep-dish pie plate. Bake at 275° for 1 hour. Turn off oven and do not open door; let meringue cool completely inside the oven.

3. For chocolate sauce, in heavy saucepan, melt butter and chocolate; stir until smooth. Stir in sugar and evaporated milk. Cook over low heat for 45-60 minutes or until thickened, stirring occasionally. Remove saucepan from the heat; stir in the extracts and the salt. Cool to room temperature.

4. Spread ice cream into meringue crust. Fold whipped cream into cooled chocolate sauce. Spread over ice cream layer; freeze until firm. **Yield:** 8 servings.

✿✿✿ Cranberry Crumb Cake

(Also pictured on page 189)

Sue Ellen Smith, Philadelphia, Mississippi

This comforting cake is light, easy to prepare and perfect with a cup of coffee. The berry flavor comes through in every sweet-tart piece...and the streusel topping looks so pretty.

 Uses less fat, sugar or salt. Includes Nutrition Facts and Diabetic Exchanges.

        1 cup all-purpose flour
    1/2 cup plus 1/3 cup sugar, *divided*
        2 teaspoons baking powder
    1/2 teaspoon salt
        1 egg, lightly beaten
    1/2 cup fat-free milk
        1 tablespoon orange juice
        1 tablespoon canola oil
    1/4 teaspoon almond extract
        2 cups fresh *or* frozen cranberries, chopped
TOPPING:
    1/4 cup all-purpose flour
        3 tablespoons sugar
        2 tablespoons cold butter

1. In a large bowl, combine the flour, 1/2 cup sugar, baking powder and salt. Combine the egg, milk, orange juice, oil and extract; stir into dry ingredients. Spoon into an 8-in. square baking dish coated with nonstick cooking spray. Combine cranberries and remaining sugar; spoon over batter.

2. For topping, combine flour and sugar in a small bowl; cut in the butter until crumbly. Sprinkle over cranberries. Bake at 375° for 35-45 minutes or until edges begin to pull away from sides of pan. Refrigerate leftovers. **Yield:** 9 servings.

Nutrition Facts: 1 piece equals 212 calories, 5 g fat (2 g saturated fat), 31 mg cholesterol, 203 mg sodium, 40 g carbohydrate, 1 g fiber, 3 g protein. **Diabetic Exchanges:** 2 starch, 1 fat, 1/2 fruit.

Cran-Apple Cobbler, p. 220

Crustless New York Cheesecake, p. 217

Banana Cream Brownie Dessert, p. 224

Just Desserts

Save room for comforting cobblers, rich and creamy cheesecakes, sensational souffles, eye-catching trifles or any of the decadent confections here. They're sure to make meals extra special.

Cranberry Walnut White Fudge, p. 223

🎗🎗🎗 Peanut Butter Snowballs

Wanda Regula, Birmingham, Michigan

These creamy treats are a nice change from the typical milk chocolate and peanut butter combination. Put these snowballs in candy boxes or tins, and you'll have yummy holiday gifts for friends and neighbors.

- **1 cup confectioners' sugar**
- **1/2 cup creamy peanut butter**
- **3 tablespoons butter, softened**
- **1 pound white candy coating**

1. In a mixing bowl, combine sugar, peanut butter and butter; mix well. Shape into 1-in. balls and place on waxed paper-lined baking sheet. Chill for 30 minutes or until firm.

2. Meanwhile, melt the candy coating in a double boiler or microwave-safe bowl. Dip balls and place on waxed paper to harden. **Yield:** 2 dozen.

🎗🎗🎗 Chocolate Souffles

Jeannette Mango, Parkesburg, Pennsylvania

Baked in individual custard cups, these chocolaty delights are wonderful with Christmas dinner. For variety, try sprinkling fresh raspberries or chocolate curls on top.

✓ Uses less fat, sugar or salt. Includes Nutrition Facts.

- **7 teaspoons plus 2/3 cup sugar, *divided***
- **1/2 cup packed brown sugar**
- **1/3 cup cake flour**
- **1/2 cup baking cocoa**
- **2 teaspoons instant coffee granules**
- **3/4 cup water**
- **4 squares (1 ounce *each*) semisweet chocolate**
- **3 egg yolks, beaten**
- **6 egg whites**
- **1/2 teaspoon cream of tartar**
- **1 teaspoon confectioners' sugar**

1. Spray seven 10-oz. souffle dishes with nonstick cooking spray. Sprinkle 1 teaspoon of sugar into each dish, tilting to coat the bottom and sides; set aside.

2. In a saucepan, combine 1/3 cup sugar, brown sugar, flour, cocoa and coffee granules. Stir in water until blended. Bring to a boil; cook and stir for 1 minute (mixture will be thick). Remove from the heat. Stir in chocolate until melted. Stir a small amount of hot filling into egg yolks; return all to the pan, stirring constantly. Cool to room temperature.

3. Let egg whites stand at room temperature for 30 minutes. In a mixing bowl, beat egg whites until foamy. Add cream of tartar; beat on medium speed until soft peaks form. Gradually add remaining sugar, 1 tablespoon at a time, beating on high until stiff peaks form. Gently fold a fourth of the egg white mixture into chocolate mixture; fold in remaining egg white mixture.

4. Spoon the batter into the prepared souffle dishes. Bake at 325° for 25-35 minutes or until a toothpick inserted near the center comes out clean. Cool on wire racks. Dust with confectioners' sugar. Refrigerate leftovers. **Yield:** 7 servings.

Nutrition Facts: 1 serving equals 313 calories, 8 g fat (4 g saturated fat), 91 mg cholesterol, 57 mg sodium, 58 g carbohydrate, 5 g fiber, 7 g protein.

★★★
Light Lemon Cheesecake

Deborah Lobe, Olympia, Washington

My family loves cheesecake but not the fat that usually comes with it. This pretty, fruit-topped alternative offers a smooth texture and luscious taste without the guilt.

✓ Uses less fat, sugar or salt. Includes Nutrition Facts and Diabetic Exchanges.

   3/4 cup reduced-fat cinnamon graham cracker crumbs (4 whole crackers)
   3 packages (8 ounces *each*) fat-free cream cheese
   2 packages (8 ounces *each*) reduced-fat cream cheese
1-2/3 cups sugar
  1/8 teaspoon salt
   9 egg whites
  1/4 cup lemon juice
1-1/2 teaspoons vanilla extract
   1 teaspoon grated lemon peel
   8 strawberries, sliced
   2 medium kiwifruit, peeled and sliced

1. Sprinkle graham cracker crumbs on the bottom and up the sides of a 9-in. springform pan well coated with nonstick cooking spray; set aside. In a large mixing bowl, beat cream cheese, sugar and salt until smooth.

Add egg whites; beat on low speed just until combined, about 2 minutes. Stir in the lemon juice, vanilla and lemon peel.

2. Pour into prepared pan. Bake at 325° for 70-80 minutes or until center is almost set. Turn oven off; leave cheesecake in oven with door ajar for 30 minutes.

3. Remove from oven. Carefully run a knife around edge of pan to loosen. Cool 1 hour longer. Refrigerate overnight. Remove sides of pan. Top with strawberries and kiwi. Refrigerate leftovers. **Yield:** 12 servings.

Nutrition Facts: 1 piece equals 300 calories, 8 g fat (5 g saturated fat), 26 mg cholesterol, 522 mg sodium, 42 g carbohydrate, 1 g fiber, 15 g protein. **Diabetic Exchanges:** 2 fat-free milk, 1 fruit, 1 fat.

★★★
Strawberry Cream Puffs

Sherry Adams, Mount Ayr, Iowa

Many people think cream puffs are difficult to make, but these never let me down. They're a great way to use fresh berries.

   1 cup water
  1/2 cup butter, cubed
   1 teaspoon sugar
  1/4 teaspoon salt
   1 cup all-purpose flour
   4 eggs
CREAM FILLING:
   2 pints fresh strawberries, sliced
  1/2 cup sugar, *divided*
   2 cups heavy whipping cream
Confectioners' sugar
Additional sliced strawberries
Mint leaves

1. In a large saucepan, bring the water, butter, sugar and salt to a boil. Add the flour all at once and stir until a smooth ball forms. Remove from the heat; let stand for 5 minutes. Beat in the eggs, one at a time, beating well after each addition. Continue beating until the mixture is smooth and shiny.

2. Drop by tablespoonfuls 2 in. apart on a large ungreased baking sheet (make 10). Bake at 400° for about 35 minutes or until golden brown. Cool on a wire rack.

3. For filling, combine berries and 1/4 cup sugar. Chill 30 minutes.

4. Beat cream and remaining sugar until stiff. Just before serving, cut tops off puffs. Combine berries and cream mixture. Fill cream puffs and replace tops. Sprinkle with confectioners' sugar and serve with additional berries and mint leaves. **Yield:** 10 cream puffs.

★ ★ ★
Raspberry-Filled Meringue Torte

Rosemarie Cook, Haliburton, Ontario

My family loves to have this impressive-looking torte with holiday meals. I've relied on the light meringue recipe for as long as I can remember—it's a success every time I make it.

☑ Uses less fat, sugar or salt. Includes Nutrition Facts.

    6 egg whites
1/4 teaspoon cream of tartar
1-1/2 cups sugar
    1 cup flaked coconut
1/2 cup cornstarch
FILLING:
    2 packages (10 ounces *each*) frozen sweetened raspberries
    3 tablespoons cornstarch
    2 tablespoons sugar
    1 carton (8 ounces) frozen reduced-fat whipped topping, thawed
  10 fresh raspberries

1. Line baking sheets with parchment paper and trace five 7-1/2-in. circles on paper; set aside.

2. In a large mixing bowl, beat the egg whites until foamy. Add cream of tartar; beat on medium speed until soft peaks form. Gradually add sugar, 1 tablespoon at a time, beating on high until stiff peaks form. Combine coconut and cornstarch; fold into meringue.

3. Spread meringue evenly over each circle on prepared pans. Bake at 300° for 30 minutes or until firm and lightly golden. Cool for 5 minutes. Gently remove meringues from baking sheets to wire racks to cool completely.

4. Meanwhile, drain raspberries, reserving juice. Set the berries aside. Add enough water to juice to measure 2 cups. In a saucepan, combine cornstarch and sugar; stir in the raspberry liquid until smooth. Bring to a boil; cook and stir for 2 minutes or until thickened. Cool completely. Fold in the sweetened raspberries.

5. To assemble, place one meringue on a serving plate; top with 2/3 cup whipped topping and 3/4 cup raspberry filling. Repeat three times. Top with remaining meringue layer and whipped topping. Refrigerate for 1 hour before serving. Garnish with fresh berries. Cut with a serrated knife. **Yield:** 10 servings.

Nutrition Facts: One piece equals 332 calories, 6 g fat (6 g saturated fat), 0 cholesterol, 59 mg sodium, 66 g carbohydrate, 3 g fiber, 3 g protein.

🎀🎀🎀
Chocolate Caramel Fondue

Cheryl Arnold, Lake Zurich, Illinois

Keep the ingredients for this wonderfully rich treat on hand, and you'll be able to quickly whip up dessert when unexpected company drops by. I serve the thick fondue in punch cups so guests can carry it on a plate alongside fresh strawberries, pretzels and other dippers.

1 can (14 ounces) sweetened condensed milk
1 jar (12 ounces) caramel ice cream topping
3 squares (1 ounce *each*) unsweetened chocolate
Assorted fresh fruit *and/or* pretzels

In a large saucepan, combine the sweetened condensed milk, caramel topping and chocolate. Cook over low heat until chocolate is melted. Serve with fruit and/or pretzels. **Yield:** 2-1/2 cups.

🎀🎀🎀
Apple Pockets

Sharon Martin, Terre Hill, Pennsylvania

With this lightened-up version of apple pie, you can enjoy a traditional dessert without the guilt. The cute golden bundles are shaped using a homemade yeast dough, but it's their old-fashioned flavor that really appeals.

✓ Uses less fat, sugar or salt. Includes Nutrition Facts and Diabetic Exchanges.

2-1/4 cups all-purpose flour, *divided*
1 package (1/4 ounce) quick-rise yeast
1 tablespoon sugar
1/2 teaspoon salt

2/3 cup water
1/4 cup butter
FILLING:
    4 cups thinly sliced peeled Rome Beauty *or* other baking apples (2 to 3 medium)
1/3 cup sugar
2 tablespoons all-purpose flour
1/2 teaspoon ground cinnamon
TOPPING:
1/4 cup milk
4 teaspoons sugar

1. In a large mixing bowl, combine 1 cup flour, yeast, sugar and salt. In a saucepan, heat the water and butter to 120°-130°. Add to the dry ingredients; beat just until moistened. Stir in enough remaining flour to form a soft dough. Turn onto a floured surface; knead until smooth and elastic, about 6-8 minutes. Cover and let rest for 10 minutes.

2. Divide dough into four portions. Roll each portion into an 8-in. square. Cut into four 4-in. squares. Cut apple slices into thirds; toss with sugar, flour and cinnamon. Place 1/4 cup filling on each square; bring up the corners over the filling and pinch to seal. Secure with a toothpick if needed. Place 3 in. apart on baking sheets coated with nonstick cooking spray. Cover and let rise in a warm place for 30 minutes.

3. Brush with milk; sprinkle with sugar. Bake at 375° for 12-14 minutes or until golden brown. Remove to wire racks. Discard toothpicks before serving. **Yield:** 16 servings.

Nutrition Facts: 1 pocket equals 136 calories, 3 g fat (2 g saturated fat), 8 mg cholesterol, 105 mg sodium, 25 g carbohydrate, 1 g fiber, 2 g protein. **Diabetic Exchanges:** 1 starch, 1/2 fruit, 1/2 fat.

🎖🎖🎖
Orange Cream Cheesecake

Madonna Faunce, Boise, Idaho

With pretty layers and a silky-smooth texture, this impressive-looking cheesecake is always a joy to serve.

- 2 cups graham cracker crumbs
- 1 teaspoon ground cinnamon
- 1 teaspoon grated orange peel
- 1/2 cup butter, melted

FILLING:
- 1 package (3 ounces) orange gelatin
- 3 packages (8 ounces *each*) cream cheese, softened
- 1-1/4 cups sugar
- 1 can (5 ounces) evaporated milk
- 1 teaspoon lemon juice
- 1/3 cup orange juice concentrate
- 1 teaspoon vanilla extract
- 1 envelope unflavored gelatin
- 2 tablespoons cold water
- 2 tablespoons boiling water
- 1 carton (8 ounces) frozen whipped topping, thawed

TOPPING:
- 2 cups whipped topping
- 1/4 cup sugar
- Lemon slices, orange peel strips, kumquats and lemon balm for garnish, optional

1. In a large bowl, combine crumbs, cinnamon, peel and butter. Press onto bottom of a greased 10-in. springform pan. Refrigerate for at least 30 minutes.

2. Prepare orange gelatin according to package directions. Set aside 1/2 cup at room temperature. Chill remaining gelatin until slightly thickened, 40-60 minutes.

3. In a large mixing bowl, beat cream cheese and sugar for 2 minutes. Gradually beat in milk and lemon juice. Beat on medium-high speed 2 minutes longer. Gradually beat in orange juice concentrate and vanilla.

4. In a small bowl, sprinkle unflavored gelatin over cold water; let stand for 2 minutes. Stir in boiling water until gelatin is completely dissolved. Stir into room temperature orange gelatin. Stir into cream cheese mixture, then fold in whipped topping. Pour into crust.

5. For topping, in a large mixing bowl, beat whipped topping and sugar. Beat in chilled gelatin (mixture will be thin). Chill for 30 minutes. Gently spoon over filling (pan will be full). Refrigerate for 8 hours or overnight. Garnish with lemon slices, peel, kumquats and lemon balm if desired. **Yield:** 10-12 servings.

🎖🎖🎖
Rocky Road Freeze

Sheila Berry, Carrying Place, Ontario

For an irresistible dessert-on-the-go, put a double dip of this yummy treat in a cone. The recipe is also great for special occasions—it looks lovely in a clear-glass sauce dish.

- 1 can (14 ounces) sweetened condensed milk
- 1/2 cup chocolate syrup
- 2 cups heavy whipping cream
- 1 cup miniature marshmallows
- 1/2 cup miniature chocolate chips
- 1/2 cup chopped salted peanuts

1. In a small bowl, combine the milk and chocolate syrup; set aside. In a large mixing bowl, beat cream until stiff peaks form. Fold in chocolate mixture, marshmallows, chocolate chips and peanuts.

2. Transfer to a freezer-proof container; cover and freeze for 5 hours or until firm. Remove from freezer 10 minutes before serving. **Yield:** about 1-1/2 quarts.

Cran-Apple Crisp

Diane Everett, Newtown, Connecticut

Cranberries, walnuts and orange peel make this apple-packed dessert extra special. After the first taste, guests will be asking for the recipe...and a second helping!

 Uses less fat, sugar or salt. Includes Nutrition Facts and Diabetic Exchanges.

- 8 cups sliced peeled Granny Smith *or* other tart apples (about 5 large)
- 3/4 cup sugar
- 1/2 cup dried cranberries
- 1/2 cup chopped walnuts
- 1/4 cup all-purpose flour
- 1-1/2 to 2 teaspoons grated orange peel
- 1/2 cup packed brown sugar
- 1/3 cup whole wheat flour
- 1/3 cup nonfat dry milk powder
- 1 teaspoon ground cinnamon
- 1/4 to 1/2 teaspoon cloves
- 5 tablespoons cold butter
- 1/3 cup quick-cooking oats

1. In a large bowl, combine the first six ingredients; toss to coat. Transfer to a 13-in. x 9-in. x 2-in. baking dish coated with nonstick cooking spray.

2. For topping, in a small bowl, combine the brown sugar, whole wheat flour, milk powder, cinnamon and cloves. Cut in butter until mixture resembles coarse crumbs. Stir in oats. Sprinkle over apples. Bake, uncovered, at 350° for 40-45 minutes or until golden brown. **Yield:** 15 servings.

Nutrition Facts: 1 serving equals 202 calories, 7 g fat (3 g saturated fat), 11 mg cholesterol, 51 mg sodium, 35 g carbohydrate, 2 g fiber, 2 g protein. **Diabetic Exchanges:** 1-1/2 fat, 1 starch, 1 fruit.

Chocolate Mint Eclair Dessert

Renee Ratcliffe, Charlotte, North Carolina

My college roommate gave me this recipe, which I lightened up a bit. I think the combination of mint and chocolate is perfect for the holiday season.

 Uses less fat, sugar or salt. Includes Nutrition Facts and Diabetic Exchanges.

- 23 whole chocolate graham crackers
- 3 cups cold fat-free milk
- 2 packages (3.3 to 3.4 ounces *each*) instant white chocolate *or* vanilla pudding mix
- 1/2 teaspoon mint *or* peppermint extract
- 3 to 4 drops green food coloring, optional
- 1 carton (8 ounces) frozen reduced-fat whipped topping, thawed

CHOCOLATE FROSTING:
- 1 tablespoon butter
- 2 tablespoons baking cocoa
- 2 tablespoons plus 1 teaspoon fat-free milk
- 1 teaspoon vanilla extract
- 1 cup confectioners' sugar

1. Coat a 13-in. x 9-in. x 2-in. dish with nonstick cooking spray. Break five whole graham crackers in half; line the bottom of pan with three half crackers and six whole crackers.

2. In a bowl, whisk milk and pudding mix for 2 minutes. Whisk in extract and food coloring if desired. Fold in whipped topping. Spread half over graham crackers. Top with a another layer of three half and six whole crackers. Top with remaining pudding mixture and graham crackers (save remaining half cracker for another use). Cover and refrigerate for 2 hours.

3. For frosting, melt butter in a saucepan. Stir in cocoa and milk until blended. Remove from the heat; stir in vanilla and confectioners' sugar. Spread over dessert. Cover and refrigerate overnight. **Yield:** 15 servings.

Nutrition Facts: 1 piece equals 244 calories, 7 g fat (3 g saturated fat), 3 mg cholesterol, 296 mg sodium, 41 g carbohydrate, 1 g fiber, 4 g protein. **Diabetic Exchanges:** 2 starch, 1 fat, 1/2 fruit.

✿✿✿ Coconut Angel Squares

Betty Claycomb, Alverton, Pennsylvania

I have so many fast-to-fix dessert recipes, but this one is truly special. It tastes like a coconut cream pie but requires only a fraction of the work.

- 1 prepared angel food cake (8 inches), cut into 1/2-inch cubes
- 1-1/2 cups cold milk
- 2 packages (3.4 ounces *each*) instant coconut cream pudding mix
- 1 quart vanilla ice cream, softened
- 1 carton (8 ounces) frozen whipped topping, thawed
- 1/4 cup flaked coconut, toasted

1. Place cake cubes in a greased 13-in. x 9-in. x 2-in. dish. In a mixing bowl, beat milk and pudding mixes on low speed for 2 minutes. Add ice cream; beat on low just until combined.

2. Spoon over cake cubes. Spread with whipped topping; sprinkle with coconut. Cover and chill for at least 1 hour. Refrigerate leftovers. **Yield:** 12-15 servings.

✿✿✿ Strawberry Graham Dessert

Audrey Huckell, Wabigoon, Ontario

My mother passed this yummy recipe on to me, and I've been serving it to my family for years. The strawberries and cream cheese make it easy to dress up ordinary gelatin.

- 1 cup graham cracker crumbs (about 16 squares)
- 2 tablespoons butter, melted
- 1 package (3 ounces) strawberry gelatin
- 1 cup boiling water
- 1 package (16 ounces) frozen sweetened sliced strawberries, thawed
- 1 tablespoon lemon juice
- 4 ounces cream cheese, softened
- 1/2 cup confectioners' sugar
- 1 teaspoon vanilla extract

Dash salt
- 1 cup heavy whipping cream, whipped

Fresh strawberries and mint, optional

1. In a small bowl, combine cracker crumbs and butter; set aside 1 tablespoon for topping. Press the remaining crumb mixture onto the bottom of a greased 8-in. square baking dish. Bake at 325° for 10-14 minutes or until golden brown. Cool on a wire rack.

2. In a large bowl, dissolve gelatin in boiling water; stir in strawberries and lemon juice. Refrigerate until partially set, about 1-1/2 hours.

3. In a small mixing bowl, beat the cream cheese, sugar, vanilla and salt until smooth. Fold in whipped cream. Spread half over cooled crust. Cover and refrigerate remaining cream mixture.

4. Pour the gelatin mixture over the filling; refrigerate until firm. Top with the remaining cream mixture. Sprinkle with the reserved crumb mixture. Refrigerate overnight. Garnish with fresh strawberries and mint if desired. **Yield:** 9 servings.

🎗️🎗️🎗️
Crustless New York Cheesecake

(Also pictured on page 208 and on front cover)

Mrs. George Parsell, Flushing, New York

With an array of fresh fruit on top, this rich and decadent dessert is stunning. Your guests will be amazed at how much they enjoy a cheesecake that doesn't have a crust.

    1-1/2 cups sugar
        3 tablespoons cornstarch
        3 cups (24 ounces) ricotta cheese
        2 tablespoons lemon juice
        2 packages (8 ounces *each*) cream cheese,
          softened
      1/2 cup butter, softened
        4 eggs, lightly beaten
        1 teaspoon vanilla extract
        2 cups (16 ounces) sour cream
        3 tablespoons all-purpose flour
Assorted fresh fruit

1. In a large mixing bowl, combine the sugar, cornstarch, ricotta and lemon juice until smooth. Add cream cheese and butter; mix well. Add eggs and vanilla; beat on low speed just until combined. Add sour cream and flour; beat just until combined. Pour into a greased 9-in. springform pan. Place pan on a baking sheet.

2. Bake at 325° for 70-75 minutes or until edges are lightly browned and top is dry to the touch (the center 5 inches of cheesecake will not be set). Cool on a wire rack for 10 minutes. Carefully run a knife around the edge of pan to loosen; cool 1 hour longer.

3. Refrigerate overnight. Remove sides of pan. Garnish with fruit. Refrigerate leftovers. **Yield:** 12-16 servings.

🎗️🎗️🎗️
Baked Barley Pudding

Judy Berarducci, Port St. Lucie, Florida

This homey dessert has the same sweet and satisfying flavor as traditional rice pudding. The custard-like treat bakes up firm, golden and irresistible.

    1-1/4 cups water
      1/2 cup uncooked medium pearl barley
      1/4 teaspoon salt
        2 cups milk
        1 cup heavy whipping cream
      1/2 cup sugar
        2 eggs
        1 teaspoon vanilla extract
      1/2 cup golden raisins
      1/4 teaspoon ground cinnamon

1. In a saucepan, bring water to a boil. Stir in barley and salt. Reduce heat; simmer, uncovered, for 15 minutes, stirring occasionally. Add milk; cook over medium-low heat for 10 minutes or until barley is almost tender, stirring frequently. In a bowl, whisk the cream, sugar, eggs and vanilla; gradually stir into the barley mixture.

2. Spoon into eight greased 6-oz. custard cups. Sprinkle with raisins and cinnamon. Place custard cups in two 9-in. baking pans. Fill both pans with boiling water to a depth of 1 in. Bake, uncovered, at 350° for 30-35 minutes or until a knife inserted near the center comes out clean. Store in the refrigerator. **Yield:** 8 servings.

Editor's Note: Pudding will appear layered when baked.

2 packages (3 ounces *each*) raspberry gelatin
2 cups boiling water
3 cups fresh *or* frozen raspberries
2 cups graham cracker crumbs (about 32 squares)
1/4 cup packed brown sugar
1/2 cup butter, melted
1-1/2 cups cold milk
1 package (3.4 ounces) instant vanilla pudding mix
1 package (8 ounces) cream cheese, softened

1. In a large bowl, combine the raspberry gelatin and boiling water; stir until the gelatin is dissolved. Fold in the raspberries. Refrigerate for 1 hour or until syrupy. In a small bowl, combine the graham cracker crumbs, brown sugar and butter. Press into a greased 13-in. x 9-in. x 2-in. dish.

2. In a large mixing bowl, beat the milk and pudding mix on low speed for 2 minutes. In another mixing bowl, beat cream cheese until smooth. Gradually add pudding. Spread over crust. Spoon gelatin mixture over the top. Chill until set. Refrigerate leftovers. **Yield:** 12-15 servings.

Raspberry Icebox Dessert

Magdalene Dyck, Burns Lake, British Columbia

After tasting this lovely dessert at a church social, I had to get the recipe. I was thrilled to learn how easy it is to make.

Rainbow Gelatin Cubes

Deanna Pietrowicz, Bridgeport, Connecticut

These eye-catching cubes are fun to serve...and to eat! I vary the colors to suit the occasion—pink and blue for a baby shower, school colors for a graduation party, etc. Kids of all ages gobble up these treats.

☑ Uses less fat, sugar or salt. Includes Nutrition Facts and Diabetic Exchanges.

4 packages (3 ounces *each*) assorted flavored gelatin
6 envelopes unflavored gelatin, *divided*
5-3/4 cups boiling water, *divided*
1 can (14 ounces) sweetened condensed milk
1/4 cup cold water

1. In a large bowl, combine one package flavored gelatin and one envelope unflavored gelatin. Stir in 1 cup boiling water until dissolved. Pour into a 13-in. x 9-in. x 2-in. dish coated with nonstick cooking spray; refrigerate until almost set but not firm, about 20 minutes.

2. In a large bowl, combine the condensed milk and 1 cup boiling water. In another bowl, sprinkle two envelopes unflavored gelatin over cold water; let stand for 1 minute. Stir in 3/4 cup boiling water. Add to the milk mixture. Spoon 1-1/4 cups of the creamy gelatin mixture over the first flavored gelatin layer. Refrigerate until set but not firm, about 25 minutes.

3. Repeat from beginning of recipe twice alternating flavored gelatin with creamy gelatin layers. Chill each layer until set but not firm before pouring the next layer on top.

4. Make final flavored gelatin; spoon over top. Refrigerate for at least 1 hour after completing last layer before cutting into 1-in. squares. **Yield:** about 9 dozen.

Nutrition Facts: 2 cubes (prepared with sugar-free gelatin and fat-free sweetened condensed milk) equals 26 calories, trace fat (0 saturated fat), 0 cholesterol, 27 mg sodium, 4 g carbohydrate, 0 fiber, 2 g protein. **Diabetic Exchange:** 1/2 fruit.

Chocolate Meringue Cups

Ellen Govertsen, Wheaton, Illinois

Looking for something low in cholesterol that will satisfy your sweet tooth? Give this airy cloud of cocoa meringue and chocolate mousse a try! It's well worth the effort.

✓ Uses less fat, sugar or salt. Includes Nutrition Facts and Diabetic Exchanges.

    4 **egg whites**
    1 **teaspoon vanilla extract**
1/2 **teaspoon salt**
1/2 **teaspoon white vinegar**
    1 **cup sugar**
    2 **tablespoons baking cocoa**
CHOCOLATE MOUSSE:
    1 **cup fat-free milk**
    1 **egg**
1/4 **cup plus 2 teaspoons corn syrup,** *divided*
1/4 **cup baking cocoa**
    3 **squares (1 ounce** *each***) semisweet chocolate**
    4 **ounces reduced-fat cream cheese**
    2 **teaspoons unflavored gelatin**
1/4 **cup plus 1 tablespoon cold water,** *divided*
    1 **teaspoon vanilla extract**
    4 **egg whites**
3/4 **cup sugar**
1/4 **teaspoon cream of tartar**
  15 **peppermint candies, crushed**

1. In a large mixing bowl, beat egg whites until foamy. Beat in the vanilla, salt and vinegar; beat on medium speed until soft peaks form. Gradually add sugar, 1 tablespoon at a time, beating on high until stiff peaks form. Sift cocoa over egg whites; fold into egg whites.

2. Drop 15 heaping tablespoonfuls onto parchment-lined baking sheets. Shape into 3-in. cups with the back of a spoon. Bake at 275° for 45 minutes or until golden brown. Turn oven off; leave meringues in the oven for 1-1/2 hours.

3. In a large saucepan, combine milk, egg, 1/4 cup corn syrup and cocoa. Cook and stir over medium heat until mixture reaches 160° and coats a metal spoon. Remove from the heat. Add chocolate and cream cheese; stir until melted.

4. In a small saucepan, sprinkle gelatin over 1/4 cup water; let stand for 1 minute. Cook and stir over low heat until gelatin is dissolved. Stir gelatin and vanilla into chocolate mixture. Cool.

5. In a heavy saucepan, combine egg whites, sugar, cream of tartar, and remaining corn syrup and water. Cook over low heat and beat with a hand mixer on low until mixture reaches 160°.

6. Pour into a large mixing bowl; beat on high until soft peaks form. Fold into chocolate mixture. Chill for 1-2 hours or until mixture mounds.

7. Just before serving, spoon mousse into meringue cups; sprinkle with peppermint candy pieces. **Yield:** 15 servings.

Nutrition Facts: 1 filled cup equals 201 calories, 4 g fat (2 g saturated fat), 19 mg cholesterol, 153 mg sodium, 40 g carbohydrate, 2 g fiber, 5 g protein. **Diabetic Exchange:** 2-1/2 starch.

❧❧❧ Cran-Apple Cobbler

(Also pictured on page 208)

Jo Ann Sheehan, Ruther Glen, Virginia

This cranberry-packed cobbler is the crowning glory of many of our late fall and winter meals. In fact, we prefer this dessert to pie for our Thanksgiving and Christmas celebrations.

2-1/2 cups sliced peeled apples
2-1/2 cups sliced peeled firm pears
    1 to 1-1/4 cups sugar
    1 cup fresh *or* frozen cranberries, thawed
    1 cup water
    3 tablespoons quick-cooking tapioca
    3 tablespoons red-hot candies
  1/2 teaspoon ground cinnamon
    2 tablespoons butter
TOPPING:
  3/4 cup all-purpose flour
    2 tablespoons sugar
    1 teaspoon baking powder
  1/4 teaspoon salt
  1/4 cup cold butter, cubed
    3 tablespoons milk
Vanilla ice cream

1. In a large saucepan, combine the first eight ingredients; let stand for 5 minutes. Cook and stir over medium heat until mixture comes to a full rolling boil, about 18 minutes. Transfer cran-apple mixture to a greased 2-qt. baking dish; dot with butter.

2. In a small bowl, combine the flour, sugar, baking powder and salt. Cut in butter until mixture resembles coarse crumbs. Stir in milk until a soft dough forms.

3. Drop topping by heaping tablespoonfuls onto hot fruit. Bake at 375° for 30-35 minutes or until golden brown. Serve warm with ice cream. **Yield:** 6-8 servings.

❧❧❧ Toffee Brownie Trifle

Wendy Bennett, Sioux Falls, South Dakota

Here's a convenient yet tempting way to dress up a packaged brownie mix. Your family is sure to love it!

    1 package fudge brownie mix (13-inch x 9-inch pan size)
2-1/2 cups cold milk
    1 package (3.4 ounces) instant cheesecake *or* vanilla pudding mix
    1 package (3.3 ounces) instant white chocolate pudding mix
    1 carton (8 ounces) frozen whipped topping, thawed
    2 to 3 Heath candy bars (1.4 ounces *each*), chopped

1. Prepare and bake brownies according to package directions for cake-like brownies, using a greased 13-in. x 9-in. x 2-in. baking pan. Cool completely on a wire rack.

2. In a large mixing bowl, beat the milk and pudding mixes on low speed for 2 minutes. Fold in whipped topping. Cut the brownies into 1-in. cubes; place half in a 3-qt. glass trifle bowl or serving dish. Cover with half of the pudding. Repeat layers. Sprinkle with chopped candy bars. Refrigerate leftovers. **Yield:** 16 servings.

🎖 🎖 🎖
Kentucky Peach Cobbler

Maybellene Griffin, Beattyville, Kentucky

I've made this unbelievably easy cobbler for years. Soon after my son moved away from home, he called to ask for the recipe.

6 medium ripe peaches, peeled and sliced
  (about 4 cups)
2 tablespoons butter, softened
1-1/4 cups sugar, *divided*
1 teaspoon vanilla extract
1 cup all-purpose flour
2 teaspoons baking powder
Dash salt
1/2 cup milk
1/2 cup cold water
Vanilla ice cream

1. Arrange peaches in a greased 11-in. x 7-in. x 2-in. baking dish. In a large mixing bowl, combine butter and 1/2 cup sugar. Beat in vanilla. Combine the flour, baking powder and salt; add to creamed mixture alternately with milk. Pour over peaches; sprinkle with remaining sugar.

2. Pour cold water over the top. Bake at 350° for 35-40 minutes or until golden brown. Serve warm with ice cream. **Yield:** 6 servings.

🎖 🎖 🎖
Bavarian Apple Tart

Mary Anne Engel, West Allis, Wisconsin

When I shared this tart at my card club, everyone commented on the wonderful taste. Afterward, there wasn't a leftover in sight! No one guessed that the delicate crust, creamy filling and sweet topping came from a lightened-up recipe.

✓ Uses less fat, sugar or salt. Includes Nutrition Facts and Diabetic Exchanges.

1/3 cup butter, softened
1/3 cup sugar
1/2 teaspoon vanilla extract
1 cup all-purpose flour
1/8 teaspoon ground cinnamon
FILLING:
1 package (8 ounces) reduced-fat cream cheese
1/4 cup sugar
1 egg
1-1/2 teaspoons vanilla extract
TOPPING:
4 cups thinly sliced peeled Granny Smith *or* other tart apples (about 2 medium)
1/3 cup sugar
3/4 teaspoon ground cinnamon

1. In a large mixing bowl, cream the butter and sugar. Add the vanilla, flour and cinnamon. Press onto the bottom and 1 in. up the sides of a 9-in. springform pan coated with nonstick cooking spray.

2. In a large mixing bowl, beat the cream cheese and sugar until smooth. Beat in egg and vanilla just until combined. Spread over crust.

3. In another bowl, toss the apples, sugar and cinnamon; arrange over filling. Bake at 400° for 40 minutes or until apples are tender and crust is golden brown. Cool on a wire rack. Store in the refrigerator. **Yield:** 12 servings.

Nutrition Facts: 1 piece equals 213 calories, 9 g fat (5 g saturated fat), 42 mg cholesterol, 113 mg sodium, 30 g carbohydrate, 1 g fiber, 4 g protein. **Diabetic Exchanges:** 2 fat, 1-1/2 starch, 1/2 fruit.

🎗🎗🎗
Berry Cream Dessert

Deb Sandoval, Colorado Springs, Colorado

When I was in high school, my best friend's mom used to make this lightened-up berry dessert…and I fell in love with it. Now I surprise my family with this treat on special occasions.

✓ Uses less fat, sugar or salt. Includes Nutrition Facts and Diabetic Exchanges.

- 1 package (3 ounces) strawberry gelatin
- 1 package (3 ounces) raspberry gelatin
- 2 cups boiling water
- 2 cups cold water
- 1 carton (8 ounces) strawberry yogurt
- 1 carton (8 ounces) raspberry yogurt
- 2 cups sliced fresh *or* frozen unsweetened strawberries
- 1 carton (12 ounces) frozen whipped topping, thawed

Additional fresh strawberries, optional

1. In a large bowl, dissolve strawberry and raspberry gelatin in boiling water. Stir in cold water and strawberry and raspberry yogurt until blended. Chill until syrupy, about 1 hour.

2. Fold in strawberries and whipped topping. Spoon into individual dishes. Chill until firm, about 4 hours. Serve with berries if desired. **Yield:** 16 servings.

Nutrition Facts: 3/4 cup (prepared with sugar-free gelatin, reduced-fat yogurt and reduced-fat whipped topping; calculated without garnish) equals 95 calories, 3 g fat (3 g saturated fat), 2 mg cholesterol, 46 mg sodium, 13 g carbohydrate, 1 g fiber, 2 g protein. **Diabetic Exchanges:** 1 fruit, 1/2 fat.

🎗🎗🎗
Chocolate 'n' Toffee Rice Pudding

Joann Vess Hilliard, East Liverpool, Ohio

I can't think of a more comforting dessert than this creamy rice pudding, which gets its crunch from toffee bits.

- 3 cups milk
- 3 cups cooked rice
- 1/2 cup packed brown sugar
- 3 tablespoons butter
- 1/4 teaspoon salt
- 1 teaspoon vanilla extract
- 1/4 cup flaked coconut, toasted
- 1/4 cup English toffee bits *or* almond brickle chips
- 1/4 cup miniature semisweet chocolate chips
- 1/2 cup whipped topping
- 7 maraschino cherries

1. In a large saucepan, combine milk, rice, sugar, butter and salt; bring to a boil over medium heat. Cook for 15 minutes or until thick and creamy, stirring occasionally. Remove from heat; stir in vanilla. Cool.

2. Spoon half of the pudding into dessert dishes. Combine the coconut, toffee bits and chocolate chips; sprinkle half over the pudding. Repeat layers. Refrigerate until serving. Top with whipped topping and cherries. **Yield:** 7 servings.

🎀🎀🎀 Rhubarb Pudding

Virginia Andersen, Palermo, North Dakota

My mother gave me the recipe for this old-fashioned pudding that has tangy rhubarb flavor. My husband and daughter really enjoy it, and it's a great way to use up day-old bread.

   8 slices bread, lightly toasted
1-1/2 cups milk
   1/4 cup butter, cubed
   5 eggs, lightly beaten
   3 cups chopped fresh *or* frozen rhubarb, thawed
1-1/2 cups sugar
   1/2 teaspoon ground cinnamon
   1/4 teaspoon salt
   1/2 cup packed brown sugar

1. Remove crusts from bread; cut into 1/2-in. cubes. Place in a greased 1-1/2-qt. baking dish.

2. In a large saucepan, heat milk over medium heat until bubbles form around sides of pan; remove from the heat. Stir in butter until melted. Pour over bread; let stand for 15 minutes.

3. In a large bowl, combine the eggs, rhubarb, sugar, cinnamon and salt; stir into the bread mixture. Sprinkle with the brown sugar. Bake at 350° for 45-50 minutes or until set. Serve warm. Refrigerate leftovers. **Yield:** 8 servings.

Editor's Note: If using frozen rhubarb, measure rhubarb while still frozen, then thaw completely. Drain in a colander, but do not press liquid out.

🎀🎀🎀 Cranberry Walnut White Fudge

(Pictured on page 209)

Wanda Green, Woodland, California

A visit to several Oregon cranberry farms inspired this unusual, fruit-filled white fudge. The recipe ended up earning first place at our county fair. I like to make batches for family and friends at Christmastime.

✓ Uses less fat, sugar or salt. Includes Nutrition Facts and Diabetic Exchanges.

   1 teaspoon plus 1/2 cup butter, *divided*
   2 cups sugar
3/4 cup sour cream
   1 package (10 to 12 ounces) vanilla *or* white chips
   1 jar (7 ounces) marshmallow creme
   1 teaspoon vanilla extract
   3 cups coarsely chopped walnuts
   1 cup dried cranberries, coarsely chopped

1. Line an 8-in. square pan with foil and butter the foil with 1 teaspoon butter; set aside. In a heavy saucepan, bring the sugar, sour cream and remaining butter to a boil over medium heat. Cook and stir until a candy thermometer reads 234° (soft-ball stage), about 15 minutes.

2. Remove from the heat. Stir in the chips, marshmallow creme and vanilla until smooth. Fold in walnuts and cranberries. Pour into prepared pan. Let stand at room temperature until cool.

3. Using foil, lift fudge out of pan. Discard foil; cut fudge into 1-in. squares. Store in an airtight container in the refrigerator. **Yield:** 3 pounds.

Nutrition Facts: 1 serving equals 632 calories, 36 g fat (12 g saturated fat), 36 mg cholesterol, 124 mg sodium, 74 g carbohydrate, 2 g fiber, 10 g protein.

Test Your Thermometer

Before using your candy thermometer to make Cranberry Walnut White Fudge or another recipe, take a few moments to test your thermometer for accuracy.

To do so, bring water to a boil; the thermometer should read 212°. If it rises above or does not reach 212°, don't worry—simply add or subtract the difference to the temperature called for in the recipe.

When you're finished using the candy thermometer for your recipe, allow it to cool before washing it to avoid breakage.

🎀🎀🎀
Banana Cream Brownie Dessert

(Also pictured on page 208)

Julie Nowakowski, LaSalle, Illinois

I always keep the ingredients for this luscious dessert on hand because I make it often for potlucks and other get-togethers. After one bite, you'll understand why!

- 1 package fudge brownie mix (13-inch x 9-inch pan size)
- 1 cup (6 ounces) semisweet chocolate chips, *divided*
- 3/4 cup dry roasted peanuts, chopped, *divided*
- 3 medium firm bananas
- 1-2/3 cups cold milk
- 2 packages (5.1 ounces *each*) instant vanilla pudding mix
- 1 carton (8 ounces) frozen whipped topping, thawed

1. Prepare brownie batter according to package directions for fudge-like brownies. Stir in 1/2 cup chocolate chips and 1/4 cup peanuts. Spread into a greased 13-in. x 9-in. x 2-in. baking pan. Bake at 350° for 28-30 minutes or until a toothpick inserted near the center comes out clean. Cool on a wire rack.

2. Slice bananas; arrange in a single layer over brownies. Chop the remaining chocolate chips. Sprinkle 1/4 cup chopped chips and 1/4 cup peanuts over bananas.

3. In a large mixing bowl, beat the milk and pudding mixes on low speed for 2 minutes. Fold in whipped topping. Spread over the top. Sprinkle with remaining chips and pecans. Refrigerate leftovers. **Yield:** 12-15 servings.

🎀🎀🎀
Blackberry Cobbler

Leslie Browning, Lebanon, Kentucky

With this lightened-up but comforting treat, my family and I can watch our weight and still enjoy dessert. Other kinds of berries or even fresh peaches are just as delicious in this old-fashioned cobbler.

 Uses less fat, sugar or salt. Includes Nutrition Facts and Diabetic Exchanges.

- 1/2 cup sugar
- 4-1/2 teaspoons quick-cooking tapioca
- 1/4 teaspoon ground allspice
- 5 cups fresh *or* frozen blackberries, thawed
- 2 tablespoons orange juice

DOUGH:
- 1 cup all-purpose flour
- 1/3 cup plus 1 tablespoon sugar, *divided*
- 1/4 teaspoon baking soda
- 1/4 teaspoon salt
- 1/3 cup reduced-fat vanilla yogurt
- 1/3 cup fat-free milk
- 3 tablespoons butter, melted

1. In a large bowl, combine the sugar, tapioca and allspice. Add blackberries and orange juice; toss to coat. Let stand for 15 minutes. Spoon into a 2-qt. baking dish coated with nonstick cooking spray. In a large mixing bowl, combine the flour, 1/3 cup sugar, baking soda and salt. Combine the yogurt, milk and butter; stir into dry ingredients until smooth. Spread over berry mixture.

2. Bake at 350° for 20 minutes. Sprinkle with remaining sugar. Bake 25-30 minutes longer or until golden brown. Serve warm. **Yield:** 10 servings.

Nutrition Facts: 1 serving equals 199 calories, 4 g fat (2 g saturated fat), 10 mg cholesterol, 135 mg sodium, 40 g carbohydrate, 4 g fiber, 3 g protein. **Diabetic Exchanges:** 1-1/2 starch, 1 fruit, 1/2 fat.

Lemon Surprise Cheesecake

Karen Chesnut, Clarksburg, California

This creamy dessert is bursting with lemon flavor, from the crust to the filling to the topping. Build up the edges of the cheesecake to keep the lemon filling right where you want it.

1-1/2 cups lemon cream-filled sandwich cookie
crumbs
2 tablespoons sugar
1/4 cup butter, melted
LEMON FILLING:
2/3 cup plus 2 tablespoons sugar
5 tablespoons cornstarch
1 cup water
2 egg yolks, slightly beaten
1/3 cup lemon juice
2 tablespoons butter
1 teaspoon grated lemon peel
CHEESECAKE LAYER:
1 envelope unflavored gelatin
1/2 cup lemon juice
3 packages (8 ounces *each*) cream cheese,
softened
3/4 cup sugar
1 cup heavy whipping cream, whipped
2 teaspoons grated lemon peel

1. Combine the cookie crumbs and sugar; stir in butter. Press onto the bottom of a lightly greased 9-in. springform pan. Place on a baking sheet. Bake at 350° for 8-10 minutes or until crust just begins to brown. Cool pan on a wire rack.

2. In a large saucepan, combine sugar and cornstarch. Stir in water until smooth. Cook and stir over medium-high heat until thickened and bubbly. Reduce heat; cook and stir 2 minutes longer. Remove from the heat. Stir a small amount of hot filling into egg yolks; return all to pan, stirring constantly. Bring to a gentle boil; cook and stir 2 minutes longer. Remove from the heat. Gently stir in the lemon juice, butter and peel. Cool to room temperature without stirring.

3. In a small saucepan, sprinkle gelatin over lemon juice; let stand for 1 minute. Heat over low heat, stirring until gelatin is dissolved. Remove from the heat.

4. In a large mixing bowl, beat cream cheese and sugar. Gradually beat in gelatin mixture until combined. Fold in the whipped cream and lemon peel.

5. Spoon three-fourths of cheesecake mixture into crust; build up edges slightly. Chill for 5 minutes. Spoon lemon filling over cheesecake layer to within 1/2 in. of edges. Top with remaining cheesecake mixture. Cover and refrigerate overnight.

6. Carefully run a knife around edge of pan; remove sides of pan. Refrigerate leftovers. **Yield:** 12 servings.

20 chocolate cream-filled chocolate sandwich
   cookies, *divided*
 2 tablespoons butter, softened
 1 package (8 ounces) cream cheese, softened
1/2 cup peanut butter
1-1/2 cups confectioners' sugar, *divided*
 1 carton (16 ounces) frozen whipped topping,
   thawed, *divided*
15 miniature peanut butter cups, chopped
 1 cup cold milk
 1 package (3.9 ounces) instant chocolate fudge
   pudding mix

1. Crush 16 cookies; toss with the butter. Press onto the bottom of ungreased 9-in. square dish.

2. In a large mixing bowl, beat the cream cheese, peanut butter and 1 cup confectioners' sugar until smooth. Fold in half of the whipped topping. Spread over crust. Sprinkle with peanut butter cups.

3. In another mixing bowl, beat the milk, pudding mix and remaining confectioners' sugar on low speed for 2 minutes. Fold in remaining whipped topping. Spread over peanut butter cups. Crush remaining cookies; sprinkle over the top. Cover and chill for at least 3 hours. **Yield:** 12-16 servings.

🏵 🏵 🏵
Peanut Butter
Chocolate Dessert

Debbie Price, LaRue, Ohio

For me, the perfect dessert combines the flavors of chocolate and peanut butter. When I came up with this rich treat, it quickly became my favorite. I can fix the no-bake recipe in a jiffy.

🏵 🏵 🏵
Jeweled Gelatin Torte

Kimberly Adams, Falmouth, Kentucky

My mother served this special gelatin torte for all of our holiday dinners when I was young. I still love the colorful stained-glass look of the Jell-O cubes and the dainty ladyfingers in this elegant dessert.

 1 package (3 ounces) cherry gelatin
 3 cups boiling water, *divided*
 2 cups cold water, *divided*
 1 package (3 ounces) lime gelatin
 1 package (3 ounces) orange gelatin
 1 cup pineapple juice
 1 package (3 ounces) lemon gelatin
1/4 cup sugar
36 ladyfingers
 1 carton (8 ounces) frozen whipped topping,
   thawed

Citrus slices and fresh mint, optional

1. In a small bowl, dissolve cherry gelatin in 1 cup boiling water; stir in 1/2 cup cold water. Pour into a 9-in. x 5-in. x 3-in. loaf pan coated with nonstick cooking spray. Repeat with lime and orange gelatin, using two more loaf pans. Refrigerate until firm, about 1-1/2 hours.

2. In a small saucepan, bring pineapple juice to a boil. Stir in lemon gelatin and sugar until dissolved. Stir in re-

maining cold water. Refrigerate until syrupy, about 45 minutes. Meanwhile, line the sides and bottom of a 9-in. springform pan with ladyfingers; set aside.

3. Cut cherry, lime and orange gelatin into 1/2-in. cubes. Pour lemon gelatin mixture into a large bowl; fold in whipped topping. Gently fold in gelatin cubes. Pour into prepared pan. Refrigerate until set. Garnish with citrus and mint if desired. **Yield:** 10-12 servings.

✿ ✿ ✿
Black Forest Trifle

Peggy Linton, Cobourg, Ontario

When I want a dessert that's fit for a feast, I turn to this eye-catching, irresistible trifle. The five-ingredient recipe uses a convenient brownie mix and cherry pie filling.

- 1 package brownie mix (13-inch x 9-inch pan size)
- 2 packages (2.8 ounces *each*) chocolate mousse mix
- 1 can (21 ounces) cherry pie filling
- 1 carton (16 ounces) frozen whipped topping, thawed
- 4 Skor candy bars, crushed

1. Prepare and bake brownies according to package directions; cool completely on a wire rack. Meanwhile prepare mousse according to package directions.

2. Crumble brownies; sprinkle half into a 4-qt. trifle dish or glass bowl. Top with half of the pie filling, mousse, whipped topping and candy bars. Repeat layers. Cover and refrigerate for 8 hours or overnight. **Yield:** 16 servings.

✿ ✿ ✿
Apricot Rice Custard

Elizabeth Montgomery, Taylorville, Illinois

This creamy treat drizzled with apricot sauce makes a comforting dessert...or even a refreshingly different breakfast. The custard is simple to fix and so yummy.

- 1 cup uncooked long grain rice
- 3 cups milk
- 1/2 cup sugar
- 1/2 teaspoon salt
- 2 eggs, lightly beaten
- 1/2 teaspoon vanilla extract
- 1/4 teaspoon almond extract
- Dash ground cinnamon
- SAUCE:
- 1 can (8-1/2 ounces) apricot halves
- 1 can (8 ounces) crushed pineapple, undrained
- 1/3 cup packed brown sugar
- 2 tablespoons lemon juice
- 1 tablespoon cornstarch

1. In a large saucepan, cook rice according to package directions. Stir in milk, sugar and salt; bring to a boil. Reduce heat to low. Stir 1/2 cup into eggs; return all to the pan, stirring constantly. Cook and stir for 15 minutes or until mixture reaches 160° or coats the back of a metal spoon (do not boil). Remove from the heat; stir in extracts and cinnamon.

2. For sauce, drain apricot syrup into a small saucepan. Chop apricots; add to syrup. Stir in remaining sauce ingredients; bring to a boil. Boil for 2 minutes, stirring occasionally. Serve sauce and custard warm or chilled. **Yield:** 8-10 servings.

General Recipe Index

This handy index lists every recipe by food category, major ingredient and/or cooking method, so you can easily locate recipes to suit your needs.

✓Recipe includes Nutrition Facts and Diabetic Exchanges

Alphabetical Index

*This handy index lists every recipe in alphabetical order,
so you can easily find your favorite recipes.*

✓ Recipe includes Nutrition Facts and Diabetic Exchanges